Main

RACE-BAITER

RACE-BAITER

HOW THE MEDIA WIELDS DANGEROUS WORDS TO DIVIDE A NATION

ERIC DEGGANS

palgrave
macmillan

First published in 2012 by PALGRAVE MACMILLAN® in the U.S.—a division
of St. Martin's Press LLC, 175 Fifth Avenue, New York, NY 10010.

Where this book is distributed in the UK, Europe and the rest of the world, this
is by Palgrave Macmillan, a division of Macmillan Publishers Limited, registered
in England, company number 785998, of Houndmills, Basingstoke, Hampshire
RG21 6XS.

Palgrave Macmillan is the global academic imprint of the above companies and
has companies and representatives throughout the world.

Palgrave® and Macmillan® are registered trademarks in the United States, the
United Kingdom, Europe and other countries.

ISBN: 978–0–230–34182–1

Library of Congress Cataloging-in-Publication Data

Deggans, Eric.
    Race-baiter : how the media wields dangerous words to divide a nation / Eric
Deggans.
      pages   cm
    Includes index.
    ISBN 978–0–230–34182–1
    1. Journalism—Social aspects—United States. 2. Prejudices in the press—
United States. 3. Television broadcasting of news—Objectivity—United States.
4. Television and politics—United States. 5. Journalism—Objectivity—United
States. 6. Prejudices in mass media—United States. I. Title.
PN4888.S6D44   2012
302.23'0973—dc23

                                                            2012016687

A catalogue record of the book is available from the British Library.

Design by Letra Libre

First edition: October 2012

10 9 8 7 6 5 4 3 2 1

Printed in the United States of America.

To Barb, Zoe, Jessica, Sophia, and Marcus

Your love and support makes it all worthwhile

CONTENTS

ACKNOWLEDGMENTS

IT TOOK A VILLAGE TO MAKE THIS BOOK A REALITY, AND I WANT to use this space to thank everyone who helped out, inspired, or otherwise contributed to making my first outing as an author come to fruition. I will apologize in advance to anyone I inadvertently omitted or lumped in with a group; blame my omnipresent absent-mindedness (there's a reason my nickname growing up in Gary was "Absent-Minded Professor") and the distraction of actually completing this project.

Many thanks to Bob Andelman and Julie Buckner Armstrong, two authors whose early encouragement was crucial in convincing me that I could pull this off. My Los Angeles pal Janice Rhoshalle Littlejohn was also amazing in this regard, as was Jennifer L. Pozner, who offered sage advice and editorial suggestions early on. Thanks also to Russ Crumley, who suggested the book's early title, and the folks in our little writers' group who looked over the early proposal, including Jon Wilson, Anda Peterson, and Tom Hallock.

My agent Uwe Stender has been an amazing, supportive (and accessible!) advocate; his advice and encouragement has been invaluable. Many thanks also to former boss and ex-colleague Dave Scheiber, who joined Bob in highly recommending Uwe.

Palgrave editor Emily Carleton has been a friendly, enthusiastic advocate as well as an amazing creative partner. Thanks also to Christine Catarino, Victoria Wallis, and the other wonderful folks at Palgrave Macmillan who provided excellent work in finishing and marketing the book you now hold.

Special thanks to all my homies at the *Tampa Bay Times* (the newspaper formerly known as the *St. Petersburg Times*), which has been my creative and professional home for 16 years and counting. My most amazing editor Jeanne Grinstead has been impossibly supportive and was beyond understanding when this project took over my life. Her advocacy and support cannot be overstated.

More kudos to my colleagues at the newspaper, especially those in the Entertainment and Features departments who put up with my distraction during the writing process: Steve Spears, Kelly Smith, Colette Bancroft, Janet Keeler, Mike Wilson, Steve Persall, Sean Daly, John Fleming, Lennie Bennett, Sharon Wynne, Laura Reiley, Lane DeGregory, Jeff Klinkenberg, Michael Kruse, Ben Montgomery, Leonora LaPeter Anton, Jim Verhulst, Bill Duryea, Kelly Stefani, Michelle Stark, Peggy Anders, Maggie Duffy, Patti Ewald, Lyra Solochek, Craig Pittman, Angie Holan, Carrie Pratt, Paul Jerome, Barbara Moch, and everyone else in the newsroom who offered an encouraging word.

Extra special thanks to *Tampa Bay Times* editor Neil Brown and Times Publishing Company Chairman/CEO Paul Tash for hiring me so many years ago, championing my career, and allowing me to use so much of my newspaper work as the backbone for this book.

My colleagues at NPR have been invaluable in expanding my critical voice and providing enthusiastic support for my ideas—most especially, my amazing editor and tireless champion Sara Sarasohn (I'm working on that sitcom script, lady!). Thanks also to Felix Contreras, Steve Drummond, Keith Woods, Neda Ulaby, Laura Bertran, Margaret Low Smith, David Folkenflik, Audie Cornish, Steve Inskeep, Michele Norris, Michel Martin, Scott Simon, and all the cool folks there who help make my commentaries so fun and engaging.

Many thanks to other friends who encouraged me and offered book-writing advice, including Roland Martin, Andy Borowitz, Connie May Fowler, Byron Pitts, Jeff Jarvis, Kelly McBride, Adam and Tanya Coovadia, Sam and Laura Henderson, Mike Stoici, Ray Arsenault, James Schnur, Sylvia Martinez Mullenix, Linda Tropp, and Amy Alexander.

Thanks also to everyone who allowed me to interview them for this book, especially those who knew how much I disagreed with them and yet talked to me anyway.

My parents have been an amazing source of inspiration and nurturance. So many thanks to my mother, Carolyn Williams, my dad, Chuck Deggans, and my stepmom, Hue Deggans. You guys have no idea how much your dedication to my education and well-being have helped me succeed in life and how much your love continues to motivate me (shout out as well to my aunt

Cynthia Somerville, who housed me during my first newspaper internship and made my career as a journalist possible).

And the biggest thanks here goes to my wife, Barb, and my own children, Zoe, Jessica, Sophia, and Marcus. You all tolerated many months when I was little more than a shadow around our home, spending every spare moment in the office hammering at this manuscript. That you allowed me the space to finish this work says so much about how supportive you all have been.

I love you all more than I can express.

INTRODUCTION

MAKING ALL THE RIGHT ENEMIES

THE FIRST AND ONLY TIME I MET FOX NEWS CHANNEL STAR BILL O'Reilly, he looked at me like I owed him money.

The situation was, I will admit, an uncomfortable one. He and a publicity executive at Fox News had already turned down an interview request for this very book, despite the fact that he inspired the title. And though he planned several stops around my St. Petersburg, Florida, home base to tout his own new book in early 2012, sharing a cup of joe with me was not particularly high on his to-do list.

That's because we have, as a therapist might say, a bit of history.

At various times on his top-rated evening cablecast, O'Reilly has called me "dishonest," "racially motivated," and "one of the biggest race-baiters in the country" for criticizing the way he talks about race on his program.

So as I planned this tome on how race issues and prejudice play out in media, I wanted to talk with O'Reilly. And he didn't want to talk with me.

Fair enough. But when the top-rated anchor came to give a speech in nearby Sarasota, organizers emailed me an invitation to a small press conference he was holding before the event. *We have history,* I warned. *He probably won't be happy to see me there.*

Sure enough, when we gathered in a small "greenroom" area deep inside the bowels of the Van Wezel Hall, tight smiles were the order of the day. Two reporters from local papers and two high school students flanked me at a small, round table where O'Reilly was going to field questions. After talking with the anchor about my presence, the president of the group presenting the lecture series had one question: "Will you be civil?"

"Of course," I replied. "As long as he is."

Until this day, most all of our disagreements had occurred in media. After I wrote a story for the *St. Petersburg Times* in 2002 panning a prime time special he put together for the Fox broadcast network—titled "Wallowing in Corruption," the piece chided him for blaming rappers for social ills in ways classic rockers never were—he complained about the newspaper so much that my email filled with caustic messages from his fans.

When I sat on a 2008 panel discussion at a symposium in Minneapolis convened by the anti-consolidation media watchdogs Free Press, he sent a producer to interview me on camera, ambush-style, asking why I hadn't appeared on his show. "Bill hasn't asked me," I answered. Never heard back.

And I once got a call out of the blue from a producer on his show wanting to know what political party I was registered under and whether I had given any money to political candidates. "I'm a registered Democrat and I'm a journalist," I told the producer. "So I don't have any money to give anyone."

He would later note in one of his shows that he couldn't "find one TV critic . . . who isn't a liberal or registered Democrat," without detailing his research methods.[1] If he relied on phone calls like the one I got, I bet he didn't get many answers.

But nothing seemed to get under his skin like the controversy over comments he made on his onetime radio show back in 2007 about Sylvia's Restaurant, a well-established, black-owned soul food eatery in Harlem.

Recalling an experience dining there with Al Sharpton, O'Reilly told listeners: "I couldn't get over the fact that there was no difference between Sylvia's Restaurant and any other restaurant in New York City. I mean, it was exactly the same, even though it's run by blacks, primarily black patronship, it was the same. That's really what this society is about here in the U.S.A.; there's no difference."[2]

Later in the show, during a conversation with fellow pundit Juan Williams, he noted, "There wasn't one person in Sylvia's who was screaming, 'M-Fer, I want more iced tea.' . . . It was like going into an Italian restaurant in an all-white suburb in the sense of people were sitting there, and they were ordering and having fun. And there wasn't any kind of craziness at all."

The liberal watchdog group Media Matters posted a transcript with the most disturbing lines highlighted, sparking coverage in the Associated Press, the *New York Daily News,* and CNN. I wrote on it too, noting how those words sounded like an awful backhanded compliment, as if he walked into the doors of Sylvia's expecting a scene from a bad rap video.

O'Reilly blamed Media Matters for omitting the middle part of his show, where he discussed his grandmother's racism, how she had never really known a black person, and how her attitude was rooted in fear translated into "irrational hostility."

Indeed, the full audio of his remarks veered between some statements that sounded insulting—saying "I think black Americans are starting to think more and more for themselves. They're getting away from the Sharptons and the Jacksons and the people trying to lead them into a race-based culture"— to more conciliatory notes about how some prejudice exists because white-controlled media pass along harmful images of black people.

What seemed obvious, then and now, is that we don't have a great vocabulary for talking about any of this. And too often, instead of having a respectful dialogue, we fight.

All of which I wanted to discuss with O'Reilly in Sarasota. But my first question, asking why he called *me* a race-baiter, didn't get much response.

"I don't have that quote in front of me," he said. "I'm not going to answer quotes that I said four years ago. 'Cause I don't know what the context is. I can't answer the question because I don't know. If you have a transcript, I'll take a look at it."[3]

But you said back then that white people couldn't talk to black people about issues of race, I answered. Do you feel the same way now?

"All I know is I did a commentary on a restaurant in Harlem, Sylvia's, where I was very complimentary about the restaurant and what went on there . . . [and] I got shattered by ideologues who were just looking to take things out of context," he said. "I think it's a press problem, not a people problem."

Then why did he air a commentary blaming Rev. Jeremiah Wright, Media Matters, civil rights activist Jesse Jackson, and me for helping create a climate where "good people are being driven away from constructive dialogue that might advance racial harmony"? And why did every example of dubious "race-baiting" he cited feature allegations of prejudice against white people?

If we're all equal, can't white people make mistakes, too?

Later, I asked about the track record of his employer, Fox News, in closely covering issues that may heighten fear of black people, including fellow anchor Sean Hannity making the case that Derrick Bell, the first African American to become a tenured professor at Harvard University's law school, was a radical extremist closely linked to President Obama.

"We put Geraldo on [that]," O'Reilly said, smirking dismissively while referencing his on-air discussion with Geraldo Rivera. "I don't think it's important. I don't have any beef with what Barack Obama did back then."

So what do you think of the way other people on your channel talk about these issues? When Glenn Beck calls Barack Obama a racist or others say equally insensitive things, aren't they making cross-racial dialogue more difficult, too?

"I do what I do," he said. "I don't have any power . . . I told Beck he was out of line. He apologized on my show. As far as the other stuff goes, they say what they say."

To be honest, I wasn't that surprised. People used to having one-sided conversations sometimes have trouble when the setting is different.

Back in 2005, writing as media critic for the *St. Petersburg Times* (now known as the *Tampa Bay Times*), I pulled together a column highlighting the racially tinged language O'Reilly used in describing those stuck in New Orleans without food and water amid post-Hurricane Katrina flooding.[4]

The Fox News anchor had joined other conservative pundits such as Beck and Rush Limbaugh in making oddly coded, often racially tinged observations about the thousands who begged relief workers for supplies as a GOP-controlled presidential administration fumbled basic disaster assistance.

"So every American kid should be required to watch videotape of the poor in New Orleans and see how they suffered [after Hurricane Katrina], because they couldn't get out of town," thundered O'Reilly on his Fox News Channel show, *The O'Reilly Factor*.[5] "And then, every teacher should tell the students, 'If you refuse to learn, if you refuse to work hard, if you become addicted, if you live a gangsta-life, you will be poor and powerless just like many of those in New Orleans.'"

I called him, Limbaugh, Beck, and Pat Robertson on their language, noting about O'Reilly specifically: "The larger implications of his words also are obvious. These often poor, often black hurricane victims brought all this misery and death on themselves, because they weren't motivated enough to succeed in America."[6]

The same day, O'Reilly cited my column as his "most ridiculous item of the day," calling me "a dishonest, racially motivated correspondent writing for perhaps the worst newspaper in the country."[7]

Forget about a meaningful discussion on opposing views or allowing people of color the space to initiate debate; instead, opponents are instantly dismissed with a term whose toxic meaning shuts down all discussion: *race-baiter.*

But sometimes, such a slur—coming from the right people—feels less like a criticism than a badge of honor, communicating mostly one thing:

You're on the right track.

Flash forward a few years, and you see the same tactic spread across an entire chunk of major media outlets.

According to Media Matters, Fox News anchor Megyn Kelly's *America Live* show devoted at least 45 segments over two weeks in 2010 to allegations that the Justice Department under President Barack Obama was refusing to prosecute black people.[8] The spark of this story: a decision to narrow prosecution of New Black Panther Party members who had been cited for standing around a polling place, one holding a nightstick, during an election.

Kelly defended the stories in an emotional, vitriolic, on-camera argument with Kirsten Powers, a Democratic analyst employed by Fox News who suggested the coverage was excessive.[9] Dave Weigel, writing for the *Atlantic* magazine's Daily Dish blog, accused Kelly of sowing race-based fear and mistrust of the Department of Justice among white viewers "under the guise of journalism."[10]

On the other hand, MSNBC, which offers a slate of pundits favoring liberal and Democratic party ideals, faced criticism for years over a lack of diversity in its anchor lineup. In mid-2011, they hired African American civil rights activist Al Sharpton as host of a 6 P.M. show and developing black pundits such as Georgetown University professor Michael Eric Dyson, *Washington Post* columnist Eugene Robinson, and Tulane University professor Melissa Harris-Perry as guest and weekend anchors.

But there was still concern that the channel was overlooking journalists of color. And MSNBC moved slowly to deal with pundit Pat Buchanan, a former advisor to Richard Nixon and Ronald Reagan whose 2011 book, *Suicide of a Superpower,* posited that one element of America's decline could be found in its growing ethnic diversity, sparking protests. Eventually, after he'd been absent from their air for four months, MSNBC announced in February 2012 it was parting ways with Buchanan.[11]

Glenn Beck, once Fox News's biggest rising star, hyped several "scandals" that seemed rooted in racial issues. Often, he specialized in demonizing people of color—from insisting President Obama "has a deep-seated hatred of white people"[12] to alleging that Obama intends to create a "thugocracy" of a "civilian national security force" that reports only to him[13] (the then-candidate actually used the phrase while speaking about strengthening volunteer organizations such as the Peace Corps and veterans helping other veterans during his 2008 campaign).[14]

Even after leaving Fox News in mid-2011 and starting his own online video platform, GBTV, Beck continued his flights of race-based, divisive paranoia, insisting a race war was underway in America or sure to break out if Barack Obama lost the 2012 election.[15]

It's worth noting that Beck was never publicly penalized or sanctioned by Fox News for such divisive words and tactics (instead, when Beck accused the nation's first black president of racism, Fox News senior vice president of programming Bill Shine told the TVNewser website that Beck "represented his own views, not those of the Fox News Channel").[16] But the racism comment inspired protestors to target Beck's sponsors, making it tougher for Fox to earn money off his ratings until his departure from the channel in mid-2011.

The powder keg exploded in late July 2010, when conservative activist Andrew Breitbart posted edited videos of Department of Agriculture employee Shirley Sherrod speaking at a National Association for the Advacement of Colored People (NAACP) banquet.[17] Clipped to make it seem that she admitted refusing to help a white farmer in her current job, the videos became electrifying fodder for pundits to decry reverse racism at the NAACP and anti-white bias in the Obama administration.

That is, until the civil rights group released the *full* video to show that Sherrod was talking about an incident 24 years in the past, when she worked for a non-profit agency helping poor, mostly black people keep their farms. In the full video, she admitted realizing the error of her ways; eventually, she worked for years to help the white farmer save his land from bankruptcy.[18]

In February 2011, Sherrod sued Breitbart, saying in a statement that the lawsuit was "about how quickly, in today's Internet media environment, a person's good name can become collateral damage in an overheated political debate."[19] Breitbart's sudden death on March 1, 2012, returned her story to the headlines as obituaries recapped the details of the case.

In an interview with me in January 2012, about five weeks before his death, Breitbart refused to back down. "She still harbors a culturally Marxist point of view," noted the blogger about Sherrod, after saying that his original piece was intended to show that the NAACP uses language about white people that would be considered scandalous if the positions were reversed. "You do not hear in the full video a woman who does not revert from her black-versus-white point of view . . . She says it's not about black versus white, it's about rich versus poor. That's a Marxist paradigm. That is an NAACP paradigm."[20]

So who exactly was penalized here for trying to speak honestly about their own race prejudice?

In the end, along with an avalanche of criticism, Breitbart earned loads of buzz, media attention, and website clicks generated by a scandal that shunted the president's historic signing of a financial reform bill that week to the edges of the news cycle.

THESE ARE JUST A FEW EXAMPLES of what this book will dissect: the powerful ways modern media often works to feed our fears, prejudices, and hate toward each other, garnering sizable audiences, advertising dollars, and political power in the process.

It wasn't always this way. Before the rise of niche outlets such as cable TV, satellite radio, websites, and social media platforms, big media outlets made their money by seeking to serve huge, diverse audiences and selling advertisers access to them, creating a shared cultural dialogue in the process.

When Capt. "Hawkeye" Pierce left Korea on the last episode of CBS's hit comedy *M*A*S*H*, or Bill Cosby's Cliff Huxtable saluted the nation's first observance of Martin Luther King Jr. Day on *The Cosby Show*, offices across the country were consumed with talk of what had happened the night before. Mass media was the country's open hearth, where big media companies worked hard to unite audiences in feeding their own massive bottom lines.

But today's fastest-growing media platforms now focus on smaller segments of the audience—the plumpest parts of a seriously fragmented viewing/reading/listening public. And one way to ensure that those audience segments develop fierce loyalty is to feed them messages demonizing other outlets and the groups who might gather there.

It may sound cynical. But in a fragmented media culture, hate sells.

In certain pockets of media, the same tactics once used to mobilize political parties and committed voters are now used to secure audience share and unique website visitors. Even as the election of the first black president forces us all to re-evaluate how we think about race, gender, culture, and class lines, some areas of modern media are working overtime to push the same old buttons of conflict and division for new purposes.

It may seem that such arguments are leveled disproportionately against right-leaning media outlets such as Fox News Channel, but perhaps that's because conservatives have refined this success-by-segmentation strategy to a fine art, led by some of the best communicators in the business. On the liberal side, MSNBC's efforts to emerge as a left-leaning alternative are balanced by its connection to an old-school broadcast entity, NBC News.

Small wonder, then, that former vice president Al Gore's cable channel Current TV began in 2011 courting an audience to the left of MSNBC, backed by expatriates from that channel such as Cenk Uygur and, for a short time, Keith Olbermann.

While MSNBC and Current develop their liberal visions, conservative media outlets have already built a powerful alliance of radio, TV, Internet, and book publishing. This mighty megaphone links popular radio hosts such as Rush Limbaugh and Michael Savage with TV (and radio) guys such as O'Reilly and Beck, along with online platforms such as Breitbart.com, Tucker Carlson's *Daily Caller,* and Matt Drudge's The Drudge Report.

The result can be a finely tuned echo chamber, in which consumers *feel* like they're experiencing many different perspectives and information sources while they are, in fact, immersed in a media ecosystem endlessly recycling the same limited ideas.

While claims that National Public Radio skews its news reports to liberal interests are overblown—despite the resignation of two top executives there in 2011 after an embarrassing, secretly recorded video surfaced of a key fundraising official insulting the tea party movement—the organization does focus much of its programming on an intellectual, college-educated, liberal arts–oriented audience.[21] And none of its non-news hosts or personalities could be described as conservative.

To decode a media outlet's focus and perspective, look at how it makes money and who holds the most visible jobs. Those answers reveal what kind of audience they seek and how they plan to monetize it, once assembled.

NPR shows targeted to an audience comfortable with the gentle progressivism of the liberal arts world feel light-years removed from the in-your-face cultural combat aimed at the typical politically conservative Fox News viewer. That hasn't kept NPR from struggling with its own diversity issues, particularly its lack of visible African American male contributors following the controversial firing of pundit Juan Williams in late 2010. (Full disclosure: I regularly contribute to NPR shows, both as an analyst and as an author of freelance commentaries on TV.)

In the public broadcasting universe, where outlets depend on donations from the audience and corporate benefactors to fill their budgets, a different group of fans is targeted for a different kind of media experience. Among public radio's News/Talk audiences, 92 percent attended college, 70 percent held at least a college degree, and 71 percent lived in households earning at least $50,000 annually, according to the 2011 edition of radio ratings service Arbitron's *Public Radio Today* report.[22]

Cable TV may be the most obvious venue for these synergies. Fox News Channel founder Roger Ailes learned long ago that there was a sizable chunk of the cable news audience that was older, white, male, conservative, and generally irritated with the coverage offered by traditional media outlets.

Ailes likely knew ratings and influence could come from building a televised version of the right-wing-oriented talk radio world crafted by Limbaugh and longtime radio news announcer Paul Harvey—where classic American values ruled and most issues boiled down to very simple cases of good vs. evil.

Look around the dial now, and you see that concept blown up in a thousand different directions. On CNN's sister channel HLN, anchor Nancy Grace suggests a world where lawbreakers are corroding society and viewers help her hold the justice system accountable.

O'Reilly tackles a host of targets, from terrorists and gangsta rappers to the public officials and newspapers that he claims coddle them. Even left-leaning MSNBC anchors such as Ed Schultz and Chris Matthews join in this game, pouncing on right-wing political candidates and pundits with a ferocity that can sometimes make a reasoned discussion impossible.

The political news website *Politico* discussed all this in a July 2010 column: "Like all news sites, we are aware that conflict clicks. More traffic comes from an item on Sarah Palin's 'refudiation' *faux pas* than from our hundreds of stories on the complexities of health care reform or Wall Street regulation."[23] (Palin used the non-word "refudiate" to describe how "peaceful Muslims" should oppose construction of a mosque near the site of the 9/11 attack on the World Trade Center.)

It's all built around simple dynamics of propaganda and audience building: Fear of the other. Anger over your own perceived victimization. And a need to blame *someone else* for bad times.

It can be a profitable racket. According to *Forbes* magazine, Beck made $32 million from March 2009 to March 2010 across his range of media platforms, including a popular radio show, a best-selling book, a series of concert-style personal appearances, and the Fox News Channel show he would leave in 2011.[24] In May 2012, *Forbes* listed Beck's earnings for the 12 months prior as $80 million.[25]

When Keith Olbermann walked away from his MSNBC show in January 2011, he was midway through a four-year, $30 million contract, according to Howard Kurtz of the *Daily Beast* and *Newsweek*.[26] But fans need not fret: When he started his new job as the lynchpin of Current TV's prime time lineup, Olbermann got a raise, moving from $7 million annually to a paycheck of $10 million per year, according to the *Hollywood Reporter*.[27] (He was fired from that job in April 2012 after clashing with his bosses.)

Back in 2008, as Fox News's biggest star, O'Reilly signed a contract worth a reported $10 million annually.[28] Fox News announced in April 2012 that O'Reilly signed a new multi-year contract, but no salary figures were disclosed.[29] Arianna Huffington's liberal *Huffington Post* website was purchased by AOL in early 2011 for $315 million, during a year analysts estimated it might earn revenues of $60 million.[30]

Clearly, there's big money in exploiting an already divided audience.

SOME FOLKS IN BIG MEDIA may see their divisiveness as a harmless business strategy. But building success by exploiting audience divisions brings repercussions far beyond a ratings spike or a few hurt feelings.

Consider these questions:

- Why is the cable news outlet Americans regard as the most partisan and least trustworthy—according to opinion polls—also considered the most trustworthy, the most watched, and the most profitable?[31] Behold the paradoxical success of Fox News Channel.

- Why does modern media seem to find itself trumpeting race-based scandals with regularity, from the furor over GOP presidential candidates linking black people to discussions on food stamps to the non-existent racism of Shirley Sherrod and the shooting death of an unarmed black teen in Florida by a white Hispanic volunteer watchman? Does the politicized focus of some media outlets make it harder to talk across differences and find understanding, even as it feeds those companies' bottom lines?

- Why has coverage of race issues in the 2012 presidential campaign been so fitful, focused mostly on gaffes and claims of hidden-message, "dog whistle" politics? Could one reason be that the corps of journalists convened to cover the campaigns is seriously lacking in diversity? Why does this evoke memories of the Obama/Clinton primary race four years earlier, when coverage sometimes stumbled around questionable ideas about race and gender?

- Why do so many so-called reality TV shows feature such insulting portrayals of ethnicity and gender roles? In particular, unscripted shows seem to reinforce the notion of a world filled with outdated mores where women will do anything to get married (despite actual marriage rates dropping), Italians and people of color live down to the worst stereotypes about their respective cultures, and no problem is too demeaning to film for a national audience.

- Why hasn't network television found an adequate way to reflect the diversity of the country in its big-budget, scripted series? Why are so many characters of color reduced to figures known derisively as "black best friends," either wholly devoted to supporting the white lead characters or so devoid of ethnic identity that they raise suspicions that producers simply cast minority actors in roles originally written for white people?

- Why didn't the media figures who promised to spark a national dialogue on race and poverty in the wake of Hurricane Katrina actually follow through on that pledge? Did the lack of dialogue on the roots of poverty lead to greater misunderstandings when the collapse of the housing bubble in 2009 sent so many working-class and middle-class people into poverty?

Even the term "race-baiter," defined by *Merriam-Webster's Collegiate Dictionary* as "one who makes verbal attacks against members of a racial group," has evolved with the times.

A bit of quick research by friend and librarian James Schnur at the University of South Florida (along with his graduate student Sylvia Martinez Mullenix), discovered "race-baiter" references dating back to the 1920s, referring to hatred whipped up by white people against racial and cultural minorities. But these days, the term is just as likely to be used to accuse those *fighting* racism of unjustly referencing the issue to win a fight.

"It's this presumption that everything's fine if we could just stop talking about it," said David Leonard, an associate professor specializing in ethnic studies at Washington State University, Pullman. "That was the argument which was also made in the 1950s and the 1960s. And we would look back at that now and say 'Are you nuts?'"[32]

At its core, the struggle over the term centers on disagreement over one idea: that America is mostly past its problems with institutional racism.

Consider employment and poverty figures: In 2010, the poverty rate for black people was at nearly 30 percent, nearly three times the rate for white people, with black children three times as likely to be poor as white children.[33] In January 2012, unemployment rates for black people stood at 13.6 percent, nearly twice the 7.4 percent rate for white folks.[34]

And factor in one more thing: In a survey of more than 1,200 GOP voters in Mississippi and Alabama during mid-March 2012 by Public Policy Polling, 48.5 percent of respondents said they believe President Obama is a Muslim, despite four years spent debunking this inaccurate myth.[35]

In a world like this, accusations of race-baiting feel more like an uncomfortable attempt to change the subject.

"It reflects a very narrow understanding of racism that really only accounts for prejudice," said Leonard. "Talking about institutional racism is seen as someone bringing up issues of racism unnecessarily. In [some] people's minds, the arguments are what lead to divisiveness and not the inequalities already present . . . [and] that basically reaffirms the privilege of whiteness."[36]

As digital technology nibbles away at big media's dominance, many outlets have responded by amplifying the divisions that separate Americans by race, class, gender, sexual orientation, and location. The ongoing fragmentation of media—with Facebook, Twitter, iPods, YouTube sites, and

Internet-accessible smartphones allowing users to create their own, custom-tailored media worlds—has only made it all worse.

And the audience has had few guides for cutting through the clutter.

Until now.

This book is an attempt to decode the ways media outlets profit by segmenting Americans. I call it the Tyranny of the Broad Niche: what happens as the biggest pieces of an increasingly fragmented audience are courted at the expense of many others.

At a time when singular figures such as Barack Obama, Sarah Palin, Hillary Clinton, Ellen DeGeneres, and Oprah Winfrey are shattering cultural and gender boundaries, the media establishment is too often scurrying behind public sentiment.

There may be only one cure for this increasing balkanization: changing the audience itself. It's time to build a more savvy crowd that demands more from its media products and rejects the tactics of division. Judging by the feedback I've gotten from readers, Twitter followers, and Facebook friends, there's a hunger for more evenhanded material and some guidance for sorting the news from the noise.

For some, this message doesn't seem so important. Particularly if your culture is one of the broad niches used as a target audience, it can feel like media outlets are simply working harder to tell it like it is—relating news and perspectives that feel correct because they are more closely tailored to your tastes and outlook than ever before. (Comic Stephen Colbert calls this phenomenon "truthiness," or the certainty of following your feelings and emotion over actual facts.[37])

But for a look at the other side of that coin, I often describe an old print advertisement published in some black-focused magazines in the 1970s, showing a young black boy with a towel pinned on his back, looking into a mirror and imagining himself as the world's greatest superhero.

The jarring twist: The heroic face that looked back at him from the mirror belonged to a white man.

The problem with superserving the biggest niches is that those whose culture and background don't fit those spaces wind up further marginalized. Just ask the French government, which saw vicious riots tear through its ghettoized suburbs in 2005 as disenfranchised, unemployed, and disaffected youth banded together in a massive display of civil unrest.[38] When people feel they no longer have a stake or influence in the wider society, they have nothing to lose.

With luck, tearing down the button-pushing techniques of segmented media can create a social space where all children can imagine themselves as heroes, no matter what they look like.

One thing we'll have to agree on first, however, is how to talk about this stuff at all. I'll explore these ideas more fully in later chapters, but for now, it's worth noting a few simple rules I always try to follow when discussing such topics.

No one owns these subjects. Some people of color have lots of direct experience with prejudice, poverty, and racism, but that doesn't make us infallible—or even necessarily better judges of these issues than white people who have studied and thought a lot about the same subjects.

Instead, I think everyone engaging in such discussions need to put their outrage meter on low and focus instead on having an open, respectful discussion. For me, motives count for a lot. All I ask is some sense that we are both making honest arguments free from opportunism, grandstanding, or willful ignoring of facts.

So talking about race difference shouldn't be about claiming the moral high ground, and every opinion rendered in good conscience is worthy of respect.

Falling prey to prejudices doesn't make you a racist. Because we have quite rightly demonized the worst elements of racism and prejudice in modern life, it is easy to believe that all such ideas are ugly things, the province of people who walk around believing they are intellectually or morally superior to others by the accident of their birth.

But many modern prejudices are seductive and appealing. They explain the world in ways that are predictable and easy to understand, and they reinforce existing worldviews.

In short: Good people can believe unfortunate things—either through lack of experience, lack of data, or a simple mistake. And believing those things doesn't always make someone worthy of the damning label "racist." And discussing these issues doesn't automatically equal playing some kind of dishonest "race card."

It's about scrubbing our media outlets of practices that turn audiences against each other and echo unfair ideas about too many of us.

Referencing race does not necessarily equal racism. For some people, especially folks who haven't thought too much about these issues, any reference to race in controversial circumstances equals racism. But it is possible to talk about race issues—for example, wondering about the racial subtext in some unscripted reality TV shows—without actually being prejudiced against another racial or ethnic group.

This work is never done. Too often, it feels like some people celebrate an advance in diversity or social justice issues simply for the relief it provides. Under that kind of thinking, the election of a black president isn't just a major landmark for the history of American government; it's a justification to shut down discussion of institutional racism. After all, if a black man can be elected president, surely America is done with racism and institutional prejudice?

In an odd way, that kind of thinking has helped keep the nation's first black president from talking very much about race issues at all. Between political opponents who accuse him of playing the victim and others who assume his election means we can finally stop having these conversations completely, Barack Obama has been pushed into keeping silent about the biggest achievement in race relations since the passage of the Civil Rights Act: the story of how a black man named Barack Hussein Obama actually got elected president of the United States of America.

I can't wait to read the book that President Obama writes when he's finally out of the Oval Office and out of politics.

On matters of race, our issues have simply grown more complex, more subtle, and more filled with "truthiness." Especially when there's so much money to be made by turning us against each other.

As real-life events prove the old adage that any child in America really has the potential to be president, it's time our media caught up. Along the way, we can all learn enough about real communication to keep the next race/gender/orientation-based scandal from becoming a searing bonfire of misunderstanding.

Even Bill O'Reilly can learn this lesson, at least a little bit. In July 2010, he aired a brief segment taking note of how I challenged CNN's eagerness to blame Fox News while covering the attempted discrediting of Sherrod, though he didn't condemn Breitbart or his colleague Beck for indulging the same race-baiting he once accused me of perpetrating.[39]

Of course, this acknowledgement came during a segment pronouncing a "media war" underway in America, with mainstream news organizations such as NBC and the *New York Times* denounced as liberal adjuncts of the Obama White House. O'Reilly placed Fox News Channel and an unnamed "bunch of Internet concerns" on the other side, "skeptical about President Obama and liberalism in general."[40]

Once again, the message to his viewers was clear: Trust us, and not them. Not necessarily because Fox News has high-quality information, but because the other guys are dishonest, politically biased, and misleading their audience.

Here, I hope to explore the lessons I've learned from writing critically about race, social issues, and society for more than a dozen years, unraveling the potent tangle of messages that so often pit us against each other.

Along the way, I hope to turn us all into race-baiters of a sort: those working together to insist on a new way of communicating from a media structure too addicted to controversy, division, and conflict to make it happen alone.

Perhaps, at long last, it's time for the audience to save media from itself.

ONE

FOX NEWS CHANNEL VS. MSNBC

*Downgrading All Journalism in the
Race to Win a Political Fight*

SITTING IN MY OFFICE ON A THURSDAY NIGHT, WATCHING TV COV-
erage of an emotional rally in Sanford, Florida, to protest the shooting death
of 17-year-old African American high school student Trayvon Martin, it felt
like I was seeing media history made before my eyes.

Martin, a teen visiting with his father from South Florida, was killed by
a self-appointed neighborhood watchman named George Zimmerman on
February 26, 2012. The teen was unarmed, holding just a bag of candy and a
bottle of iced tea. The shooter—identified as a white male in the initial police
report, but actually a Hispanic man with a Peruvian mother and Caucasian
father—said he shot Martin in self-defense after the youth attacked him.[1]
Weeks after the incident, among the few undisputed facts was a tragic reality: A young black teen was dead, and the man who killed him hadn't been
arrested.

And so on March 22, 2012, Rev. Al Sharpton also was making a small
bit of media history: as a civil rights activist leading a rally that would draw
thousands to a tiny town about 20 miles northeast of Orlando, just before
anchoring his MSNBC show, *PoliticsNation,* from the grounds of the rally,
and leading chants demanding local police arrest Zimmerman and fire the
current police chief.[2]

"Early today, Trayvon's parents, attorney, and I met with the Justice Department here," said Sharpton, who got involved with the case soon after 911 tapes of Zimmerman's call to police that fateful night were released. On the call, Zimmerman reported a suspicious person at the subdivision who turned out to be Martin.[3]

Sharpton, who learned on the morning of the March 22 rally that his 87-year-old mother had died in Atlanta, scoffed at news that the town's police chief, Bill Lee, temporarily removed himself from the job amid the growing media coverage and protests.

"Temporarily?" the activist asked, before turning to interview Martin's mother, father, and family attorney. "Temporarily is not enough. This man needs to be removed permanently. And let's not lose sight of the fact that Trayvon Martin's killer, George Zimmerman, still walks free."[4]

In a sense, this was the Al Sharpton every news junkie was used to seeing. For those troubled by his activist past, Sharpton was hitching his wagon to another high-profile, racially charged case. To those who saw how effectively he marshaled public attention and media coverage, it was proof that the reverend could help bring worldwide focus to a killing that might have gone unnoticed.

TV viewers were also used to seeing opinionated hosts weigh in on criminal cases in process. But in that moment on his MSNBC show, Sharpton brought all those roles together in one instant: an opinionated anchor leading an hour-long crusade on a major cable news channel while advocating for the victim's family, leading a rally, and even collecting money on their behalf from the rally crowd (according to the Associated Press, Sharpton kicked off the donations with a $2,500 pledge, joined by $10,000 gifts from radio host Michael Baisden and TV judge Greg Mathis).[5]

As an advocate, Sharpton raised a host of important issues: Was Martin singled out for attention by Zimmerman for his race? Did police move too slowly to investigate the killing? Had the teen been a victim of "Walking While Black"—having the unfortunate luck to draw attention from an armed volunteer watchman just because he was a young black man?

But Sharpton's involvement at the heart of the Martin case raised questions for media critics, too.

I talked about it on CNN, appearing on media critic Howard Kurtz's show *Reliable Sources* on March 25, 2012: "The problem is that MSNBC has to cover this as a news organization and as I said, we're getting to the point where George Zimmerman is starting to speak up, the man who shot Trayvon Martin. He has an attorney. He has a side. Is he going to feel like he can talk to NBC News or MSNBC and be treated fairly when one of their signature on-air personalities has spent weeks talking about how he should be arrested and he should be in jail?"[6]

When NBC News was later criticized for the way it edited audio of Zimmerman's 911 call to police—cutting out a moment when the dispatcher asked Martin's race, so it appeared the volunteer watchman offered the information on his own—the network apologized privately to reporters and fired the producer and a reporter connected to the story, while assuring media critics and the public the omission was a mistake.[7]

But, in part because of Sharpton's role at MSNBC, some critics asked if the network's editing actions were deliberate. For news professionals, that sounded far-fetched, but sometimes journalism is a game of appearances as much as reality.

And it raised an uncomfortable question: Where does the line between news channel and opinion channel really lie?

MSNBC spokesman Jeremy Gaines replied to these questions with an email: "When Rev. Sharpton joined MSNBC, it was with the understanding that he would continue to do his advocacy work," Gaines wrote me, three days after the rally in Sanford. "We're fully aware of that work and we have an ongoing dialogue. His participation in these events is very public and our audience is completely aware of where he stands on the issues. It's because of this work and his decades of activism that Rev. Sharpton brings such a unique perspective to our line up."[8]

It's a position that sounded an awful lot like treading water, taking advantage of the notoriety and attention that comes from having an anchor at the forefront of the hottest story of the year without addressing the implications of making a major face at MSNBC also a face for the family at the center of a still-contested murder case.

And, of course, at the heart of all these issues were questions of racism.

One reason the Martin story became an international issue—I saw stories about Sanford's police chief stepping down in French, Australian, and English newspapers—is because of the early work by journalists of color: columnist Charles Blow at the *New York Times*, Trymaine Lee at the *Huffington Post*, Roland Martin at CNN, and Sharpton and Melissa Harris-Perry at MSNBC. Though Martin was killed on February 26, national media outlets didn't begin talking about his story until more than a week later, as his family began speaking to the press, wondering why their son's killer hadn't been arrested.

Ryan Julison, a Florida-based public relations expert, was asked to help spread word about the case by an attorney for Martin's family. He found initially that getting national media attention was tough, and said he used early stories by Reuters and *CBS This Morning* to push local media into attending a press conference held by the family on March 8.

Julison had also worked to publicize the cases of a drum major at historically black Florida A&M University who died amid allegations of hazing, and a homeless African American man assaulted by the son of a lieutenant in the Sanford police department.[9]

"The race issue certainly plays heavy in the media, but it depends on how clean and how easy the story is to tell," said Julison. In his other race-related cases, he noted, the victims were less sympathetic: a twentysomething college student who willingly joined the school's marching band and a homeless black man who struggled with drug addiction. But Martin, a black teen with no history of violence and no weapon on his person, was a seemingly uncomplicated case.

"The media wants to frame a story that's easy to tell," he added. "Unarmed teen, shot down by an armed—at the time we thought he was white—neighborhood watch guy, that's an easier frame. Race is explosive and it certainly is a huge determining factor in coverage, but it depends on how it is framed and told."

Still, Julison said, other major national TV news outlets were hesitant to spend much time on the story until March 16, when audio of 911 calls from Zimmerman and residents at the subdivision were released. Local police had resisted making the calls public until Sanford mayor Jeff Triplett ordered their release; when they were revealed, the drama of the audio expanded the story.[10]

The city's police chief had said that Zimmerman didn't know Martin's race, but the audio revealed the volunteer watchman had told the 911 dispatcher that the youth "looks black"; Zimmerman seemed to continue following the teen after a dispatcher told him it was not necessary; and calls from neighbors revealed high-pitched screams that sounded like a young person, stilled after a gunshot.[11]

"I remember having conversations with [ABC News reporter] Matt Gutman and [NBC News correspondent] Kerry Sanders; they were struggling to get the story on the air," Julison said of the days before the 911 audio was released. "The 911 tapes gave them the ammunition they needed. It hit the *Today* show and hit everywhere; it set the table. We were on the morning shows and the evening news shows every day."[12]

More than anything, the audio provided some objective evidence that the parents' suspicions might be right, the public relations expert added. "They provided the emotion. People wanted to side with us, and this gave them the reason to . . . The media takes the racial dynamic, because it incites people to pick a side."

For some, it was proof of how stereotyping and prejudice in society can cause more than hurt feelings or offended sensibilities.

Associated Press writer Jesse Washington, an African American who covers race and ethnicity, wrote a moving column about explaining the "black male code" to his son, warning the 12-year-old that others' fears of him, simply because of his race and gender, could be deadly if he didn't learn how to carry himself in a non-threatening way.[13]

Even conservative news outlets such as Fox News Channel seemed a little stunned by the circumstances, at first.

As Sharpton was speaking to thousands in Sanford on March 22, Bill O'Reilly opened that evening's edition of *The O'Reilly Factor* by talking about how the liberal watchdogs at Media Matters aired radio ads critical of conservative pundit Rush Limbaugh. O'Reilly didn't get to Trayvon Martin until more than halfway through his show, asking fellow anchor and attorney Megyn Kelly about the police chief stepping down.[14] Later that evening, on his 9 P.M. show, Fox News anchor Sean Hannity would ask, "Is it possible it's a horrible accident?"

Then Geraldo Rivera stepped in it. Big time.

In an emotional appearance on the news channel's *Fox and Friends* show the day after the Sanford rally, Rivera zeroed in on Martin's clothing, implying that the hooded sweatshirt the teen wore made him look worthy of suspicion.

"I am urging the parents of black and Latino youngsters, particularly, to not let their children go out wearing hoodies," the anchor said, offering comments he later admitted even his son found shameful. "I think the hoodie is as much responsible for Trayvon Martin's death as George Zimmerman was."[15]

Angry that the anchor seemed to be blaming the victim, advising people of color to simply accept the stereotypes others have of them, critics drowned Rivera in nasty replies. Roland Martin, a pundit for CNN and black-centered cable channel TV One, concluded the man had "lost his mind."[16] Actor Wil Wheaton (*Star Trek: Next Generation*) tweeted: "Hoodies don't kill people. Paranoid racists with guns kill people." And the website Mediabistro dug up a photo of O'Reilly and Rivera, purportedly from 2007, sitting at a baseball game wearing—wait for it—hooded jackets and/or sweatshirts.

But liberating as it was to clobber Rivera for his insensitivity, his comments revealed an important question:

Should people, especially those who don't have power, such as racial minorities and women, change to conform to the system?

Or should the system change for them?

Too often, when ideologies clash in big media—especially on race and social issues—these are the questions at hand, buried beneath the jockeying for viewers, impact, and prominence.

Does America mostly work for everybody—which means that people who face adversity should just get over it and work harder—or is the system embedded with inequity, sexism, and racism that require tireless vigilance and constant advocacy to change?

These are faultlines entire media industries have been built on, from Fox News's tireless echo of conservative, middle-aged, middle-class white sensibilities (the system mostly works) to Pacifica Radio's string of progressive stations and shows, including flagship series *Democracy Now*'s challenge of America's corporations, militarism, and dominance by the wealthy (the system often doesn't work).

Applied to the Martin case, these divisions are easy to see. The *Orlando Sentinel* reported that white and black residents in Sanford interviewed randomly seemed split on the issue, with whites more hesitant to condemn the local police department for failing to arrest Zimmerman weeks after the teen's death. White residents more often had faith in the legal system, while black people viewed the lack of arrest as a reminder of the bad old days in Florida, when imperious police forces could disregard the rights of any person of color anytime.[17]

Even President Obama noted, "If I had a son, he'd look like Trayvon." Skilled as he was at avoiding typical approaches to talking about race, America's first black president had to admit that this situation felt a little bit personal.

Small wonder then that when Zimmerman eventually was arrested on April 11, a poll by news service Reuters and marketing firm Ipsos found that 91 percent of black people surveyed believed Martin was unjustly killed, compared to 35 percent of white people.[18]

But the racial dynamics in the Martin case seemed different and deeper than the superficial stories many national news outlets were telling.

The *Miami Herald* noted that the community where Martin was shot was a neighborhood in transition, with an influx of poorer people, people of color, and rising crime rates, raising tensions. In the year before the teen's death, there had been eight burglaries, nine thefts, and one other shooting in the area, according to the *Herald*.[19]

Some in Sanford's black community had longstanding frictions with the police department, accusing it of moving slowly to arrest the son of a police officer caught on video punching a homeless black man and of failing to adequately investigate two security guards who were eventually acquitted of killing a black man by citing self-defense.[20]

In my own work for the *Tampa Bay Times*, I wondered if some of this wasn't wrapped up in a too-simplistic notion of racism.

"We still, too often, act like racism is a switch—either you're Archie Bunker or David Duke and acting as a clear cut white supremacist, or you're not," I wrote for The Feed, my own media blog at the *Tampa Bay Times*. "But that's not how I think it works. Very often, people who would never consider themselves racist in other settings have very negative views of minorities in certain circumstances—say, if they live in a high-crime neighborhood where many offenses are committed by black or brown people."[21]

In the 45 days between Martin's death and Zimmerman's arrest, national media obsessed over the story in surprising and dismaying ways.

At the beginning, Zimmerman went into hiding and had no surrogates speaking for him. So the narrative of an innocent teen killed by an overzealous, wannabe cop seemed to hold sway. Cable news personalities such as Martin and Harris-Perry wore hooded sweatshirts on air, NBC aired video of several black on-air personalities talking about their experiences with racial profiling during the news magazine *Rock Center*, and an audio analysis by CNN broadcast on March 22 suggested Zimmerman complained about "fucking coons" during his 911 call to police.

Conservative bloggers and pundits began to complain of a rush to judgment, wondering why some news outlets described Zimmerman as a "white

Hispanic" (there are indeed white, black, and brown Hispanics, since the term describes people with family lineage from Spain, Portugal, or Latin America). They also complained that pictures of a much younger Martin were often shown alongside a mug shot of Zimmerman from a 2005 arrest.[22]

Julison said he gave reporters the only images he had: photos from Martin's funeral program. One of the only other photos of Zimmerman available before his 2012 arrest was an image of him smiling in a shirt, tie, and jacket, obtained from an unnamed source at his last place of employment by the *Orlando Sentinel* newspaper, which initially didn't give other news outlets the right to reproduce it. Eventually, after the image was distributed on several wire services, other news outlets began to use it.[23]

Some media quickly polarized along political lines. The conservative-friendly *Daily Caller* website published photos and messages from the dead teen's social media accounts featuring Martin with gold caps on his teeth, an image also featured on the popular right-wing Drudge Report website. Eventually, Fox News hosts and analysts such as Sean Hannity and Bernard Goldberg complained about the news coverage, with Goldberg insisting "they [mainstream news media] need the word 'white' to further the storyline, which is 'white, probably racist vigilante shoots unarmed black kid.'"[24]

Some of the criticisms made important points, pushing mainstream news outlets to look at NBC's editing of the 911 call and the use of photos in depicting Zimmerman and Martin. When CNN aired a story in which a different audio analyst contradicted their earlier reporting on the 911 audio, saying Zimmerman *didn't* use a racial slur after all, the conservative media watchdog Newsbusters.org noted the cable channel "had to walk back" its earlier report.[25] ABC News had similar problems when it aired surveillance video of Zimmerman entering police headquarters after the shooting; a blurry version seemed to show he had no injuries, contradicting his claims of a fight, but after the network digitally enhanced the footage days later, the image showed his head may have been injured.[26]

Still, some of the pro-Zimmerman pushback seemed to willfully ignore any racial issues, offering typical conservative accusations that "race-hustling" activists and a liberally biased media exaggerated the injustice of Martin's death.

Some commentaries veered into straight-up racism, including *National Review* columnist John Derbyshire's piece for the website *Taki's Magazine*, "The Talk: Nonblack Version," in which he advised his children to avoid large concentrations of black people and avoid helping black people in distress.[27] It was such a stark example of racism—Derbyshire claimed statistics would prove the "black stranger will be less intelligent than the white"—that the *National Review* severed all ties with him.[28]

The line between challenging so-called "political correctness" on racial issues and outright racism seemed to grow awfully thin—especially after the *National Review* was forced to jettison another contributor, Robert Weissberg, three days after dropping Derbyshire, upon discovering he participated in a white nationalist conference.[29]

Julison, the Martin family's PR expert, said the arrival of civil rights protestors such as Sharpton and Jesse Jackson helped fuel political polarization of the case, even as they brought greater attention.

"When you have civil rights activists getting involved, the story takes on a different tone," he added. "Al Sharpton helps bring attention, but the other side is galvanized because they can say 'We know where this is going.' In this situation, [Zimmerman's arrest] vindicated Sharpton in his involvement, but you also open things up to Fox News and the other side of the political spectrum. Now they have something to sink their teeth into; it did blur the issue."[30]

It was a blending of roles I had argued about with MSNBC executives and Sharpton himself months earlier. But after Zimmerman's arrest, Sharpton took a victory lap, welcoming Attorney General Eric Holder as featured speaker at the 2012 convention for his National Action Network.

Still, in many ways, my biggest concerns about his impact on the credibility of MSNBC, and TV journalists in general, were just starting to come true.

GIVEN THAT HE WAS TALKING TO A GUY who had openly criticized his hiring, the Rev. Al was pretty cordial when we finally met—on the telephone.

Always confident and supremely on message, he was ready to discuss an issue that had landed me on CNN and prompted him to skip a featured appearance at the 2011 National Association of Black Journalists' conference: his new status as the first black anchor anywhere near prime time on a major cable news channel.

"I didn't think it was the great leap that some people did," Sharpton said during our phone interview back in August 2011. "I was a little surprised that some people [objected] . . . No one objected to me doing the *Barbershop*

show on [black-centered TV network] TV One. No one objected to me doing a radio show or a column. To me, this was just a logical extension of what
I was already doing in media."[31]

But the Rev. Al Sharpton is no typical media figure.

On the surface, this would seem a victory for any advocate of diversity in
media. For years, critics had watched as the big cable TV news outlets handed
big anchor jobs to a succession of middle-aged white guys, peppered with a
few women. From MSNBC's Ed Schultz and Lawrence O'Donnell to CNN's
Eliot Spitzer, Kathleen Parker, Erin Burnett, and Piers Morgan, the long list
of featured faces on cable TV news channels in 2010 and 2011 seemed about
as diverse as your average country club cotillion.

Then, in July 2011, word leaked that MSNBC was considering Sharpton
for an hour-long show at 6 P.M., based on his success as a guest host for two
weeks that summer, filling in for vacationing Turkish American host and
YouTube sensation Cenk Uygur.[32] The departure of star Keith Olbermann
earlier that year had left the liberal-oriented network scrambling to mine
new talent for its ranks. But Uygur, whose pugnacious style drew millions of
viewers to his YouTube show The Young Turks, wasn't fitting in at MSNBC,
and by July 20, he was out the door.

News that Sharpton was about to join the ranks of punditizers at MSNBC
made noise in some quarters. Law professor and legal pundit Jonathan Turley,
known as a liberal-leaning voice occasionally willing to roil the waters with
a tart libertarian point of view, wrote that Sharpton's history—ranging from
his days championing the charges of rape made by Tawana Brawley in 1987
(found to be false by a grand jury) to tax problems—made him unfit to lead
an MSNBC show.[33]

"His selection destroys the credibility of MSNBC in its criticism of folks
like O'Reilly and Beck," Turley wrote on his blog. "It is a ratings-driven decision that does not consider impact on the credibility of MSNBC as a news
organization."[34]

Turley's opinion was echoed by voices from the left and right—from
blogger/columnist Glenn Greenwald, writing for *Salon*, to Jeff Dunetz, a
blogger on conservative activist Andrew Breitbart's Big Government website—citing Sharpton's controversial activist past or his seeming friendliness
with the Obama administration as concerns.

But the criticism stung particularly when it came from one unexpected
corner: black journalists.

As news of Sharpton's consideration began to circulate in the media, some journalists of color wondered whether the most significant anchor job for an African American at MSNBC should go to someone with no background as a journalist. On the email list of the National Association of Black Journalists, members debated the issue, trading opinions on whether Sharpton's hire was an appropriate response to an open letter the group had issued criticizing the lack of diversity in recent TV news anchor hires. The NAACP had also released a letter in July 2011 criticizing the lack of diversity in cable TV evening news shows, exemplified by prime time changes at CNN.

Richard Prince, author of Journal-isms, an online column dedicated to publishing stories on ethnic diversity and the news media, wrote: "When rumors surfaced this week that Sharpton was under consideration for the MSNBC job, one NABJ member told colleagues, without challenge, 'This would still be just another non-journalist media "celebrity" receiving a TV show based upon their name recognition, not their years of experience, training, ability and talent.'"[35]

Sharpton himself was upset enough about the comment to cancel a planned appearance at the NABJ convention that July.

For me, it was part of a bigger trend that included CNN's hiring of Eliot Spitzer, the former New York governor who resigned in disgrace after admitting liaisons with prostitutes. Hiring an anchor because he (or she) has fame and can draw viewers, regardless of their ability on television or experience navigating news and information on a national broadcast platform, just seemed a recipe for downgrading the channel's credibility in exchange for ratings points.

"It's a larger problem," I told host Howard Kurtz on his CNN show about media issues, *Reliable Sources*. "When you see somebody like Eliot Spitzer even get a show, then he has to cover the peccadilloes of a politician who is caught in a sexual scandal, all of a sudden there is a resonance there you wouldn't necessarily have if you had someone with a straight journalism background in that job."[36]

To his credit, Sharpton didn't mention any of that when we finally spoke. But he did profess surprise that all his critics—including journalists pushing for more diversity in TV news—would highlight his new job while staying silent as former radio stars such as Sean Hannity, Glenn Beck, Rachel Maddow, and Ed Schultz took over key segments of the cable TV news landscape.

Worrying about leapfrogging radio pundits over TV journalists in cable news is "a legitimate concern," admitted Sharpton. "But those of us who have been in advocacy and those of us that have been in radio are saying that they are taking people who have been in radio . . . and putting them in [TV] slots, why can't they take us? Why is there a different standard for us?"[37]

In a statement made to black-focused website *Loop21.com,* Sharpton was even more explicit, arguing that the place where political conflict occurs now is on cable TV news.[38] For an activist like himself, gaining an hour-long foothold on MSNBC was like claiming space on the civil rights battlefield.

"When you look at the last 15 years, there was a rise of the Right Wing that manifested itself through George W. Bush and later the Tea Party," he told the website in a statement. "A lot of that was driven by talk show news. The battlefield now is in the studio of radio and talk television. You can't go to the Jordan River with a Red Sea strategy, and I applaud MSNBC for their strategy."[39]

And that, simply stated, may be the biggest problem.

In a traditional journalism environment, even opinion writers are expected to obey some standards of fairness and detachment—a willingness to consider all sides while pushing for intellectual honesty and clarity.

You're expected, in other words, to be an honest broker.

But if your goal is to win an ideological battle with a group of opponents clustered in other media outlets—in Sharpton's case, right-wing and tea party movement favorites such as Sean Hannity and Glenn Beck—the fight goes beyond a clash of ideas.

For many years, critics have lambasted Fox News Channel for unfairly supporting GOP politicians and conservative political protests such as the tea party movement.

In a 2008 interview with MSNBC host Chris Matthews, former Bush press secretary Scott McClellan implied that the White House was helped by Fox News pundits and commentators who echoed their spin on political issues—including "whether intentional or not . . . misleading [the public] about the reason for going to war" in Iraq—after receiving talking points from the administration.[40]

And as followers of the then-nascent tea party movement began to hold massive protests against President Obama's fiscal policies in 2009, critics such as the liberal media watch group Media Matters documented in detail the way in which Fox News personalities and the channel itself seemed to be publicizing and helping to organize the events.

The *Los Angeles Times* reported that Fox News executives ordered Fox News personality Sean Hannity to drop his participation in a widely publicized tea party Tax Day rally on April 15, 2010, when they discovered organizers were charging attendees $20 each to see his speech, with proceeds going to fund future movement events.[41]

But what of Sharpton joining with the American Federation of State, County and Municipal Employees and other groups to hold rallies in 25 different cities protesting economic disparity on December 9, 2011?[42] Or when the MSNBC host wrote a column for the liberal-oriented *Huffington Post* website urging fans to join a branch of the Occupy Wall Street protests in their area?[43]

In the Trayvon Martin case, Sharpton sometimes pivoted from leading rallies or press conferences for Martin's parents to interviewing them and their attorneys for his MSNBC show on the same day.

Many weeks before Sharpton began his work on the Martin case, I asked MSNBC president Phil Griffin if he was concerned about having his highest-profile black host come from an activist background rather than journalism.

"When I watch Rev. Al . . . I'm proud of him on our air, and I knew what he would be, but he has surprised an awful lot of people with the fairness on that program that he does every night," Griffin said in a January 2012 interview. "Yes, he has a point of view but he brings on all types, he speaks from authority and I'm very proud of what he does. I'd rather celebrate than worry about, you know, definitions and categories and where people begin their careers."[44]

Griffin has often used the lack of official content directives from his executives—along with the presence of conservative *Morning Joe* host Joe Scarborough—as proof that his channel does not offer the kind of lockstep political advocacy critics decry in rival Fox News.

But it is also obvious that the sharply drawn opinions advanced by MSNBC personalities in the evening hours—Griffin maintains that the channel's "prime time" starts at 5 P.M. and stretches to 11 P.M.—would be difficult if not impossible for a traditional, "objective" journalist to present.

As many critics have noticed, even some anchors considered to be in MSNBC's newsier afternoon hours, such as Tamron Hall, Martin Bashir, and

Thomas Roberts, have taken to expressing opinions during their shows and in promos.

So what about an anchor who goes beyond offering sharp opinions? What can be said about a cable news channel host who organizes protest marches, supports protest movements, and leverages a national organization to protest specific legislation when he's not on the air?

Early in his MSNBC tenure, Sharpton himself insisted that his advocacy efforts would not be supportive of specific political candidates, which would violate the tax-exempt status of his National Action Network[45] and, presumably, NBC News standards (the ethical guidelines developed by the network's news division also apply to its sister cable news channel).[46]

"A civil rights group can't endorse candidates," Sharpton told me in August 2011. "Glenn Beck and others have done their activism marches while they have been affiliated with [a cable news channel] and I will continue what I do with National Action Network. None of it is partisan political."[47]

But the question of whether such activity is obviously partisan may be in the eye of the beholder.

For many consumers of TV news, cable news channels are morphing before their eyes from reporting vehicles to political/punditry operations.

And what does that do to the notion of an objective truth?

IT'S NO SECRET THE PUBLIC HAS LITTLE LOVE for journalists these days.

In fact, recent polls indicate the public has serious and growing doubts about journalists' adherence to their core mission: the delivery of fair and fearless reporting on the heart of important issues.

And we may have the partisan cable news channels to thank for it all.

The Pew Center for People and the Press released a report in September 2011—ten years after news organizations across America notched some of their greatest triumphs reporting on the terrorist attacks of 9/11—documenting some of the most negative public opinions about journalists since its tracking began 26 years ago.[48]

The report did find that respondents trusted information from national news organizations more than information from state governments, Barack Obama's presidential administration, the federal government, business corporations, and Congress.[49]

But when asked whether news organizations are often influenced by powerful people and organizations, 80 percent of respondents agreed. On the question of whether news outlets tend to favor one side, 77 percent agreed.

Regarding mistakes, 66 percent said news outlets' stories are often inaccurate and 72 percent said these organizations try to cover up any errors.

And on the subject of political bias, the public was also clear: 63 percent felt news outlets were politically biased in their reporting.

This was a tremendous slide from 1985, when 55 percent of respondents said news organizations tend to get their facts straight, 34 percent said stories are often inaccurate, and only 45 percent said news organizations were politically biased.[50]

Such numbers could spell serious trouble for modern news outlets. But the Pew Center's information also revealed that 66 percent of respondents said they get most of their news from television, with the Internet pulling a distant second at 43 percent.[51]

Why the discrepancy? Why are so many people spending so much time getting news from organizations they distrust so much?

Once again, the Pew Center's numbers offer an answer. People trust the news sources *they* use regularly more than media outlets in general.

"When asked to rate the accuracy of stories from the sources where they get most of their news, the percentage saying these outlets get the facts straight more than doubles," read a section from the report's overview. "Fully 62 percent say their main news sources get the facts straight, while just 30 percent say stories [from sources they regularly consume] are often inaccurate."[52]

What makes the difference in such results?

One idea involves the notion of "confirmation bias," or the tendency of people to believe information that validates beliefs or ideas they already hold and reject evidence to the contrary.

In the same way that potential voters may trust politicians who represent them directly yet cite the current U.S. Congress as the least accomplished and most frustrating in modern history, TV news outlets can continue to draw viewers, despite record levels of negative opinions about them in the public at large.[53]

And there is one more notion worth consideration in the Pew Center poll on attitudes about news.

Even though the world of news media has never been more diverse—with a multiplicity of websites, weblogs, video blogs, online video channels, podcasts, email newsletters, and cable news channels joining the traditional array of newspapers, magazines, TV channels, and radio outlets available to consumers—there is one platform the Pew Center says dominates how Americans view the modern media.

The cable news channel.

"It is clear that television news outlets, specifically cable news outlets, are central to people's impressions of the news media," said the study. "When asked what first comes to mind when they think of news organizations, 63 percent volunteer the name of a cable news outlet, with CNN and Fox News by far the most prevalent in people's minds. Only about a third (36 percent) name one of the broadcast networks. Fewer than one-in-five mention local news outlets and only 5 percent mention a national newspaper such as the *New York Times, Wall Street Journal,* or *USA Today*."[54]

So it may be no coincidence that the rise in negative feelings about news outlets coincides with the rise of cable news channels, with some of the biggest dips in attitudes about accuracy, fairness, and independence coming between 2007 and 2011—the years in which MSNBC became an increasingly successful, liberal-leaning competitor to Fox News.[55]

It is also true that these negative feelings coincide with the spread of the Internet and social media—allowing news consumers to access a greater variety of reports on a single issue with more speed than ever before. In such an environment, plagiarism, fabrication, and mistakes can be exposed more quickly and more broadly than ever, leading educated news consumers to understand how even the most respected news organizations can feature major inaccuracies in their material.

But the opinion poll numbers lead to a natural question: Could the manner in which some cable news channels have become political battlefields actually help increase Americans' distrust for all journalism?

DAVID FRUM MIGHT BE THE LAST PUNDIT you would expect to sound an alarm on the damaging effects of political advocacy disguised as news coverage.

A Harvard Law School graduate who once described himself as having been a Republican "all my adult life," Frum worked on the ultra-conservative editorial page of the *Wall Street Journal* before joining George W. Bush's White House administration as his economic speechwriter.[56]

But Frum has also long displayed a lack of patience with the shortcomings of conservatism, particularly intellectual inconsistency. His departure from the American Enterprise Institute came days after he published a blog post criticizing the Republicans' unwillingness to cut deals for concessions to health care legislation pushed by President Obama. (He argued conservatives had been pushed into an untenable position by right-wing radio and TV figures.)[57]

And in November 2011, Frum wrote a commentary for *New York* magazine decrying the "alternative knowledge system" created by an array of conservative-oriented media and information outlets—from Fox News Channel and Rush Limbaugh's radio show to an array of right-leaning book publishing houses, think tanks, magazines, and websites. Titled "When Did the GOP Lose Touch with Reality?" the piece was a bracing critique warning that a "flight from reality and responsibility" could doom the Republican Party, simply because its most important political ideas were increasingly divorced from actual facts and logic.[58]

But Frum's observations about the conservative media's role in creating and fomenting these notions could just as easily apply to big, politically skewed news media outlets outside the right-wing universe—explaining why fans cleave to the messages of their preferred news outlet across the board, even as news consumers overall see their output as increasingly inaccurate and compromised.

"Extremism and conflict make for bad politics but great TV," Frum wrote. "The business model of the conservative media is built on two elements: provoking the audience into a fever of indignation (to keep them watching) and fomenting mistrust of all other information sources (so that they never change the channel). As a commercial proposition, this model has worked brilliantly in the Obama era. As journalism, not so much."[59]

Frum's words call to mind the classic slogans of cable news giant Fox News Channel: "We Report, You Decide" (perhaps compared to rivals, who may decide for you), and the phrase Fox trademarked in 1998, "Fair and Balanced Journalism" (as opposed to other outlets, which hide their bias).

"Conservatives have built a whole alternative knowledge system, with its own facts, its own history, [and] its own laws of economics," Frum's *New York* piece argued. "Outside this alternative reality, the United States is a country dominated by a strong Christian religiosity. Within it, Christians are a persecuted minority. Outside the system, President Obama—whatever his policy errors—is a figure of imposing intellect and dignity. Within the system, he's a pitiful nothing, unable to speak without a teleprompter, an affirmative-action phony doomed to inevitable defeat."[60]

Apply these notions to the corner of modern media that molds most viewers' perceptions about the news industry—the cable news channels—and it's no surprise the public lacks confidence (except, of course, in the news sources each person regularly consults).

Frum enlarged his comments to speak specifically about television during an appearance on CNN's *Reliable Sources* media analysis show in December 2011.

"TV enhances its own credibility by destroying the credibility of all other institutions, and you can see this in polls," Frum told host Howard Kurtz. "When other institutions' credibility declined, TV's credibility goes up . . . You need to create conflict and you need to create a sense of embattlement. You need to create a sense that we, this network, are your only reliable friends."[61]

Small wonder, then, that a 2010 survey by the Democratic company Public Policy Polling showed that nearly as many Americans *distrusted* Fox News (37 percent) as trusted them (49 percent). Among Republicans, that trust number stood at 74 percent, compared to only 30 percent of Democrats.[62]

A more recent Public Policy Polling survey released in January 2012 found that when asked which outlets they trust the most and least, respondents placed Fox News at the top of both lists, with the same percentage: 34 percent.[63] Among Republicans, 68 percent picked Fox News as their most trusted source; Democrats trusted NBC, PBS, and CNN in descending order (MSNBC scored sixth, with 8 percent of Democrats); and PBS was trusted by the most people (52 percent), though not trusted most by any of them.[64]

"Television news has become just as polarizing as the politicians themselves," said Dean Debnam, president of Public Policy Polling, when quoted in an overview of the poll results. "Democrats trust everything except Fox News, while Republicans trust nothing except Fox News."[65]

In the end, a firm understanding of how these channels turn political ideas into content and mobilize fans may be the average viewer's best defense.

MSNBC WASN'T ALWAYS A LOUD, LIBERAL-LEANING OPPONENT to right-centered Fox News. Instead, there was a time when chunks of its programming felt like a faded echo.

I saw the evidence myself up close during a 2003 trip to New York, where I spent time with the then–relatively new MSNBC anchor Joe Scarborough, a former member of the U.S. House of Representatives not long out of Congress who was hosting a 10 P.M. show for them called *Scarborough Country.*[66]

We were just two years past the 9/11 attacks and months into the start of war with Iraq. MSNBC was then broadcasting from studios in Secaucus, New Jersey—long before it would move to its current Manhattan location—struggling with its stance on the issues of the day. Earlier that year, the channel had fired its biggest star, former daytime talk pioneer Phil Donahue, whose self-named show had featured consistent criticism of the Bush administration's arguments for war, and MSNBC seemed determined to position itself as a patriotic window into the conflict.

By the time I arrived in the studios that May, the newsroom—often shown in the background of shots on camera—was swathed in reds and blues, and American flag stickers dotted personal computers in the room, complimenting the huge flag overhanging the studio's reception area.[67] Alongside one wall, a multitude of pictures showing soldiers were tacked up as a tribute, the inspiration and backdrop for their "America's Bravest" feature stories on U.S. fighters.

The moves seemed a response to the tenor of the times and, more specifically, the ratings. Back then, rival Fox News Channel's viewership was soaring thanks to its own patriotic war coverage, which included hiring retired Lt. Col. Oliver North as a reporter embedded with American troops and incorporating the U.S. flag into their onscreen logo.[68]

MSNBC countered with its own patriotism offensive, including promotional ads featuring a photo montage of soldiers in Iraq as a piano version of "The Star-Spangled Banner" tinkled in the background.[69] Hard as it may be for MSNBC fans to believe now, the channel that would eventually give major anchor jobs to Rachel Maddow and Al Sharpton featured conservative voices back in 2003, bringing on former Nixon aide Pat Buchanan, conservative talk radio host Michael Savage, and Scarborough, a conservative former legislator from Florida's panhandle.[70]

Even then, Scarborough, a politician more likely to poke fun at enemies than excoriate them, was chafing at the strident, right-wing rhetoric some MSNBC executives seemed to want, mimicking Fox News Channel star Bill O'Reilly.

"They wanted me to be little O'Reilly, and it wasn't a position I was comfortable with," said Scarborough five years later, as his *Morning Joe* show was climbing in the ratings and he was the only conservative host still employed at MSNBC. "Starting in about 2004, I started to move away from that . . . I wasn't really comfortable being shocked and stunned six segments a night, five days a week."[71]

Instead, once the shock of negotiating America's trauma over 9/11 and wars in Iraq and Afghanistan had subsided, MSNBC found its voice in star Keith Olbermann, who morphed his show *Countdown* from a breezy satire of the news into a pointed denunciation of the worst in right-wing politics and a support of centrist liberal ideals.

When I once asked whether such polarization of cable news has a negative effect, MSNBC anchor Lawrence O'Donnell sounded a philosophical note while resisting the notion that ideological opposition was necessarily a bad thing.

"All I can tell you, is the audience has voted," said O'Donnell, speaking during a 2010 press reception months before starting his show *The Last Word.* "The audience has said in prime time cable news, we want political opinion television and, you know, that's why they're not watching what they used to watch, and they are watching Keith. That's why they're watching Rachel. It's why they watch Fox."[72]

It's also a lot easier—and cheaper—to present opinions on a regular basis, night after night.

Fox News, created and controlled by master TV producer/onetime political consultant Roger Ailes, targets its audience with the precision of a political campaign.

Stars such as Bill O'Reilly, Sean Hannity, and Megyn Kelly offer a product clearly tailored toward right-wing constituencies, regularly championing issues political conservatives find important while peppering their discussions with easily understood heroes and villains.

For O'Reilly, it might be the notion that anti-religious elements want to eliminate Christmas celebrations as a way to "destroy religion in the public arena," as he once said on his show, which featured a segment called "Christmas Under Siege."[73] Kelly earned notoriety by insisting that the Department of Justice under President Obama may have shied away from prosecuting members of the New Black Panther Party for voter intimidation because of race, even threatening to cut off the microphone of liberal commentator Kirsten Powers when she disagreed.[74]

In both cases, the controversies aimed to evoke potent fears among white Republicans—that the country is becoming so godless it will turn its back on Christmas, or that a black president might turn his back on enforcing laws that protect white, GOP-supporting voters against black radicals.

Such coverage is consistent and relatively cheap. Viewers tune in to see O'Reilly or Hannity's take, regardless of the day's news; traditional journalists must wait for big news events or spend time digging up their own blockbusters.

Finally, in what is Ailes's masterstroke, Fox News's formatting helps weld fans to the idea that the channel is a counterweight to presumed liberal bias among traditional news outlets.

"Every other network has given all their shows to liberals," Ailes told Howard Kurtz, former media critic at the *Washington Post,* writing on tonal shifts at Fox as Washington bureau chief for the *Daily Beast* website and *Newsweek* magazine. "We [Fox News] are the balance."[75]

Fox News Sunday host Chris Wallace, a former host of NBC's *Meet the Press* and ex-ABC News journalist, echoed Ailes's thinking in a 2011 interview with *Daily Show* host Jon Stewart on Wallace's own program.[76]

The discussion crystallized two rising narratives about the state of modern news reporting. To Stewart, the problem with modern news media—especially television news and particularly the 24-hour cable news channels—is the addiction to conflict, controversy, and attention-grabbing coverage.

But to Wallace, echoing the words of Fox News founder Ailes, such sentiments were a dodge. In the Fox News universe, journalists at mainstream news outlets are planting subtle messages that downgrade conservatives.

When Stewart asked whether Wallace saw Fox News as the "ideological equivalent" to NBC News, Wallace replied: "I think we're the counterweight . . . I think that they have a liberal agenda and I think we tell the other side of the story."[77] A week later, Wallace tried to explain his comment more fully, citing coverage of local and state dysfunction during the flooding caused by Hurricane Katrina as an example of the ways in which his show didn't just criticize the federal government—then led by Republican George W. Bush—for the crisis.[78]

"I wish I had said 'the *full* story,'" Wallace said in his commentary, after noting that the *Huffington Post* slapped a giant headline on coverage of the original interview with the Stewart quote, "You're insane."[79] His implication: Even coverage of the Stewart interview showed political bias in media.

But Wallace didn't tell his viewers that the *Huffington Post* is an *openly* biased media outlet—a liberal-focused website. It would be expected to feature Stewart's criticisms of Fox News and Wallace prominently.

No matter. Wallace's update served its real purpose: to assure *Fox News Sunday* viewers that his show and his employers were the news outlets they really should trust.

Even a Fox News employee who wrote a book about how the nation's argument culture is stifling honest debate and hamstringing government—Juan Williams, whose 2011 book *Muzzled* detailed his firing from National Public Radio—declined to criticize his employer for its contributions to the political fights in media.

"One party dominance and one-sided thinking have become the rule rather than the exception in much of the media," wrote Williams, who blamed such orthodoxy at NPR for an increasing friction that culminated with his ouster in October 2010 after noting on Fox News that he got "nervous" on airplanes with people in "Muslim garb."[80]

"Things became much more polarized in terms of the media landscape over the course of the 10-year period I was at NPR and for some of the bosses at NPR, it became not just that he's doing cable TV and he's doing radio but he's not reliably defined in the NPR mold," Williams told me later, in an interview about the book.[81]

"I think they wanted to control [my] brand in such a way as to fit a specific niche in the media landscape," he added. "An upper-income, highly-educated, white, skews male audience that is the target audience for NPR."[82]

But when I asked about why, if he thinks such discourse is harmful to the country, he accepted a multi-year contract at Fox News after his NPR firing, Williams insisted the news channel wasn't a pioneer in polarizing discourse.

"I think it's the entire media structure," he said. "To my mind, if I look at the editorial page of the *New York Times* it's clearly starkly liberal. If I look at the editorial page of the *Wall Street Journal,* it's clearly starkly conservative. If I'm talking to conservatives, they say Hollywood is filled with a bunch of liberals . . . anti-family and anti-conservative. If I talk to people who are liberals, they say talk radio in this country is filled with a bunch of right wing nuts . . . This is a much larger framework than saying, oh well, Fox came on the scene and created this reality."[83]

It was interesting to note how Williams lumped the editorial pages of newspapers—which are supposed to have a political point of view—in with outlets expected to be more neutral, in the same way Wallace compared the *Huffington Post* and Comedy Central to Fox News.

My own thesis: The mainstream American news media has lots of biases, including a bias toward conflict, celebrity, impact, ratings, profitability, wealth, and the concerns of its sponsors. For most mainstream news outlets, these biases affect their news product far more substantially than any specific political bias, but they are so pervasive and accepted that the lay viewer sometimes barely notices their impact.

Additionally, journalists often are steeped in the social justice imperative of reporting. That means taking very seriously the news media's role as the Fourth Estate in American society: an aggressive watchdog of government, a voice for the average person without wealth or power, and a check on the influence and authority of major institutions such as big corporations in an effort to ensure equal treatment for everyone.

Elements of the ethics code approved by the Society of Professional Journalists speak to these ideas, urging journalists to "give voice to the voiceless," noting that "official and unofficial sources of information can be equally valid." Additionally, journalists are warned to "examine their own cultural values and avoid imposing those values on others," while "[avoiding] stereotyping by race, gender, age, religion, ethnicity, geography, sexual orientation, disability, physical appearance or social status."[84]

Altruistic as these ideas sound, in practice they can also seem a bit like left-wing ideology to a political conservative.

What Fox News's "counterweight" approach really does is take advantage of the unsettling feeling some conservatives have that the core notions motivating traditional journalists don't reflect how right-wing news consumers see the world. Ailes has created a TV universe where the way conservatives *feel* the world should work is the way it *does* work—at least for all the anchors and pundits speaking to viewers through Fox News.

Along the way, any news outlets challenging that worldview are denounced as biased and unworthy of trust, teaching the largest niche of loyal cable TV news viewers that any journalism that opposes their core values is dishonest and inaccurate.

In an environment like this, how can anyone even be sure what good journalism really is?

TWO

INFORMATION WARS

How Partisan Media Manipulate
Facts to Get Your Attention

LESS THAN TWO MONTHS BEFORE HE SUDDENLY COLLAPSED AND
died on a walk not far from his California home, Andrew Breitbart tried to
school me on how liberals use race to divide the nation.

I had called his cellphone on a whim in late January (it seems everyone who covered politics *or* media had his digits). And even though it was a
Saturday afternoon and he had somewhere to go, Breitbart spent nearly an
hour explaining why he is driven to debunk claims of racism in society.

"I'm pointing out how race is used as a weapon by the left," he said,
speaking in great bursts of excited phrases.

"I'm really mostly just the Number One cultural critic of political correctness, multiculturalism, and cultural Marxism as it infects cultural institutions like the mainstream media, Hollywood and academia," Breitbart
said. "Race arsonists out there . . . their goal is to split our country into black
versus white, straight versus gay . . . They use the news media in order to fight
to keep narratives in place in order to separate these people."[1]

Breitbart passed away at age 43 on March 1, 2012; officials in the Los
Angeles County coroner's office would later announce he died of heart failure.[2] Friends and foes alike marveled in posthumous essays about his career
or his seemingly boundless energy in pursuing cultural and political combat.

When we spoke, he used the term "racism by proxy syndrome" to describe incidents in which allegations of racial prejudice are found to be untrue, from an African American exotic dancer's contention that she was raped by white members of Duke University's lacrosse team to Al Sharpton's infamous support of rape allegations made in 1987 by Tawana Brawley, a black teen whose claim that she was sexually assaulted by six white men was rejected by a grand jury.[3]

Like other conservatives I've spoken with on these issues, he didn't seem to make any allowances for when allegations of racist attacks *were* true—like, say, when 19-year-old Deryl Dedmon, who is white, was sentenced to two life sentences on March 21, 2012, after pleading guilty to murder and hate crime charges in killing a black man by running over him in a truck.[4]

Still, Breitbart's weapon of choice when it came to fighting his war on "racism by proxy" was obvious: the new-media world of blogs, online video, independent websites, and activist, politically focused media aggregators.

"Use your videotape, use your camera, use your cellphone as a weapon," said the blogger, whose work developing the liberal-oriented *Huffington Post* and writing for the right-leaning Drudge Report—two of the online world's biggest politically oriented news websites—is the stuff of media legend. "We've been able to use new media because people come to our sites. And people come to new media because they have less trust in the mainstream media because of its inherent political biases . . . We're able to do the hard-lifting investigative journalism that the mainstream media used to do."[5]

The adopted son of upper-middle-class parents in California, Breitbart has spoken often of his early years as a liberal, partying through college and struggling to find a direction. According to his book *Righteous Indignation*, his father-in-law Orson Bean—yeah, the actor who was always on the *Tonight Show, that* Orson Bean—got him thinking about conservatism by suggesting he listen to Rush Limbaugh's radio show.

In the book, he described how "Professor Limbaugh" and other AM talk radio hosts helped convince him that conservative politics made more sense than his previous liberal beliefs (in a subsequent chapter, I'll talk more about how all those radio shows evolved, and how *they* talk about race and social issues).

Through his early jobs delivering scripts in Hollywood to getting on the Internet in early 1993, connecting with Drudge soon after, and helping

Arianna Huffington with her website, Breitbart learned the inner workings of three very important worlds: media, online technology, and celebrity.

Small surprise then, that many years later he became a new kind of combatant in the culture wars: a politically motivated, cyber-savvy information warrior.

And race was the controversial honey he sometimes used to attract attention. "The narrative is controlled by the media. The left *is* the media," Breitbart wrote in *Righteous Indignation.* "Narrative is everything."[6]

Amelia Arsenault, an assistant professor at Georgia State University specializing in new media and politics, has studied Breitbart and the other information warriors he has inspired, in hopes of writing a book on their strategies and influence.

Arsenault said Breitbart's use of race-related controversies seemed "more of a business strategy": he seeks out the most incendiary topics to drive visitors to his array of websites, in the same way newspapers of the late 1800s chased scandals to drive up their readership.

"Even back in the days of yellow journalism, you saw these large newspapers building up their model through the politics of scandal, attracting attention," she said, referring to the reputation newspapers such as William Randolph Hearst's *New York Journal* had for exaggerating stories or using lurid headlines to draw readers. "People who are driven by an ideological agenda . . . can use the politics of scandal online to drive traffic . . . I think that he tailors scandals according to how they're going to reach basically his key market. [And] the target market is white, angry disenfranchised lower middle class. The key theme is not necessarily the racial dimension, but the liberal hypocrisy."[7]

In *Righteous Indignation,* Breitbart describes how he helped twentysomething conservative video activist James O'Keefe spread the clips recorded by hidden camera that took down the Association of Community Organizations for Reform Now, better known by its acronym ACORN, back in 2009.

Already plagued by mismanagement, voter registration fraud allegations, and an embezzlement scandal, the group was the perfect target for O'Keefe and partner Hannah Giles, who visited some of their offices across the country claiming to be a prostitute and her boyfriend who were seeking help in obtaining a loan to buy a house that they would use to continue selling sex. When ACORN staffers were shown in video clips offering help for such a seemingly outlandish scheme, a media and political firestorm erupted.

Breitbart used the release of O'Keefe's videos to launch his website, BigGovernment.com, and provided the footage to Fox News so that the news channel would cover the story just as his new platform was launching.

"I went to ABC News first and I went to a very prominent person who was there at the time . . . it was John Stossel, but at the time I had to say I went to ABC News and a top-level person said to me, 'There's no way in hell, because of the politics of this place, that anybody would allow for this,'" said Breitbart, who added that he then took the footage to conservative-leaning news channel Fox News. "And that was what launched the story."[8]

It's also what fully launched Breitbart's tactics as a twenty-first-century conservative information warrior.

The ACORN story shared many of the classic elements of his biggest stories. The topic was emotionally charged for conservatives and liberals; there was plenty of video footage; the story was released nationwide on ideologically friendly outlets, increasing pressure for mainstream news outlets to cover it quickly; and the presentation was selectively edited to produce maximum outrage.

Indeed, an investigation by the attorney general's office in California found that in the videos Breitbart and O'Keefe released of their visits to three California ACORN offices, important context was often left out of the edited versions shown on Fox News and elsewhere. The report concluded that ACORN employees didn't actually violate laws, though staffers did have "highly inappropriate" conversations with the pair that were "disturbing and offensive."

"Although O'Keefe is dressed in stereotypical 1970s pimp garb in the opening and closing scenes of the videos released on the Internet, when O'Keefe visited each of the ACORN offices, ACORN employees reported that he was actually dressed in a shirt and tie," the report said. "Also, contrary to the suggestion in the edited videos, O'Keefe never stated he was a pimp."[9]

Although Breitbart and others have said that what they did was journalism, the edited ACORN videos from California seem to have left out three very important steps in the journalism process.

They didn't fully characterize their own actions. For the audience to understand what kind of transgressions were being shown in the videos, they had to know how O'Keefe and Giles were presenting themselves to ACORN staffers.

Long after the first ACORN videos appeared, major news outlets were mistakenly reporting that O'Keefe was dressed in his pimp costume when he visited the organization's offices—which makes the discussions seem all the more outlandish and awful.

It was just the sort of issue I warned about during a September 20, 2009, appearance on media critic Howard Kurtz's CNN show *Reliable Sources,* after the host asked why mainstream media outlets were so slow to pick up covering the video scandal, with some major news outlets taking days to decide on coverage.[10]

Conservative pundit Amy Holmes was an analyst for CNN when we appeared together on this segment. "If a liberal activist had walked into the [conservative think tank] Heritage Foundation, for example, and conducted the same sort of sting operation, it would have been on the front page of the *Washington Post* in a day," she said.

But I noted that journalists were, at that moment, reporting on a video they hadn't really vetted, filmed by a person they didn't know using techniques they weren't fully informed on.

Given those circumstances, I said, a measured response makes plenty of sense.

"It was unearthed by a conservative filmmaker," I said. "And who knows what his motives are? Who knows how he edited the tape? Who knows what kind of journalistic standards went into creating this?"

They didn't fully characterize the actions of the people they videotaped. In the attorney general's account of the visits—compiled after they obtained unedited video footage from the filmmakers and interviewed ACORN staffers in California, among other efforts—workers are described as trying to handle the filmmakers' odd requests in some appropriate ways.

One worker gathered lots of information on their plans and then called police. Another staffer took them to an office for a service called "Program for Torture Victims" and twice told them to seek help there (eventually, that staffer was prodded by O'Keefe and Giles into inappropriately making suggestions on how they could set up a prostitution business and how she could help). A third employee told police she thought O'Keefe and Giles were scamming her and played along as if it were a joke, falsely claiming she once had worked as a prostitute and killed an abusive ex-husband.[11]

None of this information, which might have reduced the videos' emotional impact, was initially communicated in the edited videos.

And while it may have been possible to ferret out this information by sifting through online transcripts, which were available to the public, the edited versions should have included this information, too.

They didn't give the subjects of the story a chance to respond before it was made public. Traditionally, journalists—even in sting operations—take the material they have gathered for their story and tell the subject what they have found, giving them a reasonable amount of time to respond for inclusion.

Instead, Breitbart and O'Keefe seemed to outsource that part to traditional media, releasing their videos in a way that ratcheted up the pressure for other news outlets to cover the story quickly and overlook its significant flaws.

"Videos of five different ACORN offices in five separate cities would be released on five consecutive weekdays over a full week—Baltimore, Washington, New York, San Bernadino and San Diego," Breitbart wrote in a 2009 column for the *Washington Times* dubbed "The Politicized Art behind the ACORN Plan."[12]

According to his column, the delayed release of videos was a strategic plan, designed to prompt early responses from ACORN that would be discredited by subsequent videos. "By dripping the videos out, we exposed to anyone paying attention that ACORN was lying through its teeth and that the media would look imbecilic continuing to trot out their hapless spokespeople," he wrote.

It's a tactic that makes sense in a political fight; as an old political axiom warns, "If you're explaining, you're losing."

But in media, such strategies also allowed Breitbart and O'Keefe to gin up maximum public outrage around the story before the subjects really had a chance to learn what the allegations were or what really happened, let alone provide a coherent response. Good investigative journalism gives its subjects a chance to explain their side, even if they're in the wrong.

And even though investigative journalists have often lied to their subjects to get at stories, they should not lie to the audience that consumes them.

Race hovered as a significant subtext here, as several of the ACORN employees shown in the videos were people of color, the organization was led by a black woman, and the group had a track record of activism on issues important to poor people and minorities.

Pundit Glenn Beck was a major voice criticizing ACORN's tactics for years, accusing the group of using racism allegations to "blackmail" banks into giving housing loans in a September 30, 2008, broadcast of his television show, back when he worked for CNN Headline News.

"ACORN screams affirmative action to scare lenders, then volunteers to serve as advisors," he said. "In other words, they threaten to expose people as racists unless they agree to ACORN's idea of reform. It is a scam, pure and simple."[13]

As is his style, conservative talk show host Rush Limbaugh was even more explicit about connecting fear of ACORN to scary black radicals.

"We thought that it was just liberal welfare policies and all that that kept blacks from progressing while other minorities grew and prospered," Limbaugh noted during his show on October 14, 2008. "But no, it is these wackos from Bill Ayers to Jeremiah Wright to other anti-American, Afrocentric black liberation theologists, working with ACORN, and Barack Obama is smack dab in the middle of it. They have been training young black kids to hate, hate, hate this country. And they have trained their parents before that to hate, hate, hate this country. It was a movement!"[14]

But an analysis by FactCheck.org of many allegations against ACORN found that the group's false voter registration problems stemmed from employees who "were trying to get paid by ACORN for doing no work" (because some staffers were paid according to how many people they registered), not from a conspiracy among activists trying to influence elections. The same piece also found that those who earned mortgages through ACORN programs got counseling on budget and credit issues and had lower rates of default than those who took out the subprime mortgages that caused such serious economic problems.[15]

There is little doubt that ACORN—which was created in 1970 and served, at its height, as an umbrella organization for more than 1,000 smaller groups—had lots of problems wrapped up in legitimate efforts to spread voter registration and advocate for disenfranchised people.[16]

But the corrective should have been quality journalism. Instead, low-level ACORN staffers were tricked into responding outlandishly to an outlandish situation, in videos edited so craftily that in March 2010—six months after O'Keefe's tapes were released—the *New York Times* had to publish a correction noting that four articles reaching back to September 2009 had said O'Keefe was dressed like a pimp when visiting ACORN offices.[17]

When I asked Breitbart about the significance of initially allowing people to think O'Keefe was dressed as a pimp during his visits—even he wrote in his *Washington Times* column that the video footage featured O'Keefe "dressed as a pimp"—the blogger was dismissive.

"It's like the beginning of a Borat show," he told me, referencing the mockumentary film in which comedian Sacha Baron Cohen pretended to be a Kazakhstani journalist to reveal actual bigotry and jingoism among unsuspecting subjects. Later, Breitbart noted, "You are holding him [O'Keefe] to an absurd standard."[18]

Seems to me that revealing exactly how O'Keefe presented himself while making the videos is a pretty simple standard. Regardless, the videos had their intended effect: ACORN lost its support from Congress and shut down about six months after the videos first appeared.[19]

The reaction to Breitbart and O'Keefe's work, especially in conservative circles, was likely aided by a couple of psychological factors: *attitude polarization* and *confirmation bias.*

As I wrote earlier in Chapter One, confirmation bias is the tendency for people to cherry-pick information that confirms views they already hold, particularly if the information at hand is ambiguous.[20] And attitude polarization follows from that bias, as people focus more intently on their beliefs, accepting material that supports their convictions while casting a more critical eye on evidence that debunks them.

It makes sense, then, that a tea party–friendly audience already critical of ACORN might be more willing to accept the evidence presented in these hidden camera videos, which simply confirms conspiracy theories already trumpeted in other corners of conservative-oriented media. Even after major elements of the presentation had been contextualized and criticized, the willingness to believe the original vision remained.

So Breitbart had his new media strategy for rolling out attacks on liberal political institutions.

And it was a process that Breitbart—who referenced his own attention-deficit issues repeatedly in his book *Righteous Indignation*—crafted specifically to suit our short-attention-span media age.[21]

At a time when media outlets face tremendous pressure to report big news immediately for fear of being scooped, Breitbart offered scandals blasted across multiple media platforms with a built-in ideological framework.

In the end, it was a hit-or-miss process; video clips Breitbart posted of a speech given by then-USDA worker Shirley Sherrod, which seemed to endorse anti-white prejudice, caused enough controversy to bring quick pressure for her to resign. But subsequent revelations of how the heavily edited clips failed to tell the full story eventually hurt his credibility.[22] (I'll discuss the Sherrod incident in greater detail in Chapter Three.)

But Breitbart did score big with another revelation: explicit pictures of Congressman Anthony Weiner sent via Twitter to a young woman who was not his wife, publicized on BigGovernment.com, which eventually forced Weiner's resignation.

As much as Breitbart criticized the mainstream media as a tool of liberals, he also craved its attention, well aware that he needed access to its audiences to spread his message, even as he was trying to take it down.

"In an earlier era, where media was more homogenous, you had to persuade journalists directly to give you coverage," said Tom Rosenstiel, director of the Project for Excellence in Journalism, a non-partisan, Washington, D.C., think tank. "Today, in this more varied media culture, you can get noticed by friendlier media and eventually get coverage from [outlets] who are skeptical of you, because you've reached a point of prominence . . . It's built into [mainstream media's] economic model that they present lots of points of view. They're trying to keep the audience as broad as they can. So criticism that the press is unfair or is ignoring a story because of some blind spot can be a very effective lever."[23]

There are others of varying political stripes who also practice subversive media tactics, from Michael Moore's guerrilla-style documentary films to the work of Alexandra Pelosi, another documentarian who just happens to be the daughter of the former House Speaker Nancy Pelosi.

And O'Keefe has released sting videos on his own to varying degrees of success, embarrassing NPR into dropping CEO Vivian Schiller and head of fundraising Ronald Schiller (not related) after releasing a secretly recorded video in 2011 featuring the fundraiser expressing criticism of tea party conservatives as "racist" and "Islamaphobic." (Watching a longer version of the video, it seems that some of Schiller's strongest words were quotes of other GOP officials.[24])

The filmmaker also tried luring a CNN reporter onto a boat stocked with sex toys in 2010; was arrested during an attempt to enter the offices of U.S. Sen. Mary Landrieu; and faced criticism from a former assistant, Harvard student Nadia Naffe, who filed a criminal harassment complaint against him that was later dismissed.[25]

Breitbart's successors also got a cold reception from mainstream media when they tried rolling out a story in early 2012, using video from 20 years ago to imply that the president of the United States was connected to a black law professor they characterized as a dangerous radical.

Even while pressing some of the same buttons of race, paranoia, and history, they hit a wall when they brought up the name of a man who few people outside the worlds of law and civil rights knew beforehand: Derrick Bell.

FOR FOX NEWS ANCHOR SEAN HANNITY, this was video designed to shake a presidency.

The images seemed ordinary enough: A youthful Barack Obama, a bit geeky-looking in a mid-size afro and dress shirt, stood before a crowd of fellow students at Harvard, urging them to "open your hearts and your minds to the words of Professor Derrick Bell."

Then he walked over to an older-looking black man, hugged him, and stood back as that figure began speaking. In fact, Hannity broadcast a clip within a clip; the Obama/Bell footage was part of a speech by noted attorney and law professor Charles Ogletree, who was shown saying, "Of course, we hid this throughout the 2008 campaign."

"That hug and the president's association with a radical professor like Bell is no doubt going to become a hot topic in coming days," Hannity assured the audience on his March 7, 2012, show.[26]

The anchor was trumpeting the latest scoop from Breitbart.com, released to the world less than a week after Breitbart's death. Hannity prefaced the footage with a different clip, featuring Breitbart himself at the Conservative Political Action Congress convention in February 2012 promising to release videos "to show you why racial division and class warfare are central to what hope and change was sold in 2008."

Joined by Breitbart.com editor in chief Joel Pollak and the site's editor, Ben Shapiro, Hannity made the case that Bell, the first tenured black professor at Harvard University's law school, was a radical figure whose connection to Obama was covered up by powerful friends and left unexplored by the mainstream media.

Why was Bell considered such a radical? One reason: He was a seminal figure in creating and developing the branch of legal philosophy called critical race theory.

"Derrick Bell was the Jeremiah Wright of academia," Pollak told Hannity, invoking another figure hated by conservatives, the controversial pastor of President Obama's former church in Chicago. "He had some crazy views. In fact, just two months before this [Harvard] speech was given, Derrick Bell gave a controversial speech in Chicago where he said America remains a racist country and the civil rights movement was a sham because white supremacy remains the system and we've got to transform that system radically in order to get rid of racism."[27]

Pollak would echo the same views the next day on CNN, facing another Harvard graduate, skeptical anchor Soledad O'Brien, who had a hard time believing the Breitbart bombshell amounted to much.

"What part of that was the bombshell? Because I missed it. I don't get it," O'Brien said, after the clip of Obama and Bell played. "What was a bombshell?"[28]

Pollak said the clip displayed a relationship between Bell and Obama, repeating his charge about the former Harvard professor resembling Wright. "He passed away last year, but during his lifetime, he developed a theory called critical race theory, which holds that the civil rights movement was a sham and that white supremacy is the order and it must be overthrown."

"So that is a complete misreading," O'Brien interjected. "I'll stop you there for a second—then I'll let you continue. That is a complete misreading of critical race theory. That's an actual theory. You could Google it and some would give you a good definition. So that's not correct. But keep going."

And they proceeded to argue over the meaning of critical race theory in a way that left this viewer certain of two things: Even O'Brien didn't seem totally sure what the theory was, and Pollak was advancing a vision of Bell that seemed at odds with the way many legal scholars remember him.

For media critics like me, the exchange was telling, because it revealed a lot about how Breitbart-style scoops work, even in the absence of the man himself.

While several of Breitbart's scandals have focused on the intersection of race and politics—in this case, the ultimate connection of the two in African

American president Barack Obama—they also often hinge on obscurity. They shine a spotlight on figures, organizations, or concepts the general public doesn't know particularly well, which makes it easier to redefine them in the most alarming way possible.

In this case, Bell and critical race theory stood in the cross hairs. Though Bell has written textbooks used across the country, the professor never quite attained the popular status of better-known black intellectuals such as Cornel West or Henry Louis Gates Jr. So allegations that he might be a radical could fly further, especially with conservative viewers already suspicious of both academics and President Obama.

And critical race theory (CRT) is itself a complex subject: a legal philosophy aimed at examining how institutions in any society are built and shaped by the racism of their founders, particularly legal institutions in America.[29]

Seattle University law professor Richard Delgado, who co-wrote the 2001 book *Critical Race Theory: An Introduction* with his wife Jean Stefancic, said CRT is centered on the notion that everyone sees life through the lens of their own racial history, so the institutions they create will be affected by that view.

"Much of racism is institutional and unconscious, not the old-fashioned kind of obvious racism the civil rights movement fought," Delgado said. "It's an effort to examine the relationship between race and political power and influence. It's an effort to bring traditional civil rights up to date. And to analyze how racism works today in a society where everybody condemns racism and would be shocked at the very thought that their friends might be racist. Still, we all are."[30]

That's not a definition you can easily call up on Wikipedia, leaving those wary of accepting Breitbart.com's explanation with few options, short of running to a law library.

Later, O'Brien did speak with Emory University professor Dorothy Brown, who asserted that CRT is "nothing about white supremacy," which was also not quite right.[31]

Another Breitbart-ian tactic involves defining terms early. Get an opponent to accept your definitions, and the fight is halfway won.

So in arguing with Pollak over the detail of whether critical race theory was "all about" white supremacy, O'Brien also seemed to accept the contention that such a focus would be worthy of criticism, weakening her position.

In truth, Bell did have some very controversial ideas. He did believe racism in America was a permanent state that would never be overcome, according to Delgado, a friend of the former professor, who died in October 2011.

He believed people of color only gained advances in society when those breakthroughs also advantaged white people, noting that America's segregation and racial oppression in the early 1960s made it tough for the United States to convince third world countries considering communism to align instead with democracy.[32]

And Bell had an intellectual's way of making provocative statements about race, noting that some black people admire Nation of Islam leader Louis Farrakhan, a figure long criticized for his anti-Semitic remarks, because he doesn't "mind telling off the white folks."[33]

Bell was also a passionate lawyer who fought for civil rights in the 1950s, quit the Justice Department rather than end his lifetime membership in the NAACP, and left Harvard in protest of the university's failure to grant any African American women tenure.[34] None of which is particularly easy to argue in a two-minute cable TV news segment.

Just as the ACORN stories helped Breitbart launch a new site, release of the Bell story coincided with the redesign of Breitbart.com. At the same time, Breitbart ally and syndicated columnist Michelle Malkin launched Twitchy.com, an online platform that pulls together Twitter messages, comments, video clips, and other material into long displays that outline an unfolding issue, often from a conservative perspective.[35]

But in contrast to the coverage of the ACORN videos, the Obama/Bell video drew little mainstream media attention in its early days (a search of the LexisNexis news database two weeks after the revelations indicated fewer than a dozen newspaper stories and about 14 stories on cable news channels about the subject).

PBS's investigative series *Frontline* had already featured much of the video in a 2008 documentary and reposted the video of the speech and hug on its website when the Breitbart.com analysis surfaced. The site Buzzfeed.com also obtained the footage from WGBH-TV in Boston and posted it online before Breitbart.com, though their clip lacked footage of the men actually hugging.[36]

Other media outlets also featured interviews with Ogletree, who told the *Boston Herald* his comment about hiding the video was a joke. Bell's widow defended her husband's legacy to MSNBC anchor Ed Schultz. And a

tribute website launched just after his death, professorderrickbell.com, became a clearinghouse for information about Bell and material to counter the
Breitbart.com stories, with tribute videos on his life embedded on the home
page below links to essays on his life story.

After years of seeing such charged videos spark overreaching coverage,
many news institutions regarded the Derrick Bell videos with a collective
shrug.

"My bewilderment stemmed from the question of why anyone would
consider this video to be a scoop at all," wrote NPR's media correspondent
David Folkenflik in a post for the news blog The Two Way. Later, he wrote:
"Scoops are supposed to break news or deepen our understanding in new
ways. This video flap accomplished neither."[37]

Perhaps most notably, the story didn't have Breitbart himself to push it
along, squaring off against naysayers with his animated style and the connections to land on major news outlets.

During our conversation in January, he was animated and passionate,
barely able to contain himself as I made a point he disagreed with, capable
of drowning an objection in a five-minute monologue packed with insults,
half-truths, and cogent analysis all run together.

Breitbart was a master at pushing opponents to fit the mold he wanted,
exposing the weaknesses that would make them most vulnerable to conservative criticism.

But for people of color, that often meant trying to make them fit in-
sulting stereotypes: the Angry Black Man or Woman, the Hypersensitive
Politically Correct Person, the Race-Baiter Using False Allegations to Political
Advantage, and so on.

Or, as in the Bell story, a Secret Pro-Black Radical with an Unknown
Plan for Subjugating White People—demonizing black intellectuals and devaluing figures considered important signposts of progress in racial equality.

"I don't think that anybody in the media really knows what I believe
when it comes to certain issues . . . I flummox them," Breitbart said, noting
that views such as his advocacy for gay rights kept him from achieving status
as an extreme right-wing ideologue.

"Our college campuses over a generation or two have cultivated,
through . . . Chicano studies, African American studies, queer studies . . .
these studies programs have upset the order of a classic liberal education and
turned young humanities students into weaponized, leftist cultural Marxist

weapons," he added, just getting warmed up. "They use the news media in order to fight to keep narratives in place in order to separate these people. And this has political consequences because these are then the constituencies that the Democratic party panders to."[38]

You got the sense he was mostly excited by the game of turning big media against itself—exposing what he saw as its central hypocrisies.

But Breitbart also helped accelerate a media culture in which facts are fungible as opinions, making it tough for those on opposite political sides to agree on the most basic issues—especially when it comes to the hot-button issue of race.

FOR ARI RABIN-HAVT, THERE'S A HISTORIC PARALLEL to the way Breitbart and others use race issues to galvanize a conservative media audience.

"It's been a conservative strategy since Richard Nixon to utilize race as a weapon to divide people and scare a certain segment of the population toward the conservative mindset," said Rabin-Havt, executive vice president at the liberal-oriented watchdog group Media Matters. "Breitbart and O'Keefe and those guys continue in this tradition. The difference, is they're using new media tools to get their word out quicker."[39]

Media Matters is one of the loudest voices on the left side of the political spectrum, utilizing its website, blogs, press releases, and political action initiatives to spread word about what it deems conservative "misinformation" presented as fact.

The group also documents prejudiced speech by media figures, publicizing audio clips of controversial words by Don Imus, Dr. Laura Schlessinger, Glenn Beck, Bill O'Reilly, Rush Limbaugh, and many others. They offer audio and video clips along with transcripts, studies, and news stories unearthed by a staff of more than 85 people, working in teams from 5 A.M. to 1 A.M., to ferret out the biggest hypocrisies or misstatements.[39]

According to Rabin-Havt, the group's focus on verifiable facts and recorded statements is no accident. "I like to dispute things with footnotes and research," he said, noting Media Matters's tendency toward long transcripts, audio and video clips, and lots of links to reference material. "Our style is to overemphasize the facts we're reporting."

When Imus called women from the Rutgers University basketball team "nappy-headed hos" in a joke aired on his CBS Radio show and MSNBC simulcast, a Media Matters employee caught it at 6:14 A.M. and posted both a video and a transcript to its website, according to the *Wall Street Journal*.[41] By that day's end, the group had emailed a press release on the remark to hundreds of reporters; the National Association of Black Journalists and Al Sharpton's National Action Network eventually got involved in protesting the host's history of jokes rooted in prejudice.

A few days later, Media Matters published another post detailing other incidents in Imus's history when he or his on-air cohorts used prejudiced and sexist speech, including calling Hillary Clinton a "bitch" in a joke. Eight days after the slur against the basketball team was first publicized by Media Matters, Imus had lost both his TV and radio shows (though he would eventually find a new TV home at Fox Business Network).

This is the pattern Media Matters has refined since its 2004 founding, amassing a $13 million budget in 2010 and gathering its material critical of Fox News into a 2012 book, *The Fox Effect: How Roger Ailes Turned a Network into a Propaganda Machine*. First, they expose a controversy involving a conservative media outlet or figure, then they mobilize opposition for maximum effect.

And in its most high-profile cases, racism or sexism become a heated flash point, from Schlessinger hurling the word "nigger" at a black caller several times to Rush Limbaugh calling a graduate student and activist testifying at a congressional hearing on federal requirements for covering contraception in health insurance plans a "slut" and "prostitute."

In mid-March 2012, Media Matters announced it would pony up at least $100,000 to run advertisements in eight cities criticizing Limbaugh for his comments about the Georgetown student, urging listeners to call local stations airing his show and targeting cities where he might be vulnerable.[42]

Some have criticized such campaigns for stifling free speech; even left-leaning comic Bill Maher wrote a column for the *New York Times* criticizing the reaction to Limbaugh, asking, "When did we get it in our heads that we have the right to never hear anything we don't like?"[43]

But Rabin-Havt said sexism and racism in the media should be exposed and opposed, especially when it also involves twisting facts.

"The mantra of our book is simple; pizza tastes better than broccoli," he added, criticizing conservative media outlets for being "too quick to abandon facts" in their presentations. "It's much easier to have your own views confirmed than to listen to the truth. It's people trying to have their own views confirmed taken to the extreme."[44]

But some targets of Media Matters have criticized the group for taking quotes out of context.

Fox News pundit Bill O'Reilly has leveled this accusation several times, saying they left out important parts of his discussion of a visit to Harlem restaurant Sylvia's back in 2007, making him look racially insensitive. There, I think he had a point, although the damaging comments he made—expressing surprise that the well-known restaurant didn't feature any "craziness," for instance—were still disturbing.

Conservatives also have accused Media Matters, founded by *The Fox Effect* co-author and former conservative media writer David Brock, of co-opting journalists and coordinating with the Obama White House to damage GOP causes and stars. The newspaper *Roll Call* reported that Brock's super political action committee, American Bridge 21st Century, has become an opposition research hub for the Democratic Party, raising $3.7 million in 2011 to dig up damaging information on GOP candidates that can be leaked to journalists.[45]

One of Media Matters's biggest critics is another online outlet, the *Daily Caller*, which published a multi-part series on Media Matters days before *The Fox Effect* was released. *Daily Caller* founder Tucker Carlson then spread word about the stories on Fox News Channel, where he was employed as an analyst.

The stories accused Brock of traveling with an armed aide and struggling with mental illness, working directly with people connected to the White House to place stories in the national media, and considering plans to investigate the personal lives of Fox News employees.[46] But the pieces, based largely on anonymous sources, didn't gain much traction with mainstream outlets outside the conservative media universe. ("It sounds pretty standard to me and not much of a story," Reuters media columnist Jack Shafer wrote, later calling it "bad journalism and lame propaganda."[47])

Carlson said he founded the *Daily Caller* as a "traditional online newspaper" in 2011 after "the press decided during the Democratic primary they were on the side of Obama." He maintained that his Media Matters series wasn't about taking down a political opponent or harming Brock—whom he admits to criticizing directly—but getting out a good story other media outlets wouldn't publish.[48]

The Fox News pundit also declined to call his website a conservative outlet, despite its frequent jabs at liberal politicians and media figures.

And embedded in his reasoning for establishing the *Daily Caller* was a sense that media unfairly helped Barack Obama get elected president for the groundbreaking racial implications.

"What people would say is, 'Well, look, it's not about the policies. It's about what this election says about America. It's really important for America to get past its troubled racial history and Obama is a living symbol of that,'" Carlson said, recalling conversations with unnamed political reporters on the campaign trail in 2008. "I will not concede, because I don't think it's good for America to elect a guy who is not going to be a good president."[49]

But isn't it possible that he just ran a better campaign? I asked.

"Winning is self-justifying, so the guy who is winning is presumed to have an effective campaign whereas the guy who is losing is presumed to have a bad campaign, and by the way, there's some truth in that," Carlson allowed. "I'm just saying there was this overlay on top of the whole campaign of much larger questions that really had nothing to do with Obama and McCain as individuals."

A 2008 study by the Project for Excellence in Journalism of more than 2,400 campaign stories over six weeks found that Democratic candidate Obama got a little more positive and neutral stories than negative coverage, while the GOP's John McCain received substantially more negative coverage. However, that coverage was often focused on McCain's own actions, from his risky move to suspend his own campaign and head to Washington, D.C., to address the economic meltdown in Congress to his selection of Sarah Palin as a running mate.

"[The results] offer a strong suggestion that winning in politics begat winning coverage," the report said. "Obama's coverage was negative in tone when he was dropping in the polls, and became positive when he began to rise, and it was just so for McCain as well."[50]

But Carlson's point—that Obama got elected president at least in part because of his race—imparts two important ideas about how some conservative media outlets perceive race-related stories.

First, there is the sense that political correctness has distorted the political process so much that an unqualified person of color has been elected president. That's a notion that, unsurprisingly, some people of color find insulting, as if Obama didn't earn his historic status as America's first non-white president.

And second, there is the notion that the national news media enables such distortions through its own liberal bias.

Those ideas surfaced during the *Daily Caller*'s coverage of the national outcry following the shooting death of Trayvon Martin, a 17-year-old, black high school student killed by a volunteer watchman in a Sanford, Florida, subdivision who said the unarmed youth attacked him when the two crossed paths. Martin's killing sparked nationwide protests in March 2012, as civil rights leaders such as the Rev. Al Sharpton and Jesse Jackson criticized local police for deciding not to arrest the shooter, George Zimmerman.

But as Sharpton and Jackson led huge rallies portraying Zimmerman as a gung ho policeman wannabe who may have targeted Martin because of his race, conservative media outlets began to push back, complaining that mainstream media outlets were using old pictures of the teen that made him look less threatening, while discounting Zimmerman's account of events.

The *Daily Caller* published a picture of Martin showing his gold teeth to a camera and another photo of him raising a middle finger to the lens; both pictures taken from his two Twitter accounts, according to an editor at the site. The site also published copies of Martin's tweets—one account was under the name NO_LIMIT_NIGGA—which were filled with profanity and sex jokes, as you might expect from a teenage boy.

"Our readers, and most Americans, are keenly interested in the personalities and character of the two men involved in the altercation in Sanford, Fla.," said *Daily Caller* executive editor David Martoko, author of the first story on Martin's tweets, in a quote emailed to me by a spokeswoman for the site. "This information, which was in the public domain for months before the Twitter account was disabled, fills in some of that information. We chose that photo of Trayvon Martin [showing his teeth] because it was the picture he chose to represent himself on Twitter—and also because, unlike the years-old photos of Martin that are accompanying most media reports, it represented what he looked like nearer to the end of his life."[51]

The *Daily Caller* wasn't alone. A website called Wagist posted photos from Martin's MySpace and Twitpic accounts showing his tattoos, citing a Twitter message from a friend saying "nigga needa plant" as "fairly direct evidence he may have been a small-time drug dealer."[52]

In its own display of photos, Twitchy.com made a serious mistake, publishing an image it originally said showed Martin shirtless, with his pants hanging low, underwear showing, flipping off the camera. But the photo was of a different person and the site subsequently posted an apology.

The Business Insider website also had to publish a correction when it published the same photo, which it disclosed had been obtained from Stormfront, a white supremacist website.[53] Why the site was using photos from an openly racist source was not clear.

Not surprisingly, the Project for Excellence in Journalism found in a study of press coverage in the month after Martin's death that discussion on the role of race consumed the biggest percentage of coverage on blogs: 15 percent of reports. On cable TV and talk radio, top topics were gun control and Florida's Stand Your Ground self-defense law (17 percent); suspicion about Martin and doubts of Zimmerman were about equal. Twitter was dominated by outrage at Zimmerman and sympathetic calls for justice for Martin's family.[54]

I found that TV outlets—especially cable news channels and morning television programs—count on channeling emotion to hook viewers, and so sought out the most emotional frameworks for the story (ideological news outlets such as liberal MSNBC and conservative Fox News Channel were also pushed to their sides of the political spectrum).

But as the pressure to arrest Zimmerman built throughout the month of March, the same social media tools used to spread word about Martin's death were being used by some to try to turn him into a less sympathetic figure, creating a bizarre tug of war over the legacy of a seemingly average 17-year-old youth.

In the rush to push back against Zimmerman's demonization, websites like the *Daily Caller,* Wagist, and Twitchy went too far, thugifying Martin and unfairly suggesting that a teen's tattoos, obscene gestures, or cursing might add more perspective on the events that led to his violent death.

The Martin case and the tsunami of outrage it provoked threatened a lot of the ideas at the heart of conservative media, providing a deadly example that racial profiling and prejudice may still be a problem in America. It also revealed the nation might rise up to demand a white man—or, more accurately, a Hispanic man Sanford police first assumed was white—pay a price for killing an unarmed black teen, even if the evidence is inconclusive.

Indeed, that last idea may be the worst nightmare for some in conservative media—that mainstream news outlets and civil rights protestors such as Sharpton and Jackson might unite with a black president to unfairly disadvantage white people.

Daily Caller founder Carlson made that point on Fox News during one appearance, taking on Democratic officials speaking out about the Martin case: "For people to weigh in, for professional race-baiters, like the ones you just saw on television, or the president himself to weigh in and make it a simple parable about white racism is very foolish," he said.[55]

Carlson was referring to remarks in which President Obama focused on the "tragedy" of losing a young life, noting, "If I had a son, he'd look like Trayvon."[56]

The idea of resisting the mainstream media's allegedly inherent liberal bias also inspired another combatant in the online political news media wars, the Media Research Center's conservative-oriented watchdog site NewsBusters.org.

Established in 2005, NewsBusters was developed as a faster-moving online arm of the Media Research Center (MRC), a 25-year-old think tank focused on proving liberal media bias in news media and pop culture, with an array of institutes, an online news service, an online video site, and more.

NewsBusters.org was created by website designer Matthew Sheffield, working with the MRC, after developing RatherBiased.com in 2000. Sheffield created RatherBiased.com to chronicle the missteps of then–CBS News anchor Dan Rather, helping raise questions about a flawed 2004 story on President George W. Bush's National Guard service that eventually led to the anchor leaving the network.[57]

Sheffield suggested the MRC create its own blog as an outlet for its research and quicker commentaries, according to the MRC's director of media analysis Tim Graham. By early 2012, Graham said, NewsBusters was posting up to 25 items a day.

(Full disclosure: NewsBusters has criticized my work in the past, including a column on Breitbart's Shirley Sherrod posting and an NPR interview in which I criticized caustic political speech after the shooting of U.S. Rep. Gabrielle Giffords.)

"In a sense, we're the ombudsmen of the conservative movement; we are reacting when our side is mangled or misinformed," Graham said. "We don't pretend to be objective. The problem is [that] we have a news media which pretends to be objective."[58]

NewsBusters joined criticism that helped push NBC into investigating how it unfairly edited audio of Zimmerman's 911 call; eventually, the network reportedly fired the producer responsible for the edits and apologized. The site also criticized the *New York Daily News* and *Miami New Times* for publishing unverified claims by a neo-Nazi that his group would patrol the streets in Sanford, Florida, where Trayvon Martin was shot (police said the group hadn't done so).

But while Media Matters posts have ended pundits' careers, NewsBusters can focus on items where media figures simply express ideas opposing conservatives.

One post criticized CNN for including comic actor and host John Fugelsang on a panel where he wasn't labeled as a liberal and he called Rick Santorum a "homophobe."

Another analysis criticized NBC News for promoting "left wing activism against the GOP" by covering protests that drew more than 200 women to the state capitol in Texas, pushing back against plans by legislators to end a program providing health care to 130,000 women.[59]

A spin through the NewsBusters posts indexed by "race issues" in mid-March revealed a similar lean toward debunking claims of racism by people of color ("CBS Plays Up Voter Suppression Charge in Pennsylvania; Ignores Voter Fraud"), exposing anti-white actions by people of color ("'African Americans For Obama' Revived; Media Double Standard Obvious"), and criticizing attempts to link the gay rights struggle to black people's classic fight for civil rights ("John Heilemann: 'Objections to Gay Marriage Similar to 1960s Laws against Interracial Marriage'").

"We're the outsiders; Media Matters is the insiders," Graham said, explaining their differing focus and results. "They're inside the liberal media and we're the barbarians at the gate . . . conservatives need one outlet which will report things that the media wants to ignore."[60]

But even Carlson, who earns his living slinging opinions on TV, thinks the back and forth between ideologically opposed media may eventually keep us all from agreeing on even basic facts.

"To me, that's sort of—that's end of civilization at that point," he said. "I mean, I'm definitely pleased there's no longer a left wing monopoly on the news . . . We ought to have all kinds of different viewpoints [in media] and I think that's where we are now. But I sort of sense what you're saying may be true a little bit and I hope it's not."

And despite his status as owner of a political news website, Carlson thinks online platforms share some blame.

"The Internet allows people to tailor their news consumption so precisely that it's possible that people will never run into views they disagree with, and that's a distressing possibility," he added. "You ought to be challenged."[61]

THREE

FOX NEWS CHANNEL'S FOCUS ON SCARY BLACK PEOPLE LEAVES RACE RELATIONS AS COLLATERAL DAMAGE

STANDING BACKSTAGE AT A PACKED CONVENTION HALL INSIDE the Manchester Grand Hyatt hotel in San Diego, Shirley Miller Sherrod looked less like a fiery symbol of the modern media's struggle over race and prejudice than a confused grandmother who was a bit overwhelmed.

Dressed in a tasteful dark pantsuit with a red blouse, her husband Charles Sherrod by her side, the woman who had morphed in one day from national embarrassment to heroic symbol of political victimization moved gingerly. Journalists from big organizations sidled close—one from the *Washington Post*, another from CNN—hoping for a quick word before she took the stage to tell her story.

Her tale: how big media's argument culture and those who feed its insatiable tastes nearly destroyed her good name.

On that crisp July morning, she was minutes away from taking the stage on the first full day of the National Association of Black Journalists 2010 convention. It had been just ten days since conservative blogger Andrew Breitbart blew her world apart, releasing a selectively edited video that presented this sixty-something African American woman as a so-called "reverse" racist who moved slowly to help a white farmer facing foreclosure when she worked for the U.S. Department of Agriculture.[1]

The comments came from a speech she made before an NAACP chapter months earlier; in the excerpts Breitbart posted, Sherrod admitted hesitating to help a farmer facing foreclosure because he was white. "I didn't give him the full force of what I could do," she said in one of two clips featured on Breitbart's site.[2]

That was all Breitbart, a longtime critic of the NAACP, needed to hear. He was already angry the group had passed a resolution asking tea party members to repudiate racist elements in their ranks, saying their justification—that black lawmakers claimed tea party protesters slung racial epithets at them during a health care protest—never happened.

So he offered Sherrod's words as an example of racism at an NAACP event. "She decides that he should get help from 'one of his own kind,'" the blogger wrote in an entry posted July 19, 2010, titled, "Video Proof: The NAACP Awards Racism—2010." "She refers him to a white lawyer."[3]

That first day, the videos sparked an avalanche of blog posts and a smattering of mentions across big media, including a demand from Fox News Channel star Bill O'Reilly that Sherrod resign. The next day, O'Reilly complained that network news broadcasts didn't cover the story.[4] He shouldn't have worried: By week's end, her case would consume 14 percent of all stories in major news outlets, second only to coverage of the nation's worsening economy.[5]

But the reason behind the growing story was that 24 hours after Brietbart's initial post—amid CNN's coverage featuring the white farmer in Sherrod's story speaking up for her—the NAACP released the full video of her speech, revealing the point to be the *opposite* of the initial impression. Sherrod had actually told a story of overcoming her initial prejudice, working for years to help farmer Roger Spooner keep his land.[6]

Speaking for more than 40 minutes in an admittedly rambling style, Sherrod described how her father was killed in 1965 by a white man who went unpunished, despite three witnesses; explained that his murder led her to stay in the South, despite hating its oppressive racial climate; and related how, in their first encounter, Spooner seemed bent on showing he was superior to her, even while asking for help.

Over time, Sherrod realized the white lawyer she'd left Spooner to work with was letting him down in the same way black farmers had been victimized. "Working with him made me see that it's really about those who have versus those who don't," she said in a later segment of the speech. "And they could be black, and they could be white; they could be Hispanic. And it made me realize then that I needed to help poor people—those who don't have access the way others have."[7]

The true story didn't emerge soon enough to save Sherrod's job with the USDA; officials there pressured her to leave within hours of Breitbart's revelations (though they eventually offered her another job, which she never took).[8] The NAACP, which had originally released a statement noting "she mistreated a white farmer in need of assistance," backtracked and admitted "we were snookered by Fox News and Tea Party activist Andrew Breitbart."[9]

Facing an excited crowd of black journalists less than two weeks later, Sherrod had become an entirely different sort of symbol than Breitbart had intended.

At the Hyatt in San Diego, Sherrod stood before media professionals who had tracked both her vilification and vindication closely, concerned by the rush to judgment and aura of prejudice hovering at the edges of the incident. Nearby, CNN anchor Don Lemon, who had helped the channel spread her side of the story even before the NAACP released the full video, joined in for a roundtable discussion opening the black journalists' convention.

That panel, which also featured questions from NBC News correspondent Mara Schiavocampo and me, would be broadcast on several news channels and featured on NBC's *Today* show, among other places.

"Everyone's so afraid . . . [it] takes me back to when my father had been shot and the teacher who took us from the school to the hospital was afraid to drive through the little town because of the repercussions," Sherrod said, recalling the day her dad was shot to death by a white man.[10] "[But] God knows. He knows. And right will win the end."

She may have seemed a little confused backstage, but when Sherrod strode out before the crowd, welcomed by a blast of admiring applause, the resolve that helped her survive decades of activism in the Deep South showed itself. Steely-eyed, she criticized President Obama for not knowing his history and vowed to file a lawsuit against Breitbart for destroying her good name.

And when I asked what media outlet she blamed most for the firestorm that cost her a good job and peace of mind, Sherrod answered without hesitation.

"It wasn't all media, it was Fox [News]," she said, brushing aside the news channel's statements that it didn't report substantially on the scandal until after she had resigned.[11]

"I don't know all that Fox was doing behind the scenes to get the effect they were looking for, which was to get me to resign," she said. "I started receiving hate mail right away . . . They had to know what they were doing."[12]

Of course, Fox News Channel and some of its highest profile personalities didn't see it that way. Noting that its news journalists didn't report on the video until Sherrod had already resigned—though its website and Fox Nation blog did—officials at Fox News denied contributing to the end of her career in government.[13]

Howard Kurtz, then media critic for the *Washington Post*, reported that Fox News senior vice president Michael Clemente cautioned his staff to be careful about the Sherrod story on the day Breitbart's post surfaced. "Can we get confirmation and comments from Sherrod before going on air," Clemente's email read, according to Kurtz's story (notably, a level of reporting Breitbart himself didn't undertake). "Let's make sure we do this right."[14]

Of course, several of Fox News Channel's opinion shows chewed over the circumstance of a government employee seeming to express anti-white racism until the NAACP's full video was released.

But Sherrod seemed to be speaking of an even deeper dynamic.

She was highlighting the penchant for reverse racism stories and fear surrounding people of color cultivated by Fox News over a long period. This fed an atmosphere in which Breitbart could strike at the NAACP.

When USDA officials asked her to resign, long before anything but the misleading video was known publicly, Sherrod said it was because they feared Fox News host Glenn Beck would feature the story on his popular 5 P.M. show.[15]

Back then, Beck was arguably the news channel's second-biggest star, drawing worldwide attention in 2009 for accusing President Obama of being an anti-white "racist."[16] Later that year, he claimed the scalp of Van Jones, a low-level African American White House advisor who had once been an extreme left-wing activist. He was forced to resign after long months of criticism by Beck when his name surfaced on a petition saying government officials may have allowed the 9/11 attacks to occur.[17]

Small wonder White House officials feared a replay of Jones's death by a thousand cuts when the Sherrod controversy surfaced.

Even as the case against Sherrod was crumbling, Fox News Channel's biggest star Bill O'Reilly complained that network TV newscasts were ignoring the story, along with a long list of other controversies he said were similarly overlooked by media outlets "reluctant to do damage to a very liberal president."[18]

That tally, outlined on O'Reilly's July 20, 2010, "Talking Points Memo" segment, included: Jones's resignation, the Justice Department's handling of a New Black Panther Party member standing with a baton at a Philadelphia polling place during the 2008 election, hidden video taped by conservative activists of staffers from the civil rights group ACORN allegedly giving tax advice to a man and woman posing as a pimp and prostitute, a State Department official comparing Arizona's revamp of illegal immigration enforcement laws to Chinese human rights abuses, and Obama's then-nominee to head Medicare and Medicaid saying a quality health care system essentially redistributed wealth in society.[19]

But all three network TV evening newscasts did cover Sherrod's resignation and the misleading video the day O'Reilly's commentary aired, according to the Tyndall Report, an online database of network TV news stories.

Jones's resignation did get some coverage on the network morning news shows, but he left his job at midnight on a Saturday during Labor Day weekend, a time when newsrooms are typically short-staffed. The Tyndall Report site also showed that the ACORN sting video got coverage on all three network newscasts in September 2009.

But there was one other, inescapable characteristic common to the stories on O'Reilly's "not covered" list: All but one involved issues relating to black or Latino people—from Van Jones's demonization as a secret Marxist in the White House to the hobbling of ACORN, an organizationally challenged group that often worked to register voters in minority neighborhoods.

For Sherrod, her experience at the center of a race-related media firestorm left her convinced of one thing: Fox News's pugnacious take on race issues helped light the kindling that turned Breitbart's blog post into a raging wildfire.[20]

So I asked how she felt when O'Reilly, who apologized on air for jumping to conclusions about her, then noted that she still "may well see things through a racial prism."[21] (In his world, it seems, white people have no racial prism of their own.)

"I still, every day of my life, have to be able to know when [racism] is there," Sherrod said, frustration gathering in her voice. "I don't go out looking for it, but if it's there, I need to be able to recognize it. And I saw it in what they did; in what Fox did and what Breitbart did."[22]

Her bottom line: After more than 60 years living as a black woman in the South, she knew prejudice when she saw it.

"I knew it was racism when it happened to me," Sherrod added. "Nobody had to tell me that."[23]

ANDREW BREITBART ALWAYS SEEMED WILLING to have a contentious conversation.

I found that out during an interview for this book, when I called the conservative firebrand and iconoclastic blogger on a Saturday afternoon, hoping to schedule a time when we could talk about Shirley Sherrod and the online campaign that seemed to blow up in his face, generating loads of criticism and a lawsuit.

As I noted in Chapter Two, we talked just a few weeks before he would pass away unexpectedly, collapsing during a walk not far from his home in California.

But there are two things I learned quickly about Breitbart in that call: he was ready to talk at any moment and never admitted defeat, insisting that he "stands by what I've done" in spreading the initial videos of Sherrod's speech, saying his true target was the NAACP.[24]

"[It wasn't] the Sherrod incident, it was the NAACP incident," Breitbart insisted, shifting the focus from the story of a woman mischaracterized to criticism of a civil rights institution he says has gone bad. "They've created an entire paradigm to invent racism on the right in order to intimidate people into silence."

For media critics like me, Sherrod's story was a cautionary tale of how even an unfair charge can move at the speed of the Internet, from online sites such as Breitbart's BigGovernment.com, The Drudge Report, and FoxNews.com to O'Reilly, Sean Hannity, Glenn Beck's radio program, CBS's New York affiliate, and *Fox and Friends* before the full truth can possibly be known.[25] In this process, the last stop is often the hard news reporting conducted by mainstream broadcast networks and newspapers, as journalists deliver the facts on an issue *after* cable news pundits have already indicated how the audience should feel about it.

That's a progression noted by none other than Breitbart himself, who first spoke to me on these issues in 2011, describing how aligning with a TV pundit like Glenn Beck, then on Fox News Channel, could help migrate stories from his network of blogs into the mainstream media.

"Glenn Beck turns content into something [huge], in terms of its life," said Breitbart, who, as previously noted, got a taste of that explosive, worldwide attention after giving Fox News footage from the ACORN sting videos.[26]

"He took the ACORN stories and brought them to life . . . stories that would have died on the vine," said Breitbart, who would later have a massive falling out with Beck. Breitbart accused the host of "throwing him under the bus" when Beck changed course and criticized the edited Sherrod clips on his Fox News TV show once the full truth emerged.

"As effective as new media is, I don't think the ACORN stories would have had the same effect had they not [also] been on television," Breitbart said.[27]

Angry that the NAACP had passed a resolution asking tea party leaders to denounce racism within their own ranks, the blogger decided the civil rights group had, in effect, called the entire tea party movement racist.

"I said to [NAACP president] Ben Jealous, if you're going to manufacture and lie about the tea party, I can go through events to show racism in your midst," Breitbart told me. "I get to sit through your event and find moments that are more racially charged [than] the invented issues that you are trying to manufacture in order to destroy the tea party on behalf of the Democratic party."[28]

But days after the NAACP asked the tea party leaders to act against racism, Mark Williams, a conservative talk radio host and leader of the Tea Party Express, posted on his blog a supposedly satirical letter to Abraham Lincoln from Jealous, headlined "Colored People Change Minds About Emancipation."

One quote from Williams's post: "Freedom means having to work for real, think for ourselves, and take consequences along with the rewards. That is just far too much to ask of us Colored People and we demand that it stop!" Williams and the Tea Party Express were quickly expelled from the National Tea Party Foundation.[29]

That happened days before Breitbart's videos of Sherrod were posted to his website.

Citing Sherrod's ongoing lawsuit, Breitbart wouldn't tell me who edited the video of her speech to the NAACP or whether he had access to the full video when he posted his initial commentary.[30]

Which means Breitbart either knew he was leaving out important context in Sherrod's story, or he didn't do enough reporting to know what she had really said during her entire speech. In either case, the fact that so many media platforms passed along information so flawed was an unsettling and ominous development for journalism and the culture at large.

Breitbart's success with both the Sherrod and ACORN tapes highlighted how unprepared civil rights groups were for the power of the right-wing media structure once it took aim at them.

And one reason these tactics worked so well is because the biggest outlet for conservative news and opinion, Fox News Channel, had used such stories of scary, dysfunctional people of color to build an audience skeptical of the NAACP. Fox viewers had been trained: Those who believe prejudice against racial minorities remains an important social issue are often simply hustlers looking to push their own political agendas.

To see how Fox News so artfully primes its audience for that message—in early 2012, it was crowned the most-watched cable news network for ten straight years—one only need look at another rising star in the conservative news channel's anchor lineup: onetime-baseball-player-turned-stock-trader-turned-pundit Eric Bolling.[31]

ONE OF THE SUBTLEST EARLY WARNING SIGNS of prejudice is the unearned, insulting cultural assumption.

If you're African American, it may be someone who uses street slang in speaking to you before they have heard you say a word; after all, if you're black, you must prefer being called "bro" and "homes." For a Latino person, it's the knucklehead who casually tosses around curse words in Spanish or asks about street gang life.

And there may be no better master of that form on television than Fox Business News anchor Eric Bolling.

A Chicago native and onetime baseball player, Bolling has the in-your-face attitude and get-down-to-it charisma of a former commodities trader, which he is.[32] But he's found a new life on cable news, vaulting from providing commentary in the traders' pits to a panelist's gig on CNBC's *Fast Money* and a 2008 switch to the Fox Business Network (FBN).

The name of the game in cableland is making noise. So it's no surprise that Bolling's colleagues on FBN include media personalities known for controversial failures elsewhere, including disgraced ex-MSNBC morning man Don Imus and former CNN anchor Lou Dobbs.

(Both Dobbs and Imus saw their careers hobbled by race-related incidents; Imus capped 20-plus years of race-baiting in radio and on cable TV by calling Rutgers University's women's basketball team "nappy-headed hos," while Dobbs took increasingly unfair stances against illegal immigrants in his CNN show.[33])

But in mid-2011 it was Bolling—a self-styled New York business insider in the mold of Donny Deutsch—who gained headlines for his own insulting, race-based assumptions.

And this time, his target couldn't have been bigger: President Barack Hussein Obama.

First, Bolling cracked that the president "decided that chugging a few 40s and rediscovering you're Irish" was more important than helping victims of tornado damage in Missouri, when disaster struck while the chief executive was in Ireland.[34] Few could miss his pugnacious use of a street slang term for the 40-ounce bottles of malt liquor popularized through hip hop and gang culture in the country's poorest, most ethnic neighborhoods.

A few months later, Bolling took his references to another level. Noting that President Obama was welcoming Gabonese president Ali Bongo to the White House, Bolling noted in a segment opening his Fox Business show that "it's not the first time he's had a hoodlum in the hizzouse." As he spoke, a picture of the rapper Common—an anti-gangsta artist nevertheless criticized by some conservatives—flashed on the screen.[35]

Later, Bolling repeated the tease, saying, "It's not the first time he's had a hood in the big crib." This time, a picture appeared showing Bongo smiling and flashing a big golden tooth, like a villain in a bad seventies-era blaxploitation movie.

By the time Bolling started the segment, he was speaking as if his script had been written by rapper Snoop Dogg: "What's with all the hoods in the hizzy?"[36]

True enough, Bongo's government had been accused of abuses and criminality; his presence sparked important questions for the White House. But Bolling's commentary carried the distinct tinge of something else: a signal to Fox News viewers that this wasn't just about any kind of international crime. (It's hard to imagine Bolling using the same terminology about, say, the president of Burma.) For Fox News, this was about *two* black criminals meeting to celebrate their success—and one of them was the president of the United States.

The comments stand out, mostly because neither Bongo nor Obama are known for any connection to hip hop culture, where Bolling's slang origi-nated. Instead, the anchor was sending a distinct message, connecting two prominent political leaders of color to the culture of gangsta rap (for a com-parison, imagine if a TV anchor used a cartoonish Mafia-style accent to in-troduce a story about former New York mayor Rudolph Giuliani welcoming Italy's controversial prime minister Silvio Berlusconi to Gracie Mansion).

Bolling's words drew criticism nationally. So the anchor pulled back, at least a little, admitting in an editorial note the next week that "we got a little fast and loose with the language . . . we did go a bit too far."[37]

This isn't particularly new. For years, President Obama's political op-ponents have tried to tie him to politically and socially unpopular racial images—stressing his connection to a Kenyan biological father who wasn't in his life much, questioning his citizenship, looking sharply at his African relatives, and accusing him of favoring black people in his policies and associations.

The strategy is a curious one: From Bolling's pidgin street language to former Fox News star Glenn Beck's 2009 assertion that the president main-tained a "deep-seated hatred of white people," the channels' personalities are adept at pushing the envelope of language on race issues, only to pull back when the heat of public reaction gets too great.

Beck tried to explain away his charge of Obama's racism a year later, say-ing he really meant to call the president a follower of "liberation theology," which he defined as "Marxism disguised as religion."[38] But the convoluted walk back came too late to stop an advertiser boycott that hobbled his show until he left the channel in June 2011.

Still, the liberation theology explanation followed a favorite tactic of Beck's: to pull ominous-sounding names and movements from history, tweaking and twisting their origins to serve his rhetorical purposes. In the case of liberation theology, the movement started in the 1960s and 1970s as Latin American Catholic leaders pushed the church to side with the poor in demanding fair economic, political, and social conditions.[39]

Theologian James Cone helped develop a version of these ideas for black people in the 1960s, called black liberation theology, which fused Bible teachings with the civil rights justice focus of Martin Luther King Jr. and the pro-black focus of Malcolm X.[40] Jeremiah Wright, the Chicago pastor whose incendiary sermons nearly derailed the 2008 presidential campaign of long-time parishioner Barack Obama—in one speech he urged his congregation to say "God damn America" for the way its criminal justice system unfairly hurt black people—called himself a follower of black liberation theology.[41]

But on his Fox News show, Beck linked the liberation theology movement not just to the church, but to the rantings of fringe groups such as the New Black Panther Party, playing video of the group's former chairman shouting about killing white women and babies.[42]

"Anyone who subscribes to Liberation Theology [is] perverting the message of Christianity and it goes straight to evil," Beck said on his July 13, 2010, Fox News show, about six weeks before the host would moderate his statement about Obama being racist. "It is the same way radical Islamists pervert the message of Islam."[43]

So how exactly was Beck's new Obama assessment any different than calling him a racist? Perhaps because it was an accusation delivered in phrases his fans would understand clearly, while outsiders would need several Google searches and a trip to the library to ferret out his true meaning.

Indeed, Fox News founder and chairman Roger Ailes told *Newsweek* magazine in September 2011 that Beck's racism charge "became a bit of a branding problem for us," admitting that he ordered the channel's opinion-ators to pull back on their rhetoric soon after, as the country recoiled from partisan gridlock in Washington, D.C.[44]

Still, Fox News's goal seems plain: to dismantle President Obama's reputation as a "post-racial" black politician who succeeds without invoking the typical allegations of racial oppression as more conventional leaders might. Ultimately, such tactics seek to make mainstream—in other words, white—Americans suspect that the confident-looking fellow with the Muslim-sounding name and lofty talk about hope is just another black politician looking to cash in on white guilt.

What is most remarkable is how smoothly such attitudes have been passed along to the most-watched programs on the nation's highest-rated cable news channel.

At a time when most Americans still say their primary news source is television—a 2011 poll by the Pew Center found 66 percent of respondents got most of their news from TV and the top source was Fox News, at 19 percent—Fox News Channel has developed a finely tuned ability to play on its audience's fears about black and brown criminality.[45] Whether the topic is allegations of New Black Panther activists shielded by a black president's Justice Department or hysteria surrounding an Islamic mosque and community center near the site of the 9/11 attacks in New York, few race-based conspiracy theories are too outlandish for exploration.

As one kind of proof, consider this question: How was Bolling punished for his mistakes? What sanction came after the host sparked a wide range of critical commentaries and an on-air apology?

He was rewarded with a co-host's job on *The Five*, the 5 P.M. show that replaced Beck's early evening program on Fox News Channel in July 2011—a move that for the former baseball player was akin to going from the minors to the majors. This move would be especially important to maintain his visibility following the company's decision in early 2012 to cancel Fox Business Network's prime time lineup of opinion shows, including Bolling's *Follow the Money*.[46]

As late as February 2012, Bolling was back to his old tricks, comparing African American U.S. Rep. Maxine Waters, who had just given a speech predicting she would soon chair the House of Representatives' banking committee, to troubled pop star Whitney Houston.

"Congresswoman, you saw what happened to Whitney Houston," Bolling said during an appearance on the *Fox and Friends* morning show, referencing the singer's suspicious February 11 death in a hotel bathtub (the coroner eventually ruled it a drowning due to the effects of heart disease and cocaine use). "Step away from the crack pipe, step away from the Xanax, step away from the Lorazepam, it's going to get you in trouble."[47]

Waters, who had called House Republican leaders John Boehner and Eric Cantor "demons," doesn't seem to have much in common with Houston besides her gender and race. Later, Bolling would shrug off the controversy of his remarks, saying, "I was kidding about the crack pipe . . . just kidding."[48]

But Bolling is just one among a long line of Fox News guests and anchors criticized for racially divisive work. These include anchor Megyn Kelly, who excessively covered the New Black Panther Party polling-place scandal; pundit L. Brent Bozell, who noted that "you might want to say" President Obama looks like a "skinny ghetto crackhead" during an interview; and top pundit Bill O'Reilly, who asserted that "gangsta" culture somehow led many of the people trapped in New Orleans after Hurricane Katrina to get stuck in the city.[49]

This is more than rough-and-tumble political commentary. It's prejudice as a business model, tweaking the fears of Fox News's core constituency to ensure continued attention, allegiance, and ratings.

Along the way, it divides the news audience along racial, ethnic, and age lines, even as it lines the pockets of anchors, executives, and shareholders.

TO UNDERSTAND WHY AND HOW THIS ALL WORKS, consider some numbers.

About 44 percent of American adults are over age 50, but the audience for Fox News Channel's biggest stars, Sean Hannity and Bill O'Reilly, leans older. More than two-thirds of O'Reilly's and Hannity's crowd were over age 50 in 2010, according to a report by the Pew Research Center.[50]

The dynamic was similar for liberal lights such as MSNBC's Rachel Maddow and former MSNBC star Keith Olbermann; cable news in prime time unfolds before an audience filled with older males.[51]

Let's refine that picture a bit more.

While researching a story on how early coverage of Shirley Sherrod was inflamed and distorted by racial issues, *New York Times* reporter Brian Stelter uncovered an interesting fact.

Just 1.38 percent of Fox News Channel's average prime time audience between September 2009 and August 2010 was African American. In raw numbers, that totaled 29,000 viewers among an average audience of 2.1 million.[52]

CNN was next among the big three cable networks, with 134,000 black viewers among an audience of 648,000. MSNBC drew the most: 145,000 African Americans from a crowd of 751,000 people in prime time.[53]

According to figures from the Nielsen Company, prime time ratings among viewers aged 25 to 54—a key target for advertisers—were in similar proportions a year later. In 2011, between the hours of 5 P.M. and 11 P.M., Fox News drew an average 15,000 African American viewers in this age range, compared to 51,000 for CNN and 67,000 for MSNBC.[54]

This, despite the fact that Fox News in 2012 was celebrated as the highest-rated cable news channel for ten years straight.

So now we know something else very important about Fox News's audience in prime time. It is older, a bit more male, and white.

The final piece in this puzzle comes courtesy of a September 2011 study from *Washington Post* columnist E. J. Dionne and his colleagues at the Brookings Institution think tank: *What It Means to Be an American, Attitudes in an Increasingly Diverse America Ten Years after 9/11.*

This report analyzed a host of demographic and polling data to create a complex picture of American attitudes about race and culture in the ten years following the terrorist attacks by Muslim extremists on September 11, 2001. They discovered an America increasingly divided by age, ethnicity, race, and political ideology—divisions reflected and exacerbated by ideologically focused TV news outlets.

For example, they noted that 46 percent of Americans believe that discrimination against white people has become as big a problem nationally as discrimination against racial minorities.[55] Among black people and Hispanics, that percentage shrunk to 30 percent.

For Fox News's biggest fans, that disparity was even more pronounced. Nearly 70 percent of viewers who said they most trusted Fox News Channel also said that discrimination against white people is as big a problem as discrimination against racial minorities. Among those who most trust public television, that number shrunk to 25 percent.[56]

And that dynamic isn't limited to black/white/Hispanic issues. About two-thirds of Republicans, along with Americans who identify with the tea party movement and Americans who most trust Fox News, say that the values of Islam are at odds with American values. Nearly 60 percent of Republicans who trust Fox News say American Muslims are trying to establish Sharia law in the United States—a fear some critics say is a thin veil for Islamophobia and prejudice against Muslims and is, at best, simply unfounded.[57]

Let's also note a couple of other interesting tidbits: The Brookings study found that folks from the Millennial generation—adults under 30—were twice as likely as seniors aged 65 and over to have daily interactions with black people and Hispanics. As any expert in race issues can attest, personal interaction is the surest way to dispel stereotypes about minority groups; one of the biggest challenges in combating prejudice involves the fact that most people of color, especially African Americans, live in America's biggest cities, where white people in rural areas may never meaningfully interact with them.

The 2010 Pew Center study also found that more than 70 percent of the audiences for O'Reilly, Beck, Hannity, and radio conservative Rush

Limbaugh call themselves conservative. (Among the general public, just 36 percent call themselves conservative.) And the number of Republicans who watch Fox News regularly was also growing—at 40 percent, it is double the number from a decade ago.[58]

Cable TV is a game of finding the biggest niche, the most profitable sliver of viewership to superserve. And Fox News has distilled an older, more conservative audience in prime time—a group more willing to believe that discrimination against white people is just as significant as discrimination against people of color, and a group more likely to believe that Islam is at odds with American values.

There may be no more fertile ground for the kind of race-baiting tactics Fox News has perfected over its history.

THE ROOTS OF FOX NEWS'S APPROACH TO RACE AND CONFLICT seem grounded in the history of its founder, guiding light, CEO, and chairman, former GOP operative turned media mogul Roger Ailes.

Ailes, hired by News Corp. owner Rupert Murdoch to create Fox News Channel in 1996, is said to be the only man Murdoch actually fears. He was given complete control of the news channel and Fox's 27 owned and operated TV stations nationwide when his brainchild delivered an estimated $816 million in profits in 2010.[59]

But Ailes made his early impact 40 years ago as a political consultant and media expert, impressing Richard Nixon enough when the two met backstage at *The Mike Douglas Show* that the future president hired the show's hard-charging, twentysomething executive producer to handle media for his 1968 campaign.[60]

What is also notable about Ailes's tenure as a political consultant is how many of his employers used fear of black people and controversial racial issues to win support among white voters in tough elections.

Nixon spent time in the late 1960s appealing to disaffected Democrats dismayed by President Lyndon Johnson's signing of the Civil Rights Act of 1964, riding those sentiments into the White House with the help of the 26-year-old media wunderkind Ailes. According to *Nixonland* author Rick Pearlstein, Ailes suggested Nixon hold a TV town hall and take a bluntly racist question from a "good, mean, Wallaceite [George Wallace–style] cabdriver . . . Some guy to sit there and say, 'Awright, Mac, what about these niggers?'"[61] (Wallace was the segregationist, Democrat former governor famous for trying to stop black students from integrating the University of Alabama.)

The moment would have allowed Nixon to condemn the man's language but essentially agree with his sentiment, showing frightened white voters that the candidate was willing to crack down and restore social order.

Ailes knew how, in one exchange, to pit "us"—Nixon and white voters—against "them." Amazing how little can change in four decades.

Flash forward to 1984, and Ailes was coaching GOP presidential candidate Ronald Reagan to a debate victory over Democratic nominee Walter Mondale.[62] Reagan had his own troubling history with race imagery, describing during his 1976 campaign a "welfare queen from the South Side of Chicago" who routinely defrauded the system. The references addressed white fears of shiftless black people thriving on the federal dime—Chicago's South Side was and is a predominantly black area—but reporters could never identify or find the woman, who Reagan never named (author Kaaryn Gustafson said in her book *Cheating Welfare: Public Assistance and the Criminalization of Poverty* that Reagan based his story on three outstanding instances of fraud, exaggerating the circumstances to impress audiences.[63])

Four years later, Ailes oversaw media for Republican George H. W. Bush's 1988 campaign against Democratic Massachusetts Gov. Michael Dukakis, when the GOP used the specter of black criminal William R. "Willie" Horton to make Dukakis look soft on crime. Horton, a convicted murderer, escaped from a furlough program for prisoners in Massachusetts and raped a woman, beating and stabbing her fiancé. Because Dukakis had championed the furlough program, Horton became the centerpiece of Bush's campaign speeches and widely seen television ads by independent groups.

The TV ad that most notoriously featured Horton was dubbed "Weekend Passes"; it was financed by a political action committee and produced by Larry McCarthy, a former employee of Ailes. A 1988 *New York Times* story describes how Horton's mug shot was pinned to a bulletin board next to the desk used by Bush's deputy press secretary. That same article also quotes Ailes saying, "The only question is whether we depict Willie Horton with a knife in his hand or without it."[64]

As critics began to complain that the focus on Horton was a covert racist message, Bush campaign officials, including Ailes, denied that they were doing such a thing and shifted the blame to outside groups, according to Princeton University professor Tali Mendelberg's book *The Race Card*. But

Mendelberg, citing evidence from news reports at the time, concluded that "the Bush campaign used the racial facts of the case intentionally—though subtly—as part of the overall strategy to recruit white voters without drawing the 'racist' label."[65]

After advising the elder Bush, Ailes moved on to another media figure known for using polarizing talk on race to motivate audiences: conservative talk radio star Rush Limbaugh.

Limbaugh, whose radio show has included a song parody called "Barack the Magic Negro," developed a syndicated TV show with Ailes as executive producer back in 1992.[66] But conservative talk pioneer Limbaugh had a tougher time transitioning to television than later competitors such as Sean Hannity and Glenn Beck. Though his TV show featured such scintillating material as a parody Maya Angelou poem read by black satirist Bo Snerdly (one line referred to illegal immigrants cleaning up around Bill Clinton's White House), the program was off the air by 1996.[67]

Each of these Ailes clients whipped up support among a white, often middle-class, usually male target audience by fanning the flames of racial resentment and fears of lawbreaking black people.

If you doubt Ailes's influence on every aspect of Fox News, read this quote from his close friend Limbaugh, delivered during a November 2009 ceremony when the Fox News chief received the Good Scout Award.

"One man has established a culture for 1,700 people who believe in it, who follow it, who execute it," Limbaugh told the audience, which also included a long roster of the channel's talent. "Roger Ailes cannot do everything. Roger Ailes is not on the air. Roger Ailes does not ever show up on camera, and yet everybody who does is a reflection of him."[68]

Esquire writer Tom Junod summed up Ailes's approach in a January 2011 piece titled "Why Does Roger Ailes Hate America?" He wrote:

Before the arrival of Roger Ailes, television was thought to be a unifying medium—the "electronic hearth." Mr. Ailes knew better. Mr. Ailes knew that it was the fire itself. Mr. Ailes knew that the television screen in each American home was nothing less than a battleground, and he who controlled it controlled America, no matter what the message. He didn't even have to be overtly political, because television was by definition a political medium. Roger Ailes could win . . . if the idea of a unified America lost. He could win . . . if his own subversive vision of America was realized. He could win . . .

if American life became an endless, entrenched, and above all electronic argument. And you know what?

He did win.[69]

The only question left for the rest of us: What kind of America are we left with, after Ailes's victory?

SPORTS FANS CALL IT "WORKING THE REFS," a term applied to media and politics by former Republican Party chair Rich Bond, quoted in a 1992 *Washington Post* story.[70]

The idea is that by complaining about the fairness of every call, eventually you push the referee enough that he (or she) lets a few borderline calls go your way, just to look fair.

Applied to media and politics, the term takes on much larger significance for people of color. By consistently blasting President Obama's administration and public image on issues of race, Fox News and other conservative media outlets have effectively kept the nation's first black president silent on race issues.

That also means that the landmark feat of electing America's first nonwhite president could remain a mostly symbolic achievement when it comes to improving the nation's race relations.

For proof, look no further than the arrest and subsequent reaction to Harvard professor Henry Louis Gates Jr., a longtime scholar on race and racism, who claimed that police in Cambridge, Massachusetts, overreacted by taking him into custody while investigating a report of a break-in at his home. What prompted a neighbor to call police was the sight of Gates himself attempting to enter his home after realizing he had forgotten his keys.

According to Gates, police arrested him after they knew he was the owner of the home, mostly because he grew angry when they refused to believe he had a right to be there.[71]

President Obama first responded to the incident when a reporter asked him about it at a live press conference meant to cover his massive health care bill. His answer immediately sparked worldwide headlines.

"My understanding is that Professor Gates then shows his I.D. to show that this is his house and, at that point, he gets arrested for disorderly conduct, charges which are later dropped," the president said. "I don't know, not having been there and not seeing all the facts, what role race played in [Gates's case]. But I think it's fair to say, number one, any of us would be pretty angry; number two, that the Cambridge police acted stupidly in arresting somebody when there was already proof that they were in their own home; and, number three, what I think we know separate and apart from this incident is that there's a long history in this country of African-Americans and Latinos being stopped by law enforcement disproportionately. That's just a fact."[72]

In an irony only our politically contentious times could produce, the invaluable teaching moment offered by a black Harvard professor's arrest was fumbled and forgotten, as liberals and conservatives chewed over the resultant furor from different angles.

According to the Project for Excellence in Journalism, coverage of Gates's arrest and President Obama's comments consumed nearly one-fifth of all coverage relating to African American issues in major news outlets in 2009, and almost 25 percent of all talk radio segments on race issues—a big portion of an admittedly small number.[73] And even though Gates pronounced the president's reaction "brilliant," Obama's words drew intense criticism from police groups. A Pew Research poll revealed that 70 percent of white people who heard a lot about Obama's comments disapproved of how he handled the situation, and his approval ratings among white people shrank by seven points in the days after his words hit the press.[74]

This is the moment that inspired Fox News star Glenn Beck to declare in July 2009 that the president had a "deep-seated hatred of white people" and was "racist."

Ironically, fellow Fox News star Bill O'Reilly complained about exaggerating the racial impact of public comments just a few days later, asking fellow anchor Geraldo Rivera, "What is it in America, that we still have every two seconds a racial controversy? . . . Why is this continued to be used as a sledgehammer against people in ideological battles?"[75]

One answer may be that the Gates scandal had a political dimension. The controversy exploded just as President Obama was trying to explain the intricacies of his complex health care bill to America, an effort conservatives resisted from the start. As long as citizens were arguing about race and policing in Cambridge, any conversation about health care was drowned out. And opponents who had been arguing—with little evidence—that President

Obama was a leader ready to advance the cause of African Americans at the expense of white Americans now had their smoking gun.

Small wonder, then, that when the dubiously edited video of Shirley Sherrod emerged in the blogosphere a year later, administration officials pressured her to resign before all the facts were known, and without a word of protest from the nation's first black president.

Sometimes, it seems, working the refs can produce results.

WHEN FOX NEWS CHANNEL STAR BILL O'REILLY denounced me as "one of the biggest race-baiters in the country" during a 2008 commentary on his *O'Reilly Factor* show, what surprised me most was how the anchor so neatly embodied the typical tactics used by race-baiters to disguise their own excesses.

First, his claims provided no details. In the commentary, O'Reilly provided a long list of people civil rights activist Jesse Jackson supposedly accused of being racist. But with no details included, viewers were led to assume that any charge of racism levied by certain kinds of people—liberals and black people, it seems—is bogus.

In my own case, his only evidence of my so-called race-baiting was my status as head of the NABJ Media Monitoring Committee, a group that flags unfair and prejudiced depictions of racial minorities in news coverage. The committee also suggested candidates for an annual "Thumbs Down Award," which Fox News would win later that year, along with MSNBC host Pat Buchanan.[76]

In the same way the Society of Professional Journalists advocates on free speech issues, groups such as the NABJ work to defeat prejudice and stereotyping in news coverage, reasoning that fairer reports on minorities produce more accurate stories. For us, diversity and sensitivity in news coverage is a core journalism value. Of course, O'Reilly's viewers never heard these arguments, because he made little effort to fairly depict the people he was criticizing, including me.

O'Reilly's list of offenders were exclusively liberals and people of color, with no mention of how fellow conservatives such as Rush Limbaugh, Sean Hannity, or Michael Savage also regularly deliver incendiary talk about race (can O'Reilly really think a parody song such as Limbaugh's "Barack the Magic Negro" makes it easier for racial minorities to talk to white people about race?). In his world, apparently, people of color are not allowed to speak on issues of race without facing accusations of race-baiting themselves.

Instead, white culture is presented as the benchmark of normalcy and a yardstick for appropriate behavior, without even acknowledging that white people have a separate cultural identity of their own.

And O'Reilly's segment committed the cardinal sin of race relations, tying all discussion of prejudice, stereotyping, and race issues to the explosive act of calling someone a racist.

For those of us who dissect race issues often, the term "racist" is the nuclear weapon of debate, a devastating force that shuts down all discussion. O'Reilly is right when he says many white people fear being unjustly accused of such extreme behavior, officially defined as "the belief that all members of each race possess characteristics or abilities specific to that race, esp. so as to distinguish it as inferior or superior to another race or races."[77]

After years writing on these issues, I'm convinced it's time to stop using the word "racist" to describe everyone who offers racially insensitive commentary or actions. That's because there are relatively few people who walk around believing in their bones that folks are superior or inferior because of their race. But people often act in response to stereotypes and misconceptions about other groups in ways that produce inequality. And trying to discuss those reactions is the furthest thing from race-baiting—it is an attempt to bridge the cultural divisions that segment us all.

It wasn't the first time I'd locked horns with Fox News hosts on the subject of race. On October 15, 2007, I faced off against Sean Hannity and Alan Colmes. The subject was Don Imus, whose syndicated radio show was also aired by MSNBC in the mornings, and who had made headlines by calling the players on Rutgers University's women's basketball team "nappy-headed hos" during a broadcast.

Colmes, who was supposed to be the liberal voice balancing Hannity's conservatism, insisted that Imus "satirized" the team by calling them sexually promiscuous black women who don't comb their hair. He never actually explained how a line like that might be construed as satire—a defense even Imus wasn't using at the time—but he was sure I was being unfair to a radio personality who had a 25-year history of comparing black athletes to animals and slinging around prejudiced stereotypes.

Here's a bit of the exchange, according to a transcript prepared by the liberal media watchdog Media Matters:

COLMES: The team that he allegedly insulted—I would say "satirized"—they accepted his apology. Why can't you?

DEGGANS: I think Don Imus hasn't really apologized for what he's done wrong. What he did wrong was build a 25- to 30-year broadcasting career on humor that's racist and that exaggerates stereotypes.

COLMES: Well, that's what satire is.[78]

Later, Hannity would compare Imus's joke to routines offered by Chris Rock, an African American comic who doesn't host a morning show aired on a major cable news channel.

Throughout that interview, I stressed an issue that often gets lost in these arguments over stereotypes and prejudice: history.

For me, Imus's biggest transgression wasn't a joke that crossed a line. It was a history of jokes that crossed similar boundaries, including calling African American journalist Gwen Ifill a "cleaning lady" when she worked for the *New York Times* and calling another black sportswriter at the paper, William C. Rhoden, a "quota hire."[79] Seven years before Imus lost his MSNBC job, *Chicago Tribune* columnist Clarence Page got him to raise his hand and pledge "to cease all simian reference to black athletes . . . abandon all references to non-criminal blacks as thugs, pimps, muggers and Colt-45 drinkers" and bring an "end to Amos and Andy cuts, comparison of New York City to Mogadishu and all parodies of black voices, unless they are done by a black person."[80]

Page said he was never invited back on the show again. But Imus, who had balanced hosting serious politicians and pundits with shock jock–level comedy bits bristling with prejudice and sexism, broke his own pledge—and his downfall was hastened by a growing media culture where every word said in a public setting can land online in minutes, leaving little room to deny or obfuscate.

With Imus, as with Fox News, history matters.

So it's no surprise that, one year after Imus lost both his CBS Radio and MSNBC jobs, O'Reilly was on the warpath about race issues again—this time, making the case that Jeremiah Wright's incendiary sermons accusing America of continued institutional racism left "millions of Americans of all colors . . . fed up with race-baiters and accusations of racism."[81]

In one short commentary, O'Reilly invoked all the classic arguments used to shut down discussion of race issues: asserting the primacy of white culture without stating it, setting a high bar for judging any incident to be evidence of prejudice or racism, and negating the ability of people of color to initiate talk on such subjects.

Often, people say the best way to approach race is to attempt to be "color blind"—to work hard to avoid seeing race difference and reacting to it. And because white Americans often fail to acknowledge that they have a racial culture that helps shape their attitudes and choices, the result of such color-blind efforts really means that white culture continues to dominate society and institutions.

Such "color blindness," in practice, often means burying any talk about possible prejudice or racial issues, leading us to ignore problems instead of deal with them.

"Colorblindness creates a society that denies [minorities'] negative racial experiences, rejects their cultural heritage and invalidates their unique perspectives," wrote psychologist Monica Williams in a *Psychology Today* article titled "Colorblind Ideology Is a Form of Racism." "Colorblindness has helped make race into a taboo topic that polite people cannot openly discuss. And if you can't talk about it, you can't understand it; much less fix the racial problems that plague our society."[82]

For nearly 50 years, people of color have used the victories of the civil rights movement in America to shine a light on prejudiced behavior, pressing mainstream society to rein it in. I have always suspected that conservatives such as Beck and Breitbart resent that power and seek to reclaim it for their mostly white audiences—people who are already accustomed to having their sensibilities define the boundaries of debate on every important civic issue.

O'Reilly may know what the polls cited earlier in this chapter prove: His audience already believes that prejudice against white people is as prevalent as prejudice against racial minorities. So he has receptive ears for his message that the time has come to disengage from uncomfortable conversations about race and instead demonize people—especially people of color—who do want to talk about these issues as untrustworthy "race-baiters."

Even as 2010 U.S. Census figures reveal that America is growing more diverse faster than anticipated—by 2015, racial and ethnic minorities are expected to become the majority of young people; the population of non-white people has increased in every state since the year 2000—O'Reilly advocated shutting down conversations that could help us better understand each other.[83]

I have often written that journalists should be judged by the enemies they make and the epithets they are called.

So, in this case, being called a race-baiter by the biggest star at a cable news channel that has turned racially insensitive talk into a viewership strategy feels much less like an insult.

Actually, it feels like a compliment.

FOUR

CHASING OBAMA, NEWT, BACHMANN, AND PALIN

*The Pitfalls of Race and Gender
in Political Coverage*

THE ONE THING JUAN WILLIAMS WASN'T EXPECTING WAS THE force of the crowd's reaction.

He did plan on raising a few eyebrows. Even back when he was spitballing ideas, preparing for the GOP presidential debate sponsored by his employer Fox News, the *Wall Street Journal,* and the South Carolina Republican Party, Williams knew what he wanted to ask of candidate Newt Gingrich.

And he expected it would draw an attack.

The debate, scheduled for January 16, 2012, was an important one for Gingrich, who looked like he might end his candidacy if things didn't go well in the South Carolina primary five days later. And the candidate had a history of responding to tough press questions by attacking the questioner, as he would prove days later, belittling CNN anchor John King for daring to start that channel's debate by asking about an ex-wife's public comments that Gingrich asked for an open marriage.

But Williams still wanted to ask the former House Speaker about some speech lines he felt were typical "dog whistle" politics—phrases intended to provoke deep-seated, even unconscious prejudice—such as vowing to speak at an NAACP convention on the importance of demanding paychecks over food stamps and his contention that poor children could learn a valuable work ethic by serving as janitors in their own schools.

"That's pretty explicitly racial," Williams told me, weeks later. "I do think it was intentional—and I wasn't just talking about Newt. Santorum had been up to some tricks, too. And in my opinion, it had [gone from 'dog whistles' to] become hoots and hollers."[1]

According to a *New York Times* story, Fox News executives worked with Williams to moderate the phrasing in his query, which originally used the words "demeaning" and "racially charged" to describe the food stamp rhetoric.[2]

Still, when Williams delivered the question, it came with a sting: "Speaker Gingrich, you recently said black Americans should demand jobs, not food stamps. You also said poor kids lack a strong work ethic and proposed having them work as janitors in their schools. Can't you see that this is viewed, at a minimum, as insulting to all Americans, but particularly to black Americans?"

That's when the reaction began in the crowd—a low murmur that grew into loud applause for the candidate's first words: "No, I don't see that."

Gingrich parried by noting his daughter once worked as a janitor at age 13 in Georgia and he'd heard from other supporters who valued the menial work they'd done early in life. "They'd be getting money, which is a good thing if you're poor," the former House Speaker said. "Only the elites despise earning money."

Williams had a tough time speaking over the response to that closing line, which drew sustained applause. But he refused to back down, noting that "my Twitter account has been inundated with people of all races who are asking if your comments are not intended to belittle the poor and racial minorities."

That's when the real smackdown came.

"Well, first of all, Juan, the fact is that more people have been put on food stamps by Barack Obama than any president in American history," Gingrich said, sparking applause. "Now, I know among the politically correct, you're not supposed to use facts that are uncomfortable . . . I believe every American of every background has been endowed by their creator with the right to pursue happiness. And if that makes liberals unhappy, I'm going to continue to find ways to help poor people learn how to get a job, learn how to get a better job and learn some day to own the job."

The result: a standing ovation.

"I felt the force of [the audience's] rage," Williams recalled. "I remember thinking, 'What is going on here?' I didn't realize until later, they were standing . . . I realized at that point, he had thrown red meat to this crowd. And they were responding on some angry, visceral level."[3]

Footage from part of that exchange was turned into a political ad for Gingrich. And the candidate, who entered the South Carolina race down by 10 percent in many polls, eventually won that primary by 12 points.[4]

So did the dog whistles work?

"I was struck by how, given the tumultuous response, he didn't come close to answering my question," Williams said. "And the thing that was a puzzle to me was how he used my name . . . I didn't pick it up at first. But I could hear the hissing, the way he strung it out. I guess he knew what he was doing. He wanted to call me 'boy,' making me into the 'other.' I'm so naïve, I didn't get it."[5]

Princeton University professor Tali Mendelberg wasn't surprised at the reaction, or at Gingrich's success in the South Carolina primary, though she's written a book contending that political messages gilded with racist language work best when the message isn't obvious.

In that book, 2001's *The Race Card*, Mendelberg argued that racially charged rhetoric works best in modern American politics when the language is *implicit* rather than *explicit*. As Exhibit A, she cites modern electoral politics' most successful race-baiting move: the 1988 campaign ad supporting George H. W. Bush and featuring African American murderer Willie Horton, who escaped while on a furlough program Democratic presidential candidate Michael Dukakis had championed.

So if candidates refer to welfare programs or food stamps—subjects many people, especially white voters, associate with black people—the connection to people of color can be made without overt statements. And voters can react to an idea rooted in prejudice without their conscious mind stepping in to reject overt racism.

"Gingrich calling Obama the food stamp president is an example," said Mendelberg, an associate professor of politics at Princeton University, noting that talk about doubting the president's citizenship or Christian faith also fall in the category of implicit messages on racial difference.[6]

"My research suggests that when people hear the phrase is racial, it no longer has an effect . . . except among the sub-population that has more overt racial attitudes toward people in the first place," she said. "In the past, that's primarily been males . . . explicit cues work well with white males in the south. And by coincidence, Gingrich did *really* well in [South Carolina]."

Fortunately, Mendelberg's research also indicates there's a simple solution. Outside of those voters with "overt racial attitudes," most people become more resistant to implicit racism after exposure to lots of media coverage explaining the prejudice.

"The more stories there are in media about how this is racial, the more people can realize, 'Oh this is racial,'" the professor said, noting that there's enough stigma attached to open racism these days that many people will reject it when exposed. "Remember not to overestimate the public's attentiveness to political news. The safe assumption is that the majority of people voting have seen or heard very little. They're drawing on snippets—they've seen an ad here, heard a little bit of talk radio playing in the background, people they talk to have something to say. That's the level of information for most voters."

But what happens when *journalists* have trouble recognizing the dog whistle?

Gingrich's comments on the NAACP and food stamps were made during a speech at a town hall meeting in Plymouth, New Hampshire, on January 5, 2012.

Dave Weigel, a writer for *Slate* magazine, seemed to be the first reporter to notice the importance of what Gingrich said, tweeting from the press conference: "Newt: 'I will go to the NAACP convention, and tell the African-American community why they should demand paychecks instead of food stamps.'"

That message sparked widespread attention, from liberal website the Daily Kos to Current TV anchor Keith Olbermann's Worst Persons in the World segment. But what I found most interesting was that Weigel was the only reporter in the room who noticed the alleged "dog whistle": Gingrich's linkage of race to his longstanding rhetoric about teaching people to prefer paychecks over food stamps.

A longer transcript of Gingrich's remarks reveals more of what he said:

> Now, there's no neighborhood I know of in America where if you went around and asked people, would you rather your children had food stamps or paychecks, you wouldn't end up with a majority saying they'd rather have a paycheck.

And so I'm prepared, if the NAACP invites me, I'll go to their convention and talk about why the African-American community should demand paychecks and not be satisfied with food stamps. And I'll go to them and explain a brand new Social Security opportunity for young people, which would be particularly good for African-American males because they are the group that gets the smallest return on social security because they have the shortest life span.[7]

Once word began to spread online, the story migrated to traditional news outlets, landing on the network evening newscasts by the day's end.

"I had heard him say a version of this before, and knew it was a different take," Weigel said. "He had never said before this was something he was going to tell to black voters . . . I checked the day after, did he ever say anything like that before; he never did."[8]

Dylan Byers, media reporter for the *Politico* newspaper and website, noted that journalists had heard Gingrich often talk about going to speak at an NAACP convention and, in different moments, about teaching others to prefer paychecks over food stamps.[9] Members of Gingrich's campaign staff said linking his statements to any idea of racial politicking was unfair and inaccurate.

Some campaign reporters agreed with Gingrich's people. As the Washington bureau chief for *Newsweek* and the *Daily Beast,* Howard Kurtz spent lots of time in the 2012 election cycle following the candidates around. Kurtz, who also spent many years as a media critic at the *Washington Post,* didn't believe Gingrich was indulging in racial politics with the paychecks-over-food-stamps comment, but allowed it was an issue reporters could probe more.

"There is a kind of Kabuki dance in which skilled political practitioners will send sharp-edged messages to their most ideological supporters and blame the media when they are called on it," he said, citing Gingrich's "food stamp president" line as a better example of a coded phrase hiding racial messages.[10]

"I concluded that too many journalists, for too long, have been reticent to write and speak frankly about race-related issues because they can be explosive," he added. "To shy away from honest reporting and analysis on that front is a disservice. So I've tried to practice that, now that I'm writing more directly about politics."

Still, in the moment, some might say Gingrich went from an *implicit* racial appeal to an *explicit* one, just by connecting two ideas. And even most reporters in the room, accustomed to such code-speak, didn't notice until one person pointed it out.

The same thing seemed to happen a few days earlier, when another GOP candidate, Rick Santorum, made a reference to welfare that seemed to single out black people.

The comment came on New Year's Day 2012, when Santorum was speaking at a coffeehouse in Sioux City, Iowa. NPR reported that the candidate talked about making Americans less dependent on government aid, cueing up an explosive sound bite:

"I don't want to make black people's lives better by giving them somebody else's money," he seems to say in the audio, stumbling a bit on the word "black." "I want to give them the opportunity to go out and earn the money."[11]

NPR couldn't reach Santorum for a comment before airing its story the following day. When CBS News asked him about the comment the day after the speech, Santorum speculated he might have been influenced by recently seeing a documentary film about the educational struggles of black children, *Waiting for Superman,* stressing that he wanted to help everyone.[12]

A few days later, Santorum told CNN he was "pretty confident" he didn't say "black people," noting, "I started to say a word, then sort of changed, and it sort of—blah—mumbled it, and sort of changed my thought."[13]

Once again, just one news outlet at the press conference noticed the reference—NPR—though many others jumped on the comment once their story aired. Even NPR's ombudsman, Edward Schumacher-Matos, said he heard "black people" when he first listened to the clip, then changed his mind after listening again.[14]

Keith Woods, NPR's vice president of diversity in news and operations, is also a respected African American journalist who once served as dean of the Poynter Institute for Media Studies in Florida. He told Schumacher-Matos that he didn't hear Santorum say "black people" in NPR's clip and told me that even if the candidate stumbled because he intended to say the phrase, it might not mean much.

"There's a certain element of myth that this is exceptional behavior . . . to think that somehow it's different for a politician to make a connection in his head between linking poverty and black people," Woods said, noting that journalists make those connections often in their stories and average consumers do, too (more on that dynamic in Chapter Nine). "In Santorum's case, if he slipped up and caught himself, he is an ordinary American."[15]

What bothers Woods about these issues is that they are evidence of a deeper truth. Journalists often only talk about race during a crisis.

"The problem we have is we can only believe one thing at a time," he said. "Either we are post-racial because we have a black president, or we are beset by racism on all sides, and neither is true . . . The thing I have been advocating for, since 1995, is ordinary coverage of race. So we have the ability to move it in and out of a story, even when it's not [the main subject] of what the story is about. The norm of a print newsroom is to load up and tell it in a seven-part series. You hit 'em with this big series, then you go silent again . . . these things are able to catch fire and run because we are silent on this topic the rest of the time."

And reporters can expect zero help in figuring out the truth from the candidate.

"If ever there was a moment in time when everybody is invested in not being honest, [explaining a possible gaffe] would be the moment," Woods added. "When Santorum sounds like he's saying 'black people' or Gingrich refers to the 'food stamp president,' you have this quick ignition of indignation which happens around these issues anyway. On top of that, you pour gallons of rocket fuel because it's a national election. And those people who might get burned by what they've said, have no interest in a thoughtful conversation about race."

The influence of social media is also undeniable in modern campaign coverage, extending journalists' reach while also ratcheting up the pressure to provide a steady stream of attention-getting content to websites, Facebook pages, Twitter feeds, and more.

He may have made his reputation covering war in Vietnam nearly 50 years ago, but even former CBS News anchor Dan Rather admitted to feeling the influence of online media on the reporting process, covering the GOP for businessman Mark Cuban's HDNet channel, to be renamed AXS-TV.

Sitting in a conference room at a luxury hotel in Tampa, preparing for a long day expounding on the intricacies of Florida's GOP primaries in early 2012, Rather admitted he had just started his own Twitter and Facebook pages—in part, to draw more attention to his work.

At age 80.

"Journalists can and—more than we'd like to admit—do cover the campaigns basically by staying alert to Twitter, staying alert to Facebook and viewing the debates, preferably in person," said Rather. "I don't really like this metaphor, but there were people covering the Vietnam War by staying in Saigon and going to briefings . . . now we have a deadline every nanosecond, and I'm not sure the public understands that."[16]

In this new, social media–fueled environment, he added, race issues are almost the new "third rail" of political discourse—considered dangerous to discuss head on, because any gaffe can spread "like mildew in a damp basement."

That may be why race and cultural issues often sneak into the campaign dialogue from oblique angles. Hispanic issues often arise only when talking about immigration, while GOP hopeful Ron Paul was grilled about newsletters printed under his name in the 1990s that contained racial, anti-Semitic, and anti-gay material (Paul has said he was unaware of the content).[17]

There seems little stomach for broaching the subject of race relations on its own—the way you might ask a candidate about unemployment or education—despite America's ever-increasing ethnic diversity.

"Nobody's asked the question [in a debate]: Mr. Candidate, if you're elected president, specifically what would you do to improve race relations in this country?" said Rather, who covered the civil rights movement in his early days at CBS News. "I have long believed that racial issues and how we handle them will define this country in history. Nobody in the history of humankind has ever tried to do what we have been trying in this country . . . have a constitutional republic based on the principles of freedom and democracy that is multiracial, multi-religious. Anybody who says that race is not a major consideration in our national political dialogue . . . I think is mistaken."[18]

Jay Rosen, a journalism professor at New York University, looked at the 839 questions asked during 20 GOP primary debates between May 2011 and early February 2012, seeking to understand what journalists thought the candidates should be talking about. His results were published by the *Guardian* newspaper in London.[19]

Immigration got 8 percent of the questions, gay rights (combined with abortion) got 5 percent. Racial issues didn't really show up; presumably they were in the 1 percent of unclassified questions. But questions about candidates' backgrounds stood at 27 percent and campaign strategy at 12 percent.

None of that surprised Rosen, who said that journalists often avoid accusations of bias in political coverage by focusing on what he calls the Church of the Savvy.

"[It's] how to be a sophisticated observer of politics yet remain uncommitted," he said. "You can talk about the Southern strategy and make wise learned references to Nixon and Wallace and bring up [Bush strategist] Lee Atwater and how effective that stuff was in South Carolina. Instead of saying—wait a minute this is racist politics—you're talking about the strategy. And you have the additional benefit of making journalists feel like they're practicing a kind of detachment. There's a tension between a decent and civil response to those things and the savvy inside take."[20]

And talking about race in political news stories can also be difficult because different racial groups see race in different ways.

I first broached this idea back in 2008, a month after Barack Obama's election as America's first black president, with a former schoolmate, Linda Tropp. Linda and I met many years ago when we both attended a Jewish middle school in Hammond, Indiana. (I was there because my mother, a longtime teacher in nearby Gary, Indiana, knew it was a great school—believe it or don't.)

Since our time participating in *shabbat* services and learning Hebrew, Linda has become an expert psychology researcher at the University of Massachusetts, Amherst, investigating how groups of people communicate across races and cultures.

She suggested that too little journalism or discussion about race addresses *why* different groups see race in different ways.

"Whites aren't accustomed to thinking of themselves in terms of race, or to reflect on their status as white people, unless there are demands from the social situation," said Linda, who is white. "It behooved white people to want to preserve their status; there's no reason for us to feel guilty: things are good. By contrast, there's a functional reason for black people to be dissatisfied or to see cracks in the system."[21]

But how does that play out in perceptions about race?

"If you are not confronted with discrimination on a day-to-day basis, it's that much harder to understand how people are affected by it," she said. "And if you're black and constantly affected by prejudice, it must be hard to imagine that whites don't see it. We often assign suspicion and intent to those varying perceptions. Whites might say minorities are exaggerating the problem or playing the race card, while black people might say whites don't want to see it. If we hope to get to a point of improving group relations, we need to open up our minds that people might not share our perceptions, even if it seems obvious."

I recalled standing in the press room for a GOP debate in Tampa less than three weeks after Gingrich's NAACP comments. Sitting in the rear of the press room, I spent the evening looking around. Aside from a few aides, reporters from a local Spanish-language cable news channel, and former Republican National Committee head Michael Steele, there were fewer than a dozen people of color (including me) in a room of at least 200.

Suddenly, the sporadic way in which race surfaced in the Santorum and Gingrich examples made *a lot* more sense.

Even Weigel initially defended Gingrich's use of the NAACP/food stamp link in a short story he posted online the day after the speech. "I think people misunderstood," he told me a few days after the story broke. "I really feel like what he thinks is that conservatives should be bold and say, 'Look what political correctness is doing; it puts this fence around this reform that we all need.'"[22]

When we saw each other in Tampa a few weeks later, Weigel dropped another interesting insight. Among all the voters he talked with in South Carolina, one out of every four or five brought up Gingrich's spat with Williams, saying they agreed with the notion that too many black people were willing to be dependent on public assistance.

"That line about kids not working hard enough . . . in some cases, people interpreted it as black kids on welfare not working hard enough," he said.[19]

Later, Weigel noted Gingrich's penchant for skirting the edge of racial controversy in a March 23 post for *Slate* titled "Newt Gingrich's Dog Whistle, Now Audible to Anyone Who's Ever Seen a Dog."

He recounted Gingrich's objections that week to a joke told by actor Robert DeNiro—the star asked during a re-election fundraiser attended by Michelle Obama if America was "ready for a white First Lady"—as well as his musings that Barack Obama's actions as president might give Republicans valid reason to wonder if he is Muslim.

"We see the Gingrichian version of the Southern Strategy," Weigel wrote, referencing the Republican tactic of reaching out to white Democrats in the South through anti-black racism.[24]

Perhaps the best outcome of both Gingrich and Santorum's statements is that they inspired journalists to look into exactly who *does* get food stamps and welfare in America. As CBS noted in its story on Santorum, for example, just 9 percent of Iowans who receive food stamps are black, while 84 percent of recipients are white people; nationwide in 2010, 34 percent of those receiving food stamps were white, compared to 22 percent who were African American.[25]

What might be most surprising, however, is the fact that Williams and Gingrich would have such a high-profile fight over the food stamps vs. paychecks issue at all.

After all, Williams wrote a 2006 book called *Enough: The Phony Leaders, Dead-End Movements and Culture of Failure that Are Undermining Black America—and What We Can Do about It,* criticizing established black leaders, including some at the NAACP, for profiting from a "culture of failure."

Are those ideas all that different from what Gingrich said in New Hampshire?

"I made a challenge to black America, speaking to people out of a sense of compassion and caring," Williams said to me. "I wrote it in a way that I would write a letter to my children about how they can do well in the world. That's different than trying to make out people as welfare queens or lazy bums to take advantage of government entitlements."[26]

And even though he works for a cable news channel where some personalities have accused the president of being racist or declining to prosecute crimes against black people, Williams said that some of the criticisms thrown at Obama bother him, because they seem rooted in racism.

"My problem comes when people hector him and they talk to him in ways they never did any other politician," he said. "This idea that he's a socialist or he wasn't born in this country—at some point, you start to think maybe there's a reason they persist with this stuff and maybe it is racial. Everybody gets beat up and everybody gets slammed; I just want him to be slammed like any other politician."

As a certain psychology researcher might say: Perspective certainly is everything.

THERE IS ONE SURE WAY to really snark off Julie Burton.

Show her headlines like these:

"Michelle Bachman's Evolution from Minnesota Mom to Beltway Barbie," *Huffington Post*, December 6, 2011.

"Michelle Bachman Raises the Fashion Bar for Female Politicians," the *Washington Post*'s Reliable Source column, January 5, 2012.

"Fashion Rivals: Sarah Palin vs. Michele Bachmann," *Telegraph* of London, June 29, 2011.

That's because, as president of the Women's Media Center (WMC)—a national advocacy group founded in 2005 by Jane Fonda, Robin Morgan, and Gloria Steinem—it's part of Burton's job to advocate for sexism-free coverage of women, especially when they are politicians and particularly when they are running for office.

"The influence of the media is the most powerful economic and cultural force out there," said Burton.[27]

And one of the WMC's biggest issues is the way journalists often focus on the appearance, marital status, children, and age of female candidates in ways men never face.

From radio hosts in Boston talking about Republican treasurer candidate Karyn E. Polito's "banging little body" to the *Washington Post* calling South Carolina governor Nikki Haley a "Real Housewife: fit, attractive and encased in suits that stop just below the elbow and just above the knee," the WMC works to identify ways in which media diminish women by focusing on superficial issues.[28]

Such coverage can exact a cost. The group funded a survey of 800 likely voters across the country in 2010, discovering that sexist coverage could blunt voters' tendency to vote for female candidates. The dip only disappears if the candidate responds and points out the negative treatment in the media.[29]

The results hearken back to the studies mentioned earlier about *implicit* vs. *explicit* messages. It seems that if the hypothetical female candidate makes the subtle sexism more obvious by pointing it out and criticizing it, voters can realize the dynamic at hand and reject it.

That's why the WMC created a media guide for journalists in early 2012, aimed at encouraging "gender neutral coverage of women candidates and politicians." Among the highlights: a glossary describing how words such as "ballsy," "matronly," and "nag" can be used in sexist ways and a media pledge of gender neutrality that promises, in part, "not posing questions or using language for one gender that I would not feel is equally applicable to the other."[30]

"Our co-founder Gloria Steinem talks about the Rule of Reversibility," said Burton, citing a quote from the legendary feminist that opens their media guide. "When writing about candidates [in an election], don't mention her young children unless you mention his, or say she's shrill and attractive. Don't say she's had facial surgery unless you mention if he had it. And don't ask her if she's running as a woman's candidate unless you ask the same thing of the men."[31]

That's a lesson you'd think reporters would have learned years ago.

Back in 2008, in fact, some pundits did so much apologizing, it seemed certain they must have learned something. That was the year MSNBC's David Shuster apologized for suggesting Chelsea Clinton was "sort of being pimped out" by her mother Hillary while fundraising (he was suspended) and Chris Matthews apologized for saying of Hillary Clinton that "the reason she's a U.S. Senator . . . is her husband messed around."[32]

I felt back then that we were seeing something singular. The rules had changed a bit for political reporters, especially those with high profiles, and some of the players hadn't realized it yet.

In that cycle, as Obama and Clinton fought each other for the Democratic presidential nomination, and Sarah Palin later became the second female nominee for vice president, we had a field of candidates different from those the country had ever seen before. Indeed, since their candidacies predated Campbell Brown's CNN show, Rachel Maddow's MSNBC show, Erin Burnett's CNN show, and Diane Sawyer's ascension to ABC's *World News*, the field of candidates was often more diverse than the reporters covering them.

And even those who think they're immune to the damage can change their minds.

In March 2008, Palin criticized Hillary Clinton for complaining about sexism in media coverage, noting, "When I hear a statement like that coming from a woman candidate with any kind of perceived whine about that excess criticism or you know maybe a sharper microscope put on her, I think, 'Man that doesn't do us any good.'"[33]

Flash forward to November 2009, when *Newsweek* magazine ran a cover photo featuring her in tight shorts originally taken for *Runner's World* magazine. Palin's response, posted on Facebook: "The out-of-context *Newsweek* approach is sexist and oh-so-expected by now. If anyone can learn anything from it: it shows why you shouldn't judge a book by its cover, gender, or color of skin."[34]

Suddenly, after months in the eye of the journalism storm, Palin realized there might be something to this whole media sexism thing.

In an analysis by academics Diana Carlin and Kelly Winfrey, "Have You Come a Long Way Baby? Hillary Clinton, Sarah Palin, and Sexism in 2008 Campaign Coverage," the pair listed the gender stereotypes often affixed to female candidates: seductress or sex object, mother, pet or child, and iron maiden. After detailing the various ways in which media coverage pushed both Palin and Clinton into these roles—from discussions of Palin's parenting skills to pieces about Clinton's cleavage—the authors offered a few recommendations for dealing with the stereotyping.

"Women candidates and their campaign staffs need to decide to attack sexism and attack it early and consistently," the authors wrote. "Both campaigns dismissed the sexism shown toward the other and neither was willing to give a sexism speech similar to Obama's racism address. It is possible that a candidate cannot do it herself and that at some point, a woman with considerable credibility who has not been the subject of sexist attacks, such as Madeleine Albright or Condoleezza Rice, needs to take such a speech on the road."[35]

The WMC's work seems a step in that direction, regularly alerting journalists when they cross the line from cheeky to stereotypical.

"Change comes slowly, and if we don't highlight the problems, nothing's going to happen," said Burton, who met with MSNBC president Phil Griffin and anchor Ed Schultz after the broadcaster called pundit Laura Ingraham a "right-wing slut" on his show (Schultz apologized and was suspended). "It took us 144 years to get the vote, and every single day we fight for an equal playing field."[36]

WHEN WE FINALLY MET ON THE TELEPHONE, it took Media Research Center founder L. Brent Bozell less than 15 minutes to slam the receiver down on me, angered by my insistence that he answer a simple question.

What did Herman Cain's sexual harassment scandal have to do with race?

Cain, who shone briefly as a charismatic alternative to front-runner Mitt Romney during the 2011–12 GOP presidential nomination fight, was famously undone by a drip, drip of steady revelations that he had been accused of sexual harassment by two women who received financial settlements while he ran the National Restaurant Association and a third who claimed they had a long-term affair.

Before the allegations of the affair surfaced, Bozell devoted one of his syndicated columns to the notion that Cain was being treated just like Supreme Court justice Clarence Thomas, who famously survived sexual harassment allegations during his nomination proceedings.

The column's title: "Stop the High-Tech Lynching of Herman Cain."[37]

Bozell, a hardcore conservative who once said President Obama looks like a "skinny, ghetto crackhead" on Fox News, is not one for understatement.[38]

Still, I wondered, why would you use such an awful term to describe a situation in which an aspiring politician is caught in a non-racial sex scandal?

"If the term is good enough for Clarence Thomas, and it's good enough for Herman Cain, then it's good enough for me," Bozell insisted, evoking the notion that a black person can somehow validate using a racially charged term, with no logical explanation required. "Liberal Democrats hate to see a black conservative succeed. They will do anything to bring him down."[39]

Bozell wasn't the only right-wing pundit to use such language. Rush Limbaugh and Ann Coulter—two paragons of measured political discourse—also used similar words, suggesting any criticism of a popular black conservative equaled racism, regardless of whether the issue at hand was connected to race or not.

Black men have always faced stereotypes of being oversexed and promiscuous, but Cain and Thomas both faced very specific allegations from specific women. Given that conservatives so often argue that liberals should face facts regardless of political correctness, I was briefly blindsided by right-wing pundits who insisted that in Cain's case, looking into sexual harassment allegations was the equivalent of pulling out a rope and tying him to the nearest tree.

Curiously, as I noted in a column for the *St. Petersburg Times*, when positions were reversed and conservatives wanted to take on Barack Obama, Coulter and Bozell were indignant that liberals would accuse them of racism.

In her 2011 book *Demonic: How the Liberal Horde Is Endangering America*, Coulter noted: "Just as fire seeks oxygen, Democrats seek power, which is why they will always be found championing the mob whether the mob consists of Democrats lynching blacks or Democrats slandering the critics of Obamacare as racists."[40]

Bozell made a similar comparison in 2009: "When Reagan, Bush I and Bush II were in office, nasty demonstrators—even rioters—were celebrated by the left. But when Democrats take control (Clinton, Obama), any criticism becomes angry, hateful, and now racist."[41]

On the telephone with me, Bozell insisted the lynching language was appropriate because liberal-friendly mainstream media outlets don't cover the sexual scandals of Democratic politicians with the same fervor. I wasn't sure former Democratic Rep. Anthony Weiner, who had resigned months earlier after news outlets revealed he had sent an explicit photo of himself to a college student via Twitter, would agree.

But instead, I asked: "Are you seriously saying the press didn't cover Bill Clinton's affairs, from Gennifer Flowers to Monica Lewinsky?"

CLICK! Dial tone.

It's too bad Bozell ended the call when he did. Because I wanted to ask him about a sneaking suspicion I had about Herman Cain.

That conservatives like him because he sees race—and talks about it—the same way they do.

My sense is that the biggest frustration some white conservatives have with issues of race is that many people of color see the problems and solutions so differently. And they feel unfairly accused of insensitivity and prejudice when they disagree—even if they disagree in seriously insulting ways.

How comforting would it feel, then, to have a popular black conservative assure them that racism no longer holds back poor black people?

"[Poor black people] weren't held back because of racism, no," Cain told CNN anchor Candy Crowley on her *State of the Union* show in October 2011. "People sometimes hold themselves back because they want to use racism as an excuse for them not being able to achieve what they want to achieve."[42]

That's a notion explored in a 2011 study by two researchers who found that most white people in their sample believed racism against black people had effectively ended, and anti-white racism was a bigger problem. (It was also interesting to see that some websites presented the study's results as evidence that white people *are* more discriminated against, rather than to prove that many white people *think* they are more discriminated against.)

In a column for the *New York Times* dubbed "Jockeying for Stigma," the study's co-authors Michael Norton and Samuel Sommers—from Harvard Business School and Tufts University, respectively—explained their results further.

"One outcome of granting rights to traditionally marginalized groups has been to leave many whites feeling marginalized themselves," they wrote.

"The very same developments that some would point to as evidence of progress toward equality (an African American president, a Latina Supreme Court justice) are seen by others as further evidence of the threats aligned against them."[43]

Small wonder that Cain's pronouncements fell on friendly ears, as when he visited conservative talk radio host Neil Boortz's show and called liberal Democrats who criticized his political ambitions "racist."[44] Or when Cain told CNN's Wolf Blitzer that many black people were "brainwashed" into rejecting conservatism.[45]

The Race Card author Tali Mendelberg said Cain's dismissiveness about racial discrimination toward black people distinguished him even from other African American conservatives such as Colin Powell and J. C. Watts, Republicans who nevertheless still believed that prejudice against people of color was systemic and required programs such as affirmative action to defeat.

"When it comes to the question, 'Is there still racial discrimination? Does it still have to be combated?' those kinds of issues still tend to differentiate black conservatives, who can be very conservative on issues other than race," said Mendelberg. "There was probably an additional appeal [to conservatives for Cain], who say 'He's black and he seems like he's one of us.'"[46]

A paper Mendelberg co-authored on race and public opinion last year explained the political bonds among black people a little better, noting a concept articulated by University of Chicago political science professor Michael Dawson called "linked fate"—the idea among individual African Americans that their fate is linked to the fate of their race as a whole.

"African Americans form their political opinions about political parties, candidates and public policies by using their perceptions of what is best for the entire racial group instead of what they think is best for them individually," the paper said. "The sense of linked fate is so strong that it overcomes the force of class interests for the large black middle class and the lure of cultural conservatism, which resonates with many African Americans. It is the reason why African Americans vote nearly unanimously for the Democratic party in presidential and many lower-level electoral contests."[47]

It was a sad irony that Cain, a child of the South raised in Jim Crow–era Georgia, would resort to throwing around the term lynching—a brutal act in which black people were shot, stabbed, hung, beaten, and mutilated, sometimes simply for the crime of looking at a white person in the wrong way.

In response, I suggested the problem wasn't the playing of a so-called "race card" by liberals; it was the serious ignorance of how to talk about these issues in a way that makes sense, grounding dialogue in facts and open-minded discussion, rather than a glib "truthiness" shtick based mostly on what some people wish were true.

And Cain was contrasted with another black man with a unique way of talking about race: President Obama, who has charted a course different from that of many traditional black politicians.

He is a biracial child of an African father and a white American mother, and he chose to identify as an African American. But, despite his early background as a community organizer and activist, he never tried to build his political fortunes by angrily confronting white people on race issues or shaming people into dealing with prejudice.

"No one quite knew what to do with a charismatic black leader who embraced his own personal racial identity, but refused to be spokesperson on race in America as a route to power," H. Roy Kaplan, an associate professor in the Department of Africana Studies at the University of South Florida in Tampa, told me back in 2008, just after Obama was elected president. "Even conservative black politicians and pundits spend a lot of time talking about race. Here was an effective black politician who didn't shy away from it, but didn't belabor it, either."[48]

It's an approach that confounds Obama's opponents even now, as they try turning him into the typical Scary/Angry Black Man by implying dark associations with more radical people, or insisting he is a secret Muslim, or refusing to accept he was born in this country. Or they try the other tack: devaluing his accomplishments by suggesting he won the presidency only because of his race—perhaps because so many other black people before him found it so easy?—or criticizing him for using a teleprompter.

Still, the president insists on handling such business his own way.

Even when he had to hold an April 2011 press conference to personally refute allegations he wasn't born in this country, Obama blamed the media for the persistent rumors, rather than specifically cite provocateurs like Donald Trump or hardcore conservatives who fanned the flames.[49]

More than any figure in government, President Obama highlights how race identity is a creation of modern society—a unique combination of your family history, what you call yourself, how you act in the world, and how the world sees you.

In Obama's case, because he had an African father, looks African American, married a black woman, and calls himself a black man, he *is* a black man. But he reached that place in a much more deliberate and purposeful way than most of us, which might be exactly what some people find troubling.

Simply by virtue of who he is, President Obama forces everyone in America to think a little more about race than they normally would, which may unsettle some people.

When racial issues loom—an unarmed black teen is shot dead in Florida, a black Harvard University professor is arrested in his own home, statistics reveal an unemployment rate for black people nearly twice the rate for white people—the thought arises: *What does President Obama think about this?*

Perhaps because he has other things to do, Obama hasn't answered that question very often, leaving America to sort out its own racial baggage without much help from its first black president.

"Obama is not our racial messiah," Carmen Van Kerckhove, a onetime consultant at a New York–based diversity education firm, told me just after Obama's 2008 election. "He's not the guy with all the answers. To look at him to lead us [on this] isn't realistic. He's got a few other things on his plate, you know?"[50]

FIVE

FROM SUPERNEGROES TO BBFS

Why Network TV Still Often Stars White America

THIS WAS A MOMENT SOME SAW COMING MANY MONTHS AGO.

But longtime TV producer Michael Patrick King (*Sex and the City*) still seemed surprised when he faced a crowd of television critics in Los Angeles to talk about his new CBS sitcom, *2 Broke Girls*, and they let him have it.

The problem, stated simply, was that his two lead characters, waitresses in a dive restaurant in Brooklyn, were surrounded by stereotypical support-ing characters, including a hairy, horny Eastern European cook; a jive-talking black cashier with a taste for brandy; and an Asian owner whose ethnicity, asexuality, and broken English seemed to be the butt of far too many jokes (in the pilot episode, for instance, he wants to change his name to Bryce Lee—insert kung fu fighting joke here).

The press conference, held in a spacious ballroom at the high-class Landingham Huntington Hotel in Pasadena, should have been a victory lap for King and the show, basking in high ratings thanks to a cushy timeslot after a still-blockbuster though Charlie Sheen–less *Two and Half Men* on Mondays. That night, *2 Broke Girls* would earn a People's Choice Award as Favorite New Comedy.[1]

But first, King had to handle the ire of a roomful of journalists—already cranky after more than a week spent covering similar press conferences as part of the Television Critics Association's summer press tour—and eager to confront his clumsy stereotyping.

At first, King tried a typical tactic in network TV-land: denial.

"The big story about race on our show is that so many are represented," he said cheerily. "The cast is, incredibly, not only multi-ethnic, including the regulars and the guest stars, but it's also incredibly not ageist. So the big story on our show is we sort of represent what New York used to be and is currently . . . which is a melting pot."[2]

This was exactly the wrong strategy. Because the savvy critics in the room already knew many considered the show's racial images to be a problem; earlier in the day, CBS entertainment president Nina Tassler assured journalists that she had asked King to "dimensionalize" the supporting characters[3] (network executive–speak for "ease up on the Asian jokes").

But King initially wouldn't even allow that the conversation with Tassler happened. "If you talk about stereotypes, every character when it's born is a stereotype," he said. "I mean, this show started with two stereotypes—a blond and brunette. And that implies certain stigmas as well."

But *2 Broke Girls*'s very first episode exploded the stereotypes about its white lead characters. Kat Dennings's cynically street-smart brunette Max Black was open-hearted enough to take in a new waitress, a suddenly impoverished, Paris Hilton–style rich girl played by Beth Behrs. Behrs's character, Caroline Channing, was a prissy blonde smart enough to attend Wharton Business School, loyal enough to reject an advance from Black's philandering boyfriend, and savvy enough to plan how the pair could work their way out of poverty in a year.

But four months into the show's run, the best thing King could say about supporting character Han "Bryce" Lee was that "in the last three episodes, we haven't made an Asian joke."

As anyone might expect, the dialogue did not improve from there.

"I'm gay," King said. "I'm putting in gay stereotypes every week. I don't find it offensive, any of this." Which led a journalist to ask, "Does being part of one traditionally disenfranchised group make it then carte blanche to make fun of other traditionally disenfranchised groups?"

Though I often attend the Television Critics Association press tours, this was a session I had missed, watching it unfold over Twitter as my fellow TV critics and friends sent along messages about a heated spat that seemed to explode from nowhere. Even the Twitter posts, limited to a tart 140 characters, carried enough of the room's tension and anger to make you pull out a bowl of popcorn and settle in for a seriously entertaining ride.

Writing for the *Hollywood Reporter*, TV critic Tim Goodman snarked from his @BastardMachine Twitter account: "'The big story of race on our show is so many are represented.'—King. No, the big story is your show is racist, period."

Alan Sepinwall, former TV critic for the *Star-Ledger* newspaper in Newark, New Jersey, and now at Hitfix.com, said King seemed unable or unwilling to allow that journalists might have a point.

"Not only did this not change his mind, some people said, knowing him it might make him come up with even more offensive jokes, just to push back," said Sepinwall, who approached King with conciliatory words after the session only to see the producer walk away from him, stone-faced. "But he won a People's Choice Award that night and the show's still doing well, so why should he care?"[4]

By the end of the press conference, King had jokingly implied that an Irish journalist had a sexual problem and welcomed with relief questions about a horse that appears on the show, seemingly dazed by all the negativity.

"We believe that the show is nothing but fun for the audience," the producer said. "So I'm surprised that the questions are not about fun."

He learned the hard way; there's little fun in echoing old stereotypes about ethnic characters in modern media.

KING'S TUSSLE WITH THE PRESS wasn't only notable for its hostility. It also neatly laid out the biggest problems in talking about stereotypes, prejudice, and ethnic/cultural diversity on network television.

Filling shows with minority characters isn't good enough. Just because a program is chock full of supporting characters of color, that doesn't mean they can't wind up echoing awful stereotypes. Does it really feel like progress when a show filled with characters of color includes an, um, *ambition-challenged* black guy and a dorky Asian man who can't get a girlfriend?

Characters of color can't always be defined by their ethnicity. The biggest problem with *2 Broke Girls*'s supporting characters isn't just that they started as stereotypes, it's that so much of what they do echoes those stereotypes. When characters are primarily defined by their stereotypes—the black guy who is always a smooth-talking hipster or the Latina woman who is always angry and cursing in Spanish—then you're left with hollow, limiting portrayals that do a disservice to all involved.

It's not just a black and white issue. Shows such as CBS's *2 Broke Girls* and *Rob*—a sitcom that starred Rob Schneider as a man who marries into a Mexican American family with an illegal alien cousin who tries to swindle him out of $7,200—echo a troubling trend in which horribly stereotypical Asian and Hispanic characters are accepted in ways that black characters are not. Decades of protests by African American civil rights groups may have made TV programmers more wary about how they handle black characters. But it doesn't matter which group the stereotype is aimed at; the damage remains the same.[5]

Anyone can echo harmful stereotypes. Being a member of a traditionally disenfranchised group might bring some insight. But stereotypes are seductive and easy; sexual orientation or ethnic heritage isn't an automatic inoculation from falling into such patterns, especially when they involve groups to which you don't belong.

King has faced similar criticism before: first, when people noticed that the early seasons of his smash HBO series *Sex and the City* turned Manhattan into a fantasyland of high fashion, exclusive parties, and luxurious living, with hardly any characters of color in one of America's most ethnically diverse cities. Then, his first *Sex and the City* movie was dinged for turning Jennifer Hudson into a Black Best Friend who mostly helps the white heroine get over an aborted wedding (more on this kind of character later in the chapter), and his *Sex and the City 2* was savaged for turning men in the United Arab Emirates into cartoonish *Lawrence of Arabia* throwbacks.

None of which has stopped him from carving out a career as one of the biggest producers in film and television, capable of shrugging off a roomful of critics convinced his latest project needs to "dimensionalize" its characters of color into the twenty-first century. And when CBS announced its fall schedule for the 2012–13 season, *2 Broke Girls* was moved into a prime position, Mondays at 9 P.M., as the "tent pole" supporting the network's successful comedy lineup.

When almost every story is told from one cultural perspective, it's no surprise so little price is paid for trafficking in stereotypes.

TO UNDERSTAND THE PECULIARITIES OF DIVERSITY in network television, consider the case of Boris Kodjoe.

A tall, handsome black man with a growing career in film and television—including roles in Tyler Perry's *Madea's Family Reunion* and the last two *Resident Evil* movies—Kodjoe let an interesting fact slip during a 2010 interview.

He had to be asked several times to audition for the lead role in NBC's 2010 spy drama *Undercovers,* despite the fact that superstar producer/director J.J. Abrams (*Lost, Fringe,* 2010's *Star Trek* reboot) was onboard as co-creator and executive producer.

Why? He wasn't sure they were serious about hiring a black man.

"Knowing Hollywood as I do, having made it all the way to camera tests [for other jobs] and being told they went a different way—which meant they went with a white actor—I didn't want to waste my time," Kodjoe told me.[6]

"Until the casting director called me personally; that's when I knew [they were serious]," said the actor. "It shows you how jaded I was by the traditional behaviors of Hollywood as it pertains to making casting choices. I was blinded by those limitations that had been put on me."[7]

Not that Kodjoe didn't have some reason for suspicion.

For years, network TV outlets had taken flak from critics about a decided lack of shows starring non-white characters. The year before *Undercovers*'s fall 2010 debut, among 21 new prime time shows debuting that fall on network TV, just two featured non-white characters as sole stars (excluding series such as *Modern Family* and *NCIS: Los Angeles,* where Latino or African American actors are co-stars or part of an ensemble cast). And in one of those series, Fox's *The Cleveland Show,* the lead was an African American cartoon character voiced by a white guy, Mike Henry.

In 1999, the story unfolded a little differently. Back then, when the big broadcast TV networks advanced a slate of new fall shows without a single minority character in a lead role, criticism came in a white-hot avalanche. Tough stories sprouted everywhere from *Entertainment Weekly* to PBS's *NewsHour,* and the NAACP threatened a lawsuit, leading network TV executives to create vice president–level positions supervising diversity issues (jobs, it should be noted, many non-entertainment corporations had created years before).[8]

When the dust settled, there was a sense of a hand slapped. But for all the protests and promises made, those on-camera numbers have moved slowly, more than a decade later.

These days, characters of color appear more often on network TV as members of ensembles or in co-starring roles, shoehorned into stories often with little, if any, reference to their heritage or ethnic background. Such parts are a small improvement over the heavy-handed stereotypes in *2 Broke Girls*, but show creators still often relegate minority roles to secondary positions.

The diversity issues that sparked headlines and protests ten years ago cause barely a ripple today. After years of trying and fitful conflict over failures, network TV seems to have little stomach for exploring the many ways it falls short in portraying an increasingly diverse society.

For TV and media critics, this isn't just about soothing hurt feelings or appeasing civil rights groups. The issue of diversity in fictional television instead strikes at a core truth about mass media in general and television in particular.

Seeing a wide range of people on TV teaches us about others, even as it teaches us about ourselves.

For many white viewers, television can provide an image of people of color they don't see in their daily lives. Indeed, if they live in segregated towns or areas with little ethnic diversity, all they know about black people, Hispanics, Asian Americans, and people of Arab descent may come through the media.

Stereotypes created and recycled in this media space can become reality for too many people, teaching us all to accept false limits.

Still, facing a roomful of journalists during a press conference for *Undercovers* at the TV Critics Association's summer press tour in 2010, executive producer Josh Reims initially danced around the question of whether Abrams and the production team were focused on hiring black actors as stars of the show. But given network TV's recent failure to hire people of color in starring roles—and the fact that Abrams's reputation made *Undercovers* one of the most-anticipated new shows of the season—it was inconceivable such casting occurred without serious intention.

"We went to [NBC] and said, basically, so it's out on the table. We're very interested in hiring—if we can find them—two great, diverse leads," Reims, who is white, eventually admitted to me after the press conference had concluded.[9]

But if cast diversity is seen as a positive, much-needed change, why was Reims so awkward in actually talking about it?

"It's probably fear of saying the wrong thing . . . we're so politically correct now, if you misstep, you can get crucified," said Don Reo, now an executive producer for CBS's hit sitcom *Two and a Half Men,* who also served as executive producer and creator of the only network TV sitcom to feature a mostly minority cast in fall 2009, the Fox-TV comedy *Brothers.*[10]

Reo spoke to me before *Undercovers*'s premiere; he hadn't seen the show. But as a longtime producer who worked as a white man helping two superstar African American comics develop sitcoms on family life—co-creating Damon Wayans's ABC comedy *My Wife and Kids* and executive producing Chris Rock's show on the CW and UPN networks, *Everybody Hates Chris*—he was all too familiar with the minefield of expectations and criticism that comes when white producers tell stories of minority characters.

"It's all based on the success of a breakout show," said Reo. "For a while [in 2009] there were more black people in the White House than on network television. The bottom line in television is dollars and cents. Nobody came up with a hit to match the success of *Cosby,* until Damon and I did *My Wife and Kids* . . . If they get a hit (with *Undercovers*), there will be black spies all over television."[11]

Unfortunately, the black spy trend stopped with NBC. *Undercovers* struggled from the moment of its debut in September 2010, hampered by a tough timeslot (leading off Wednesday nights at 8 P.M. against CBS's longtime success *Survivor*) and problems with its tone. "A woebegone spy drama with nary a hint of intelligence," carped the *Boston Herald,* while the *Hollywood Reporter* lamented the series was "trapped in its own lazy shortcomings."[12]

By November 2010, *Undercovers* had been canceled, ripped off NBC's schedule at the year's end with two episodes yet unaired.[13] And even the most ardent supporters of diversity had to admit that the show had lots of problems aside from the question of whether America accepted its black leads.

"I would desperately hope that no one, including network executives, would see the failure of *Undercovers* as a reflection of the race of the cast," Abrams told the website Collider.com not long after the show's cancellation. "It obviously had absolutely zero to do with that."[14]

Abrams's assessment was echoed by another experienced network TV producer, Shawn Ryan, executive producer of FX's hit *The Shield,* CBS's *The Unit,* and Fox's police drama *The Chicago Code.*

"It's kinda like the NFL, how it used to be with black quarterbacks," said Ryan, speaking to me just a few weeks before African American star Andre Braugher would be announced as a co-lead in his series for ABC, called *Last Resort.* "That barrier's been broken down, but it used to be so few [black] quarterbacks would get a shot, they really had to succeed and be superstars to work. It's the same with TV shows. You get a show like *Undercovers . . .* I don't think it was that great a show. And yet, there was a little bit of perception that NBC tried a series with black leads and America rejected it. I would argue that America rejected it for other reasons."[15]

Perhaps. But when the next TV season dawned in the fall of 2011, not a single character of color was featured as the sole star of a show among 24 new scripted series on network television.

Just like 11 years earlier.

The number improved slightly in broadcast networks' schedules for fall 2012, when one new show—Fox's *The Mindy Project,* starring former *Office* writer and co-star Mindy Kaling, who is of Indian descent—featured a person of color as a sole star. ABC's mid-season show *Scandal,* featuring African American actress Kerry Washington as the main star, also returned to the schedule, along with several new shows featuring actors of color as co-stars or members of ensemble casts.

Once again, TV lurched toward greater onscreen diversity, courtesy of a few key series. But will those experiments last?

IF ANYONE WOULD KNOW HOW THIS RACE AND IMAGE THING works on network TV, it would be Blair Underwood.

A TV star since his first big job playing attorney Jonathan Rollins on NBC's legal drama *L.A. Law* back in the late 1980s, Underwood has become one of TV's best-known African American stars.

In 2007 and 2008, he had his biggest year as an actor yet, playing key characters on ABC's drama *Dirty Sexy Money,* the CBS comedy *The New Adventures of Old Christine,* and HBO's therapy-based drama *In Treatment* (a role that earned him a Golden Globe nomination).[16]

But throughout much of 2009, Underwood didn't get another major role. It felt as if, months after the election of America's first black president, something had changed in Hollywood.

This wasn't so long after Fox's spy drama *24* cast Dennis Haysbert as a principled, stalwart African American president, signaling to viewers that events were occurring a bit beyond the current day. Now that Barack Obama had actually made it to the White House, was the supercool, urbane archetype Underwood embodied old news?

"This is an industry [where] we're marketing archetypes and whatever archetype I may be, all of '09, they weren't buying it," Underwood told me, relaxing on a sofa during an outdoor party in Los Angeles back in 2010. "I didn't work the whole year—*the whole year.* At least four times during '09, [he was told,] 'Well, you know, they like you but they want to go more *character-ry.*' That was the term. That was the euphemism: '*character-ry.*' And every time I looked at the actors cast, there was always [a black actor] who was overweight and usually comedic in type, so it was . . . 'Whatever you're selling, your archetype, your type, we're not buying that right now.'"[17]

The drought lasted long enough that Underwood thought his career might be over. "There was a time actually for about two days, literally, I was like, 'I don't know if I want to do this anymore. If this is what they're buying, they're not buying what I'm offering.'" But something told him to be patient, and NBC eventually cast him in *The Event* as a clean-cut, erudite *Afro-Cuban* president struggling to handle an insurrection by extraterrestrials hidden on Earth for more than half a century.[18]

Suddenly, with an added twist to his character's heritage, Underwood's archetype was cool again.

If a showbiz veteran like Underwood remains uncertain about his status in Hollywood, that speaks volumes.

Which begs another question: Why does this matter so much, anyway?

At a time when the nation is in deep disagreement over a host of public policy issues—the future of Medicare and Social Security, the income tax system, the role of government in helping the less fortunate, and the disproportionate levels of unemployment and poverty among people of color—there may be no more important question than how big media outlets portray racial, ethnic, and religious minorities.

Television shows us how the most influential population group in the United States—white Americans—views people of color. And by tweaking those broadcast images, TV outlets can either bring people together across their differences or keep folks separated along racial and cultural lines.

But *Undercovers*'s story highlights the most sobering element of network TV's recent diversity issues: Any progress made can vanish just as quickly, thanks to the cancellation of a few key shows.

EVEN AS AMERICA STRUGGLES WITH DIVERSITY in so many areas, the most symbolic battle remains its efforts to get right with black people.

Yawn about the legacy of long-ago slavery at your peril. There are still corners of America where black people seem to live as second-class citizens, with substandard housing, lagging public services, and limited opportunities.

One study by the Pew Research Center found that in 2009 the average white family had 20 times the wealth of the median black family and 18 times that of Hispanic households. Minority families lost twice as much wealth as white families during the recent Great Recession.[19]

And there is the nagging sense that, somehow, the nation's tangled racial history is still to blame.

The relationship between black and white remains something special in the American consciousness; I once called it "the one scab America can't stop picking."[20] It's the barometer by which we judge how the nation relates to all minorities.

And the best measure of that relationship—or at least the most visible one—is the arc of black images on the biggest stage in the world: broadcast television.

According to historian/author Donald Bogle's engrossing book *Primetime Blues: African Americans on Network Television,* the earliest images of black people came in one-shot programs and guest appearances in the 1930s, '40s, and '50s, as polished, talented singers and musicians such as Cab Calloway, Nat "King" Cole, and Ethel Waters surfaced on variety programs.

For the most part, however, black people were rarely seen in the earliest days of television. Viewers were treated to a well-scrubbed suburban landscape where minorities appeared only briefly to serve dinner or open a car door.

"There was always something good and wholesome about white culture [on TV]," said Alvin F. Poussaint, a renowned black psychiatrist and specialist in African American children, speaking in a 1991 documentary on the history of black TV images, *Color Adjustment.*[21] As a professor at Harvard Medical School who consulted on *The Cosby Show,* Poussaint spoke with authority on how images from early, white-centered TV shows focused on idyllic scenes and comfortable suburbs, indoctrinating the world.

Cultural critics use the term "social whiteness" or talk about "the privilege of being generic" in describing this dynamic, which creates an environment where white culture is the unconscious, unquestioned center, a natural home base against which all other cultures and ways of living are measured.

"It was so powerful, you kinda believed there was this life that whites led that was very wholesome and almost trouble-free," Poussaint said wistfully. "That's where the beauty was; all the good things and the pleasure [in life]."[22]

Into this environment came images more traditionally associated with early roles for African Americans on television: *The Beulah Show* in 1950 and *Amos 'n' Andy* in 1951.[23] Both shows, originally born as radio programs with white voice actors creating stereotypically fawning and simpleminded black characters, were transplanted to television with African Americans recreating and refining roles that were developed without input from any black people at all.

Beulah featured a black maid devoted to the white family that employed her; *Amos 'n' Andy* focused on two black friends moving through an all-black world filled with demeaning characters. As these shows unfolded, they presaged a slew of issues with series featuring characters of color—from the avoidance of storylines that dealt with real-life racial issues to the establishment of lighthearted sitcoms as the predominant, unthreatening venue for black roles.

Amos 'n' Andy, in particular, divided even black fans; some people were entertained by its wonderful performances, while others denounced it as a home for hopeless, damaging stereotypes.[24]

"From the days of Ethel Waters in the 1950s to the present, actors found themselves cast in parts that were shameless, dishonest travesties of African American life and culture," Bogle wrote in *Primetime Blues.* "Yet often enough, some of the actors also managed—ironically and paradoxically—to strike a nerve with viewers by turning the roles inside out. They offered personal visions and stories that proved affecting, occasionally powerful, and sometimes deliriously entertaining and enlightening."[25]

As time passed, the images changed. Throughout the 1960s, middle class black characters surfaced on television, exemplified by the Rhodes scholar/undercover agent Alexander Scott, who comic Bill Cosby played on 1965's *I Spy,* and Diahann Carroll's virtuous, widowed nurse on *Julia* in 1966.[26]

And there was a simple term for these characters: supernegroes.[27]

That name summed up their purpose: black characters scrubbed of any qualities connected to old stereotypes, such as laziness, lack of intelligence, or even bad manners. They were specifically designed to appeal to white audiences by being so accomplished, so poised, and so cool that their right to share the screen was undeniable.

(This term isn't to be confused with the so-called Magic Negro, a supporting role played by a black actor who helps the white lead character succeed through a spiritual or mystical connection to life. Think Whoopi Goldberg with Demi Moore in *Ghost,* Will Smith with Matt Damon in *The Legend of Bagger Vance,* or Morgan Freeman with Jim Carrey in *Bruce Almighty*.[28])

In some ways, these supernegroes were *just* like white characters: you saw few of their black relatives, they rarely spoke in the slang used at the time, and they had few romantic relationships with other black characters. They could not reflect contemporary black culture for fear of looking too threatening or alien.

Filmmaker Marlon Riggs explored this territory artfully in *Color Adjustment,* interviewing producer Hal Kanter, a writer for *Amos 'n' Andy* who later created *Julia.* Kanter told Riggs that *Julia* was almost an apology for the crude stereotypes in *Amos 'n' Andy,* offering the first prime time program centered on a working woman of color.[29]

But as star Diahann Carroll noted in the same film, *Julia* ultimately angered many black people, who felt the show implied that the only acceptable black people were those who left their culture behind to become bland, hyper-accomplished, non-threatening echoes of middle-class white people.

"[People] said 'She's a sellout. She's an Oreo cookie,'" Carroll said in the film. "[They complained,] 'Why doesn't this show represent the street where I spend my life [and] I spend my time?'"[30]

The '70s brought black characters who actually talked about their oppression, living in rough, impoverished neighborhoods and scrambling to get by. But shows such as *Good Times, What's Happening,* and *Sanford and Son* also reflected the typical yin and yang of black-centered shows from the time. By showcasing talented actors such as Esther Rolle, John Amos, Redd Foxx, and Jimmie Walker, these comedies gave artists a national platform to tackle storylines rooted in urban decay.

But the joke-filled formats and stereotypical characters also reduced many of those conversations to throwaway punchlines, even as black audiences recognized their own experiences between the lines, giving rise to another term describing such series: ghetto sitcoms, or "ghetto-coms."[31]

As with *Beulah* and *Amos 'n' Andy,* these "ghetto-coms" featured talented black performers transcending the often limited scripts given them by white producers. Foxx's *Sanford and Son* was even based on a British comedy, *Steptoe and Son,* adapted by *All in the Family* creator Norman Lear and his partner Bud Yorkin, who also created *Good Times* and *The Jeffersons.*[32]

Still, the small screen seemed a few steps behind the realities of life, even when producers tried to do better.

"Television doesn't lead, television follows," said Larry Wilmore, the Emmy and Peabody Award–winning executive producer of Fox's sitcom *The Bernie Mac Show* (2000–06), speaking to me back in 2001 when he was running the series.[33] A veteran of writing for Fox's sketch show *In Living Color* and NBC's *The Fresh Prince of Bel-Air,* he would later gain fame as the "senior black correspondent" for Jon Stewart's sizzling news satire *The Daily Show.*

"Television takes what we know and presents it again in a different way," he said back then. "It's an echo of culture more than anything else . . . Film, on the other hand, I feel, leads. Film is a little more visionary, and shows us things maybe we haven't seen or provokes us in ways that we haven't been provoked many times."[34]

But there was one time when network television offered a vision of race, society, and American history that was both disturbing *and* compelling, forcing the country to face its troubled history in a way that drew record audiences.

That was when America saw *Roots.*

AIRING ON ABC IN JANUARY 1977, *Roots* was the kind of show that might never see broadcast in a different age. Following seven generations of a black family, from their capture into slavery in Africa to the modern day, it was based on a highly personal book by author and journalist Alex Haley— until then best known as the writer of *The Autobiography of Malcom X.*

It would air as a "mini-series," stretched over eight consecutive days. And not only would it require a heavily African American cast, but it was a story in which the white characters would be the villains.

"It didn't sound like a good idea, doing a show where the black people are the good guys and the whites are the villains in a country that's 90 percent white," producer David L. Wolper told me in 2002 for a *St. Petersburg Times* story about *Roots*'s twenty-fifth anniversary. "We had to be very careful how we told this story."[35]

That meant white actors beloved by America would be cast in key roles, from Ralph Waite (*The Waltons*) playing an officer on a slave ship to Lorne Greene *(Bonanza)* as the plantation owner who buys Haley's ancestor, Kunta Kinte. A young drama major in his sophomore year at the University of Southern California, LeVar Burton, won the role of Kunta Kinte in his first professional audition.[36]

Wolper had a strategy for casting black actors as well. Only performers already accepted by white audiences would get the major roles, from retired sports star O. J. Simpson as the father of Kunta Kinte's African girlfriend, to *Good Times* alum John Amos as a grown Kunta, to Las Vegas mainstay Leslie Uggams as Kizzy, to Broadway star Ben Vereen as the son produced by Kizzy's rape, "Chicken" George.

"We knew black America would get what they wanted out of *Roots*," Wolper said. "The question was, what would white America do? It was a subtle philosophy. Alex [Haley] once said to me, 'If I don't get whites to watch this, then I haven't accomplished anything.'"[37]

He needn't have worried. When *Roots* finally aired, it became an unprecedented TV phenomenon; over 130 million Americans (85 percent of U.S. homes) watched at least some of the miniseries.[38] Shows in Las Vegas casinos were rescheduled to avoid airing during the program, which spawned viewing parties in nightclubs and, later, college courses to dissect its meaning.[39]

But *Roots*'s success also meant something more. In a TV environment with only a handful of channels, where disparate audiences were often forced to share the same programs, black America saw its history validated and explained in a way that put painful truths on the table for all to learn from.

"Some African Americans got so angry they couldn't speak to their white friends," Wolper said. "But some African Americans and white people bonded for a moment . . . White America saw for a moment . . . [and] appreciated what black families have gone through. *Roots* didn't really change television much . . . It changed people."[40]

But the saddest legacy of *Roots* might be how little it changed the industry. Despite Emmy Award nominations for many of the black actors on the show, including Burton, Uggams, Vereen, and Gossett (who won as best actor in a drama), few actors besides Burton got roles leapfrogging off the miniseries' success. Uggams has said she didn't work in another significant acting part for two years after *Roots.*[41]

For a brief moment, *Roots* got America talking about race, slavery, history, and genealogy in a way it never had before, but that window quickly slammed shut again, forced by an industry that remained wary of getting too far ahead of perceived public tastes.

THAT WARINESS, LIKE MOST THINGS, can be traced back to economics. Broadcast TV earns its keep by gathering friendly audiences and giving advertisers access to them. If a movie is the spectacle or freak show that draws you into a tent, television is the charismatic, welcoming pal who comes into your home and fuels a crackling dinner party.

Just ask any good salesman: It's hard to sell anything to someone who is upset or offended. Which means improving roles for minority characters on TV has always required finding non-threatening, entertaining ambassadors who can fully embody black culture without turning off white audiences.

Enter the master: William Henry Cosby Jr.

From his early days as a stand-up comic and on *I Spy*, Bill Cosby knew how to root his work in black culture while playing off universal themes. So it was no surprise he would strike a similar note when looking for a TV series to showcase his theories about teaching and child rearing, developed while he was earning a doctorate in education during the 1970s from the University of Massachusetts.[42]

According to former NBC chief Warren Littlefield, the show's producers talked Cosby out of his original idea—playing a limo driver in an hour-long drama—for a situation closer to his standup routines, developing a half-hour sitcom starring an upper-middle-class family that would be perfect for his riffs on marriage and child rearing.

Cosby became obstetrician Heathcliff "Cliff" Huxtable, living in a Brooklyn Heights brownstone with his high-powered attorney wife and children on NBC's *The Cosby Show.*[43]

Using themes pulled from his standup routines, Cosby created a show drenched in black culture where the characters rarely spoke about race. The sitcom debuted in 1984, eventually becoming the number-one rated program for five years in a row (1985 to 1990), begetting a wide array of copycats, spin-offs, and permutations.[44]

And though some said that the show's accomplished characters didn't reflect reality, Cosby insisted on the importance of showing a black family succeeding by working hard, graduating from college, and pursuing successful careers.

"I did what I did carefully thought out, putting myself in a position to teach with that TV set that education was very, very, very important," Cosby told me in a 2010 interview. "I think that from zero birth to age 12 that every black child should know the history of his race, to a point of pride, along with earning a living."[45]

In the '80s and '90s, TV shows featuring black characters expanded, in part due to the success of *The Cosby Show* (1984–92), including the spin-off *A Different World* (1987–93) and Will Smith's *The Fresh Prince of Bel-Air* (1990–96).[46] At the same time, the newly established Fox network was trying hard to get off the ground with edgy programs targeted at youth and underserved audiences.

And when it comes to national television, there are few audiences as consistently underserved as black and minority viewers.

Author Kristal Brent Zook made the connection in her 1999 book *Color by Fox,* noting that Fox pioneered a practice—later mimicked to lesser degrees by the WB and UPN networks—of counterprogramming successful shows on other networks with series targeting black and Hispanic viewers.[47]

By 1993, this meant that Keenen Ivory Wayans's black-centered sketch show, *In Living Color,* aired at 9 P.M. Thursdays against NBC's *Seinfeld*—a show often criticized for failing to feature any ethnic diversity in storylines centered on four characters in one of America's biggest melting pots, New York City. One year later, Martin Lawrence's *Martin,* Queen Latifah's *Living Single,* and a show about two police detectives of color, *New York Undercover,* were airing on Fox opposite NBC's diversity-challenged Thursday night sitcom lineup: *Mad About You, Friends,* and *Seinfeld.*[48]

NBC and Fox produced a schism among audiences that I noted in my own life. At work, black friends would dissect what happened on *Martin* or *Undercover* that week, while my white buddies would focus on *Friends*'s Ross and Rachel or the latest *Seinfeld* bit. Lawrence, Damon Wayans, and Jamie Foxx were becoming household names in black homes, while Paul Reiser, Jennifer Aniston, and Jerry Seinfeld were pop culture icons for white people and mainstream Hollywood.

Onscreen segregation, inspired by the economics of TV, was producing a similar reality in the lives of television fans.

"By 'narrowcasting' or targeting a specific black viewership . . . Fox was able to capture large numbers of young, urban viewers," Zook wrote in *Color By Fox*. "By 1993, the fourth network was airing the largest single crop of black-produced shows in television history. And by 1995, black Americans (some 12 percent of the total U.S. population) were a striking 25 percent of Fox's market. The Fox network was unique, then, in that it inadvertently fostered a space for black authorship in television."[49]

The creators and performers on these shows would become some of the biggest stars in Hollywood: Queen Latifah, Jennifer Lopez, Damon Wayans, Carrie Ann Inaba, Rosie Perez, David Alan Grier, Jamie Foxx, Charles S. Dutton, and Jim Carrey.

And these programs didn't just attract black viewers. From Arsenio Hall's late-night syndicated talk show *Arsenio* to *In Living Color* and HBO's *Def Comedy Jam*, these programs gave white America a glimpse into a world previously hidden and ultimately much cooler than their own. Which is why, as Fox moved to more mainstream programming and the WB merged with the UPN networks, the subsequent disappearance of such black and minority-centered shows from network TV felt so jarring.

"It happened slowly," Wilmore said. "Cosby was on top of the airwaves and Arsenio was the king of late night, and *In Living Color*, where I started my career, was the hippest show on television. [Back then,] if you said 'Black show,' [networks said,] 'I want to be in business with you.'"[50]

But that black TV Hollywood renaissance didn't last long. The Fox network slowly moved its black-centered shows to one day of the week, and then off its schedule entirely (by fall 1998, Fox's Thursday nights had substituted Queen Latifah's *Living Single* for *World's Wildest Police Videos*, followed by the newsmagazine *Fox Files*).[51]

The WB and UPN networks merged into the CW in 2006, eventually centering its programming on young, white females with shows such as *America's Next Top Model*, *One Tree Hill*, and *Gossip Girl*. Though some black-focused shows survived the transition, eventually they were either canceled (*Girlfriends* in 2008; *Everybody Hates Chris* in 2009), ran their course, or moved to a different network (*The Game*, canceled in 2009, resurfaced on Black Entertainment Television in 2011, where its return produced the biggest debut for a scripted series in cable TV history).[52]

And *The Cosby Show,* which left the air in 1992, would be the last black-centered scripted network TV series to be a big hit in both white and black households.

It's an odd circumstance, given how much black people watch television. The average black household has four or more television sets and watches an average seven hours and 12 minutes each day—40 percent more than the rest of the population—according to a 2011 report titled *The State of the African American Consumer* by the Nielsen Company.[53]

And there's little doubt that black audiences respond to black characters in starring roles. During the week of May 7, 2012, the top-rated program in black households was ABC's *Scandal,* a drama starring African American actress Kerry Washington, according to ratings figures from Nielsen.

Still, TV networks cancel minority-centered series without fear of losing black viewers, while fretting that packing too many characters of color into shows—even series such as *The Wire* and *Homicide: Life on the Street,* which were not explicitly about race—can risk making white viewers feel excluded, repelling them.

This is something I heard repeatedly from *The Wire* creator David Simon (a journalist who began his TV writing career on the series created from his book, *Homicide*) and the novelist Dennis Lehane (*Mystic River, Shutter Island*), who also wrote for *The Wire.* The highest-rated season of *The Wire* was its second—the one in which white characters were most prominently featured in stories split between Baltimore's docks and its poor black neighborhoods—and *Homicide* producers always suspected that their show did badly in the ratings because it had so many non-white characters.

Lehane imagined some viewers tuned in only to see "a bunch of 'Yos'" talking (referencing a dismissive term for young, streetwise black men) and flipped off. "I don't want to make it into something as simple as tacit racism," he added. "America doesn't want to think about ghettos. They would very much not like to see gang bangers and drug dealers humanized; it's too confusing."[54]

Women and viewers over age 50 get the same treatment, despite their status as two groups who watch television most. Wrapped up in chasing viewers who are hard to get—young white people, especially males—TV outlets neglect their best customers in the worst ways, like a restaurant that seats its most loyal patrons next to the bathroom.

Kathleen McGhee-Anderson, executive producer of ABC Family's black-centered drama *Lincoln Heights,* noted the irony of that situation during an interview a few years ago.

"There used to be this perception that networks thought black people will watch any show," she said. "[Proportionally], they watch TV a lot more, and if there's nothing on that reflects their experience, they're going to watch something. But that works to the detriment of having TV series where the main cast is African American. Because we'll come to the table, without having our reflection in the casts. The advertisers can advertise to us and [networks will say,] 'Why should we program to black people; they're going to watch us, anyway?'"[55]

Which leads to another problem: the lack of diversity among TV writers, producers, and network executives. If the oft-quoted adage says "write what you know," then it is small surprise that a predominantly white group of television producers would struggle to create diversely populated series and storylines that feel authentic.

According to the Writer's Guild of America, members from all minority groups comprised about 10 percent of television writers in 2009. Film was worse, with minority representation among movie writers at 5 percent.[56]

And even when people of color are in charge of images, there can be problems.

Superstar movie and TV producer Tyler Perry, whose hammerlock on black consumers' loyalty has brought record-breaking revenues for his films, created a roster of all-black comedies for the cable channel TBS a few years ago filled with the kind of broad characters that might be condemned as empty stereotypes coming from anyone else.

It was a lineup born of the ultimate act of showbiz independence. Perry crafted the role of patriarch Curtis Payne on his TBS show *House of Payne* as a modern-day Fred Sanford, an aging fire department chief who complained loudly and often about his nephew moving into his home. But then the twist was revealed: His nephew's wife was a secret crackhead.

Perry originally developed the show for a broadcast network. But when executives there balked at the program's storyline, religious references, and lack of Hollywood stars, he spent $5 million of his own cash to film test episodes himself at his production complex in Atlanta, eventually selling the show to TBS.[57]

"I looked at Oprah's formula and how she set up her talk show and said, 'Well, can that be done with a sitcom?'" Perry said to me in 2007. Earlier in the conversation, he explained, "It is a throwback to what we really enjoy, like *The Jeffersons* and *The Cosby Show* . . . That's what I wanted to have on television; a show with real stories, real subjects . . . with [actors] who looked like real Americans, not a bunch of beautiful, skinny people."[58]

By late 2011, Perry had three comedies airing on TBS. And he was at the tip of a very interesting new trend on cable television: targeting African American *female* viewers.

As 2012 began, the few television projects featuring black characters were often centered on women, from *Braxton Family Values* and *Mary, Mary* on WEtv; to *Leave it to Niecy* on TLC; to *Basketball Wives, LaLa's Full Court Life, Love and Hip Hop,* and *T.I. and Tiny: The Family Hustle* on VH1; to *The Real Housewives of Atlanta* on Bravo; and at least three films of original gospel-centered plays planned for the GMC network.

The explanation: TV outlets are recognizing that African American women are usually the primary purchase decision makers in black households, and their spending power is expected to top $1.1 trillion by 2015, said Tom Umstead, who covers diversity in the cable TV industry for the trade magazine *Multichannel News*.[59]

"I think these TV networks are realizing there's an audience out there of black women who are becoming more affluent, more educated and heading up more households than ever before," said Umstead, who documented the trend in a November 2011 *Multichannel News* piece titled "Black is Beautiful: Why Female African American Viewers Are So Hot."

"They're the ones paying the cable bills, buying the clothes and going shopping," Umstead added. "It's the perfect storm for an advertiser, if they know how to reach them."

In television, like many other places, justice comes quickest when it's paired with a chance to make money.

But all this activity in cable television led to an unexpected byproduct on the broadcast networks. As the *Baltimore Sun* noted in 2007, "for the first time in a generation, the polls on [network TV] shows favored by white and black audiences are strikingly similar."[60]

Of course, the reason for that equanimity was jarring: Broadcast TV no longer offered shows with mostly minority casts.

A ranking of top ten TV programs by the Nielsen Company for white viewers and black viewers age 18 to 49 in November 2010 told the story. On network TV, the ranking was much the same: Fox's football broadcasts stood at the top spot for both groups, though white viewers also watched Fox's musical drama *Glee* and ABC's comedy *Modern Family*.[61]

On cable, however, where more choices abound, black viewers' top ten included one NFL program on ESPN, the *Soul Train Awards* and *Black Girls Rock* on BET, and TBS's *Meet the Browns*. White viewers watched more football shows, WWE professional wrestling, the NASCAR Sprint Cup, and Fox News Channel's *America's Election HQ*.[62]

To those who only paid attention to network TV, it looked like the nation's television viewing was growing more homogenous across racial lines.

But in truth, the same economic forces that created a segregated network TV dial in the 1990s had simply moved it to a new venue: cable television.

IF DEMOGRAPHIC TRENDS ARE TO BE BELIEVED, network TV's diversity challenges may become a problem sooner than anyone expected.

The big headline: Virtually half of recent births in the United States were from minorities, with 92 percent of the country's population growth from the year 2000 to 2010 among non-white people, according to William H. Frey, a senior fellow in the Metropolitan Policy Program at the Brookings Institution.[63]

The new figures led experts to predict that non-whites would become the greatest proportion of children in America by 2015, five years sooner than demographers had predicted.[64]

This presents quite a challenge for modern media, especially network television. Minorities represented 34 percent of the population but just 22 percent of regular series characters at the start of the 2011–12 TV season, according to an annual headcount published by the Gay and Lesbian Alliance Against Defamation.[65]

Actress and writer Diane Farr had hoped to help this imbalance, developing a series idea about three pairs of people negotiating race and romance issues in modern life. The notion sprung from research for her 2011 book on interracial relationships, *Kissing Outside the Lines: A True Story of Love and Race and Happily Ever After,* featuring interviews with 20 different couples who found romance across ethnic and racial boundaries.

The book was inspired by Farr's own courtship and marriage to a Korean immigrant, Seung Yong Chung, and her experience trying to deal with prejudice, fear, and cultural misunderstandings on both sides of their families.

"It really seemed that love was the last prejudice that Americans could openly teach in their home," Farr, a second-generation American of Irish and Italian descent, told me. "Everyone really does believe everybody deserves an equal education, the right to vote and we can all share our toys in the sandbox. But once the adolescent age enters in and puberty begins, many parents in America, in private, will tell their kids, 'Yes, all people are created equal, but you can't love a black person, or you have to marry a Jewish person, or you have to marry an Asian person' . . . It's the last prejudice that exists between one generation and the next when it comes to race."[66]

Farr, a Hollywood acting veteran (CBS's *Numb3rs*, FX's *Rescue Me*, and Showtime's *Californication*), was hired by Fox in the fall of 2010 to write the script for a show featuring a black and white interracial couple, a Jewish and Asian couple, and two east Indian guys who are friends.[67]

The network eventually decided against turning the script into a series; Farr couldn't say if her shortcomings as a writer or reticence by Fox to deal with the subject matter were the ultimate culprit. But she did recall a meeting the network had with producers from all its major shows in late 2010, where executives presented demographic data on the diversification of America, urging the inclusion of non-white races in storylines to keep up with the country's browning population.

"The thing that is frightening in the aftermath of that is how many scripts I have read that were clearly written about white people and white families, where afterwards the divorced husband, the food server at the local coffee shop or the child who was clearly white before, is just [recast as a person of color]," Farr said.[68]

Of particular concern to Farr was network TV's habit of ignoring differences in interracial couples, instead of exploring the different ways romance can reach across boundaries in culture and race. In *Kissing Outside the Lines*, Farr dissects all the family strategies, hurt feelings, and hard work involved in finding acceptance with her husband's Korean relatives—the kind of story network TV rarely attempts to tell.

"I think everybody's glossing over the how-did-you-get-there part because it feels racist to ask," she said. "It's really, really jarring, because rarely in American society do you see a mixed-race couple where there's never a comment about it. So as welcoming as perhaps it seems to put a black and white couple or a Mexican and Asian couple on TV, if everybody else in the series is white, it kinda begs for comment. And without the comment, it feels gratuitous so far . . . . It's like we're hinting at the fact that we live in a post-racial America, but clearly it's not *that* post-racial."[69]

She didn't know it, but Farr was describing the full flowering of yet another trend blanketing network TV: the rise of the Black Best Friend.

The term itself is a derisive shorthand, coined to describe the limited roles available to black actresses in film and television. A 2007 *Los Angeles Times* story nailed the subject, noting such parts were "played by African American [actresses] whose characters' principal function is to support the heroine, often with sass, attitude and a keen insight into relationships and life."[70]

But television in recent years has expanded the BBF to other races and across gender lines; everyone from former *Saturday Night Live* star Garrett Morris (playing a cashier on *2 Broke Girls*) to Nepal-born Daya Vaidya (as Det. Nina Inara on the CBS police drama *Unforgettable*) is caught in the trend.

Sussing out which characters truly fit the Black Best Friend (BBF) mold can be difficult; the line between co-star, equal ensemble member, and BBF can be a fine one. But there are a few clues.

BBFs generally have few storylines to call their own, existing mostly to help the show's lead character progress or connect with audiences. Viewers rarely see anything in that character's life outside of whatever affects the star, so there's usually no spouse, kids, significant others, or relatives, outside of an occasional spotlight episode. It often means they are the only regularly seen characters of color on the show altogether.

I've even classified the BBF into four handy types:[71]

The best friend BBF. This is the traditional type, sassy and supportive, offering humor with an attitude to teach their white buddies important life lessons. Examples include Wanda Sykes on CBS's *The New Adventures of Old Christine* or Garrett Morris on *2 Broke Girls*.

The partner BBF. These characters are the perfect work pals, backing their buddy up no matter what outlandish circumstance they fall into, elevating the lead character's cool just by hanging with him (or her). Example: Ice-T on NBC's *Law & Order: Special Victims Unit*.

The spouse BBF. One way to diversify a show centered on a group of friends, for instance, is to make one of their love interests a person of color. That way, the show feels a bit more progressive without adding too many characters of color (i.e., more than one). Example: Aisha Tyler during her brief stint on *Friends.*

The adversarial BBF. On the surface, these characters are antagonists to the white hero, but they secretly want to help him (or her). Oscar nominee Taraji P. Henson plays an adversarial BBF on the CBS show *Person of Interest*—a police detective hunting down the show's lead character, a one-time CIA agent who helps avert secret disasters.

BBFS CAN SEEM THE PERFECT SOLUTION for Hollywood executives skittish about tackling race in storylines but eager to avoid the lily-white look of shows such as *Seinfeld* and *Friends*—where white characters lived in bustling corners of Manhattan curiously devoid of any non-white people.

"I would say the new glass ceiling tends to be the lead role in the show," said Shawn Ryan, creator of FX's hit police drama *The Shield.* "They do want the cast to be diverse, but there's still a lot of pressure, I think, for the main roles to probably be white. As a producer, the first thing you're saying to yourself is 'I just want the best actor in this role that is going to appeal to the most people.' And yet, I do think, if my show doesn't look at least a little bit like the real world, that's going to turn people off unnecessarily. At least in the scripted universe, I do believe the networks are making really good faith attempts at diversity."[72]

Ryan, who cast a biracial Jennifer Beals and African American actor Delroy Lindo as stars in his 2011 Fox series *The Chicago Code,* said TV networks regularly ask producers to consider diversity among supporting characters, though his biggest successes in that area have often come unconsciously.

"Delroy's character was supposed to be a white Irish guy, but he was the best actor we found," Ryan said. "I remember at the time not thinking it was a big deal when we cast Dennis Haysbert as the lead in [CBS adventure drama] *The Unit.* Then I looked around and realized, 'This is the only drama on TV with an African American lead.' I just try to be realistic."[73] Ryan would help break that glass ceiling in the fall 2012 season, hiring African American actor Andre Braugher as co-lead in *Last Resort,* his drama for ABC about a rogue nuclear submarine.

Ultimately, that's why many BBF characters fail: they're not particularly realistic. Instead, they become a diversity head fake, a Band-Aid stuck on a bigger question: How do you create images of non-white characters on network TV that feel real, don't play on destructive stereotypes, and attract enough of a white audience to make money?

"I think it's a big, hot-button issue that people are afraid to touch," Farr said. "We're closer . . . there's an acknowledgement that there's been a problem previous to this . . . But to have any actual meaningful dialogue about it or to make images, make ideas of what an American family looks like that's a little bit further than perhaps where we are as a society in private, does not seem where the networks are willing to go yet. We're moving further away from racist, but we're not there yet."[74]

Indeed, we all need a new vocabulary for the quandary network television faces, hesitant to depict a fully integrated reality, but well aware that past segregated styles will no longer suffice.

"I think there's great debate in saying [current roles are] not authentic," Farr added. "It's not the true experience. It's close. But why don't we actually discuss the elephant in the room?"[75]

SIX

HOW NEWS MEDIA BECAME A HAVEN FOR MIDDLE-AGED WHITE GUYS (AND A FEW WOMEN)

PHIL GRIFFIN JUST WANTS A LITTLE CREDIT FOR A SMART MOVE.
For years, as president of MSNBC, he heard criticism about a lack of racial diversity among the cable news channel's anchors—some of it from me—about how his liberal political bastion was nearly as devoid of ethnic diversity as its competitors.

So in mid-2011, he added Rev. Al Sharpton to his weekday lineup, anchoring a 6 P.M. show dubbed *PoliticsNation*. About seven months later, Tulane University professor Melissa Harris-Perry, a biracial woman who self-identifies as African American, became the first full-time college professor to host a regular cable TV news program, debuting her self-titled Saturday and Sunday morning show in February 2012.

Both Sharpton and Harris-Perry had been developed as personalities on the channel, serving as analysts, guest hosting for regular anchors, and, in Griffin's words, "holding the [ratings] numbers" in a way that suggested that MSNBC's audiences might accept them once they took over shows on their own.

This, by the way, is how Rachel Maddow became the biggest star in MSNBC prime time after Keith Olbermann's departure—first appearing as a guest on Olbermann's *Countdown* show, then filling in as an anchor there, and finally launching her own self-titled program. Many of MSNBC's highest-profile hires after her, from Ed Schultz to Lawrence O'Donnell, Sharpton, and Harris-Perry, followed a similar model.

"People keep saying, you know, you need diverse anchors, and I said, we're gonna develop them, because I've learned through experience; the notion that you just take somebody and put them on in a key role is, you know, a direct way to failure," the MSNBC president said, noting how competitor CNN gave former New York Gov. Eliot Spitzer a prime time show with relatively little exposure to the channel's audience; within nine months, Spitzer was gone, replaced by the channel's star anchor Anderson Cooper.[1]

"MSNBC did that for a decade, whether it was Jesse Ventura or Deborah Norville or other people, just pouring them on and seeing if it would work," Griffin added. "We'll never do that. I've learned. Experience is the greatest teacher. I've learned. But what we *did* is, we said we're going out and we're gonna find the smartest best people out there and I want this network to— *especially* this network—to reflect the country. I want to be diverse, I want . . . *but* I [also] want to be smart."

So it stung Griffin in particular when the National Association of Black Journalists (NABJ) handed its Thumbs Down award to all the major cable news channels in January 2012—just weeks before Harris-Perry's weekend show would debut—noting "their failure to assign African-American journalists to on-air roles during primetime broadcasts."[2]

Full disclosure: I was part of a group of NABJ members called the Media Monitoring Committee who sent a list of nominees for that award to the organization's board of directors almost a year earlier.

Our committee's recommendation came in early 2011, before Sharpton or Harris-Perry's shows were known. But despite Griffin's insistence that cable news prime time really starts at 5 P.M.—making Sharpton a prime time host—the fact remained that in early 2012, no major cable news channel employed a person of color, journalist or otherwise, as an anchor in the prime time hours of 8 P.M. to 11 P.M. weeknights.

Those are the marquee jobs, filled by faces and personalities who define the news networks for the public: Bill O'Reilly and Sean Hannity at Fox News, Rachel Maddow at MSNBC, Anderson Cooper at CNN. But there have been no people of color in that exclusive club for a while—the best example might be founding CNN anchor Bernard Shaw, an African American who left the network in 2001.

Instead, anchors of color were mostly stuck on weekends, a situation that many in the industry have ruefully called the "weekend ghetto."

It's no surprise that Griffin had a different take on both issues, arguing that cable news channels have evolved beyond the days of Shaw's just-the-facts news, when big media companies still controlled the nation's flow of information.

"This whole concept of journalist has to be rethought," said Griffin, while stressing that he still loves having old-school NBC News types such as Andrea Mitchell and Chuck Todd host shows on MSNBC in the after-noons before prime time. "It's so angers me that . . . I'm sorry. I don't care about journalists . . . in the straight sense. I want fair-minded, smart people [with] life experience, who understand the world, who can interpret it, and if they're journalists, great. If they come from a different background but can come on and express ideas and get it across, that's great. That's the modern world. Now, this notion . . . this notion that somehow you have to have done something to earn so-called journalist credentials? Stop. *Stop.* And I have a real problem with NABJ about this. I think it's unfair and, by the way, is Rachel Maddow a journalist? I think she is."[3]

I would argue that Maddow is a pretty fair-minded opinionator who regularly commits acts of journalism but doesn't necessarily accept the limiting designation of journalist. And, as I described in the Chapter One, there are serious risks in allowing marquee names for an organization that calls itself a cable news channel to walk away from the "honest broker" status most journalists strive to achieve.

But the back-and-forth between Griffin and NABJ also typified the dance between executives who control news organizations and groups dedicated to expanding diversity.

Because some members of groups like NABJ, the Asian American Journalists Association, the National Association of Hispanic Journalists, and the Native American Journalists Association stand to get jobs or promotions through expanded diversity initiatives, their appeals for better hiring are sometimes seen as self-serving or compromised.

And because news outlets have a long history of getting diversity wrong—and staff diversity is a key component of accurately and fairly covering people of color—journalism groups keep up the pressure to break one of the last remaining glass ceilings in TV news: the big prime time news anchor gig.

The issue resurfaced again in early 2012, when former MSNBC star Keith Olbermann was fired by Current TV, the cable channel co-founded and partly owned by former vice president Al Gore. After months of rumors that the mercurial anchor was tangling with his new bosses, Olbermann was let go in a flurry of dueling press releases in which the host was essentially accused of being too tough to work with, while he dinged his former employers for not adequately investing in the program.[4]

Olbermann was replaced quickly with Eliot Spitzer; in fact, the former New York governor started his new show, *Viewpoint,* the day that news broke of the firing. But in the excitement to detail Current TV's clash with its former star, few noticed that the self-styled "progressive" television channel now had nine hours of original talk programming each day—including three-hour morning simulcasts of radio shows by liberal talk hosts Stephanie Miller and Bill Press—in which the only non-white star host was Turkish American Cenk Uygur.

When even the ultra-liberal channels have trouble keeping up with ethnic diversity, you know there's a problem.

And survey results indicate that problems with staff diversity extend well beyond the anchors.

NABJ's fourth annual Diversity Census of local television news departments, which looks at the top six management jobs at 228 TV stations nationwide in 2011, found just 12 percent of them were held by African American, non-white Hispanic, Asian, or Native American staffers.[5] To put that in context, the 2010 U.S. Census found that 34 percent of the nation's population consisted of those ethnic groups.

When Chicago's CBS affiliate aired footage of a young black boy commenting on a shooting in his neighborhood—editing the footage to make it seem that he wanted a gun when he explained moments later that he really wanted to be a policeman—civil rights activists, journalists, and legislators again noted the importance of ethnic and racial diversity in newsrooms, to keep stereotypes from seeping into coverage.

"Today we focus on broadcast news because it is licensed to operate in the public interest by the FCC," said U.S. Rep. Bobby Rush, who discussed the NABJ's employment survey results during a panel discussion at the Congressional Black Caucus' Legislative Weekend in 2011. "This disinformation and distorted imagery must stop. It is tantamount to racial profiling by the news media and it cannot go unchallenged. It is dangerous and damaging, irresponsible and just plain wrong."[6]

Looking at overall staff numbers, the Radio and Television Digital News Association's annual census on TV and radio news diversity found similar results, covering more than 1,300 TV stations and a random sampling of 3,000 radio stations. According to this study, 20 percent of local TV staffs were ethnic or racial minorities, a rise of just 2.7 percent over the last two decades (during that same time, the minority population rose 9.5 percent). Among radio stations, the percentage of minority staffers stood at 7.1 percent.[7]

Still, TV's numbers were better than those notched by the newspaper industry. When the American Society of News Editors (ASNE) released its employment survey results for 2011, it found that job declines for staffers of color were more than double the rate for journalists in general—the fourth straight year of declines.[8]

In 2011, total newsroom employment dipped by 2.4 percent, or about 1,000 jobs. But jobs for non-white journalists dipped by 5.7 percent—about 300 jobs—which meant that nearly one out of every three jobs eliminated in 2011 belonged to a journalist of color.[9]

"The number decrease was incremental, so it's a little like a frog in a pot of boiling water," said Aly Colon, a longtime journalist and diversity consultant who wrote a report for ASNE released at same time as the staffing figures titled "The Future of Diversity in News."[10]

One of the biggest problems, Colon said, was newsroom leaders who seemed to turn away from staff diversity goals as the industry was struggling with a historic recession.

"When diversity was slightly going down, the true believers said, 'Hey, there's a problem,' and those who weren't said, 'We'll get to it later,'" he said. "But this is about the journalism that makes our world more understandable, makes our work more complete and makes it possible for us to represent the lives of the people we cover. We can't do that if diversity is not a core value. We need content that encourages people to see themselves in ways they have not been seen before."

The dips in diversity levels might not be such a problem if the proportion of non-white journalists in the newspaper industry equaled racial and ethnic groups' proportions in society. But ASNE's report also admitted that "minority newsroom employment is still substantially lower than the percentage of minorities in the markets those newsrooms serve."[11]

Which means newspapers with a paid circulation between 250,000 and 500,000 subscribers had about 20 percent of their jobs filled by non-white journalists, serving communities with an average minority population of 30 percent. Newspapers below 5,000 circulation had an average 6 percent of jobs filled by non-white staffers, serving communities where the minority population averaged 18 percent.[12]

A release from the NABJ decrying the "indefensible backsliding" of newspaper diversity efforts noted that among the more than 1,500 journalists who did land news jobs in 2011, 84 percent were white—continuing the lopsided staffing numbers made worse by the media downsizing in 2011.

"A diverse newsroom should be an economic as well as a moral imperative," said NABJ president Gregory Lee in the statement. "Diversity is a choice, and while it may be a tough choice for some in challenging economic times, it should be no less valued as managers consider bottom-line priorities. NABJ members are tired of seeing these depressing numbers annually. They demand more action on a problem that has existed for many years."[13]

So the challenge of making the country's news reporting staff match the diversity of the communities it covers is a puzzle no one seems close to solving.

Advocates of diversity say the value in having more journalists of color in important jobs should be obvious. I still recall the day, early in my tenure as a TV critic, when I saw a black news anchor challenge a white reporter after he finished a live interview with a police officer who said law enforcement planned to stop every black male they saw wearing a knit cap until they found a group of armed robbers.

"Can they do that?" the anchor asked incredulously, wondering if police had any better description of the perpetrators than "black men in knit caps."

The reporter shrugged. He hadn't thought to ask that question.

With a college professor's knack for intellectually dissecting an issue, MSNBC's Harris-Perry was careful to separate her value as an academic who has studied race issues extensively from whatever impact she might have as an anchor of color.

"It was clear to me early on, in terms of becoming a contributor [at MSNBC] that part of what they valued from my voice was my ability to talk about race in politics . . . and I think that's separate from actually being black," said the professor, who teaches African American politics at Tulane University. "It feels to me like they're going for substance and—not that race is incidental or unimportant—but that it is secondary."[14]

Still, watching Harris-Perry's early MSNBC shows, from the guide she offered to white people for talking about the shooting death of black teen Trayvon Martin, to her pleas for R&B star Beyoncé to come on her show, it's obvious she also brings a unique sensibility to the program through her race and culture.

"Certainly, Rev. Al brings a sensibility that, you know, feels like the church in a lot . . . you know, a particular aspect of the black church and of civil rights organizing," Harris-Perry said. "The blackness that I will bring does not feel like Rev. Al's, right? Because I'm not coming from an activist tradition. But there's a kind of thing we each bring from where we are situated in blackness that I think is . . . it's a contribution."

"At the end of the day, especially with stories that have cultural overtones, nobody can tell our stories like we can," said CNN anchor Don Lemon, who is black. "Just like no one can tell a white, Midwestern farm boy's story like a white, Midwestern farm boy. As an African American, you have certain cultural references that other people don't have. I've been there. And I think that's the outweighing argument for diversity in media."[15]

Lemon's history at CNN shows how he's put those ideas into practice. Back in 2010, while covering allegations of sexual misconduct against African American megachurch pastor Eddie Long, the anchor admitted on air that he had been molested, and that allegations about how Long had conducted himself with a young man who claimed to have a relationship with the clergyman sounded similar to his own experiences.

In his book *Transparent,* Lemon talked about how his connections to prominent black leaders such as Sharpton, Nation of Islam leader Louis Farrakhan, and the Rev. Jesse Jackson helped him cover the death of Michael Jackson. When challenged on whether the news media had gone overboard, the anchor defended the saturation reporting, citing polls that revealed eight out of ten black people followed the story very closely, compared to 22 percent of white people.[16] (In fact, Lemon called those criticizing the coverage "elitist.")[17]

Similar questions arose after the death of Whitney Houston in early 2012. As a pop icon whose struggles with drugs dimmed her later career, Houston had faded from interest in mainstream entertainment circles but never really left the hearts and minds of her fans in black communities across the country.

It was a telling sign that when news broke that Houston was unexpectedly found dead in a bathtub at the Beverly Hilton in Los Angeles, many of the experts called upon to explain her significance and later career were journalists of color—from Associated Press music editor Nekesa Mumbi Moody, who first reported the story of Houston's death, to Los Angeles–based journalist Kelley Carter, *Billboard* magazine editor Danyel Smith, and longtime entertainment correspondent Lola Ogunnaike.

I even contributed a little bit, helping explain why Houston deserved the deluge of post-mortem press coverage then underway on CNN's media analysis show *Reliable Sources* the morning after the singer's death. Once again, this was a news event with uneven interest across racial boundaries; according to the Pew Center, 40 percent of black people expressed interest in media coverage of Houston's death and funeral, compared with 13 percent of white people and 25 percent of women.[18]

But Lemon recalled Houston's funeral as a moment when his background provided another advantage, allowing him to explain for CNN's viewers the significance of a "homegoing" funeral ceremony from the black Baptist church.

"This is a homegoing ceremony, not a homecoming ceremony, because Whitney is going home to be with the Lord," he noted on air, reporting from the street about a block from the church where Houston's funeral would be broadcast to the world. "Today is about her, it's about honoring her family, and everyone that you see who's going to get up on that stage will do that. They're going to sing, they're going to praise. They're going to—and as we say in the black church, we're going to jump and shout and people shout and you fan them. And that's what happens. And you cry. And many people are going to laugh. And some people, you know, may get up, just impromptu."[19]

Indeed, Houston's funeral was a unique cultural moment, displaying to a worldwide audience a service steeped in the African American worship tradition. From his perch outside the service, Lemon provided a bit of guidance, explaining the intricacies of a church style he'd been involved with since his childhood.

"It was the quintessential African-American story," the anchor said. "And that was my reference—I went to church every Sunday. So when I'm on television and the white folks around me are saying 'Explain what a homegoing service is,' I'm thinking, 'Really?' When I had to explain to America what a homegoing service is, I realized my importance as an African American journalist . . . It validated the Sunday experience for every black person in this country. I said, 'Whitney Houston took the world to church today.'"[20]

Yet, Lemon was delivering his information from the street, while weekday anchors Soledad O'Brien and Piers Morgan served as the primary anchors for the service.

Sports journalists found out how important staff diversity can be when New York Knicks point guard Jeremy Lin began to shine as an unexpected star during the team's surprise seven-game winning streak at the beginning of 2012. Lin's success instantly made him the highest-profile Asian American basketball player in the country, but it also sparked an unfortunate series of missteps in media coverage.

The *New York Post*'s back sports page pronounced Lin "Amasian!" in a banner headline, encapsulating in one awful moment the problem with reporting from one limited cultural perspective. As I noted in a column shortly afterward, imagine a newspaper headline crowning an African American star like LeBron James "Negro-tastic!"[21]

The MSG Network pictured Lin's head between two halves of a split-open fortune cookie. Fox Sports columnist Jason Whitlock had to apologize for posting a joke on Twitter that made fun of Lin's presumed lack of sexual endowment.

Sports media giant ESPN also apologized after an anchor and an editor writing headlines for their mobile platforms both used the term "chink in the armor" to describe difficulties the Knicks and Lin might be having, without realizing the offensive nature of the c-word for so many Asian people. (The anchor was eventually suspended for 30 days while the headline writer, a twentysomething staffer with limited experience, was fired.)

Turns out, the Asian American Journalists Association already had a handbook for such situations, titled *All American: How to Cover Asian America,* listing three important principles for getting coverage of Asian people right: Dig harder. Make no assumptions. Don't give offense.

Let's consider that last one again: *Don't give offense.*

"For many Asian Americans, the 'C' word is the equivalent of the 'N' word," Asian American Journalists Association president Doris Truong wrote in an email to media reporter Richard Prince for his online column on media diversity, Journal-isms. "It's a freighted term that reminds us that some people don't think we belong or that we won't defend ourselves."[22]

For me, it was evidence of how tough it can be to get news outlets to learn from the progress made in depicting one ethnic group when it comes time to cover another.

The kinds of jokes and terms about sex, food, and culture that few would dare to make about African Americans were applied, seemingly with little thought, to Lin, a Taiwanese American enjoying the most impressive success of his burgeoning career in professional basketball.

It reminded me of a time, back in 2002, when a panel on NBC's *Meet the Press* was discussing then-Senate Republican leader Trent Lott's infamous remarks during Strom Thurmond's one-hundredth birthday party, when Lott quipped that if Thurmond had been successful in running for president in 1948, "we wouldn't have had all these problems over [all] these years, either."[23]

Thurmond was, of course, a candidate who ran on a segregationist platform, assuring his supporters he would fight to keep white people and black people legally separated in the South, attending different schools, patronizing different restaurants, and drinking from different water fountains.

When *Meet the Press* took on the issue as the last question in a segment on the impact of race in Southern elections, the pundits discussing the issue were host Tim Russert and columnists Bob Novak, William Safire, Joe Klein, and David Broder—all middle-aged white men.

And while Broder and Klein criticized Lott's comments, Novak pushed back hard: "He's at a damn birthday party," said the columnist. "I mean, this is the kind of thing that makes people infuriated with the media, is they pick up something that's said at a birthday party and turn it into a case of whether he should be impeached."[24]

It took the mainstream media so long to pick up on the story that Howard Kurtz hosted a segment on *Reliable Sources* to wonder why—again, with no black pundits speaking.[25]

Sitting at home, watching the discussions, I had an answer: There wasn't a person of color on hand to explain how troubling it feels to hear a U.S. senator imply that the demeaning, damaging period of racial segregation from America's past was a wonderful idea—even in jest.

A more recent study by the National Hispanic Foundation for the Arts found that diversity figures for the Sunday network TV news shows hadn't improved much, even a decade later.

Over nine months of broadcasts from March to November 2011, the group found just 3 percent of 380 people appearing as guests and/or pundits on ABC's *This Week*, CBS's *Face the Nation*, *Fox News Sunday*, and NBC's *Meet the Press* were Hispanic people of any race. Women were just 22 percent of guests, while black people stood at 8 percent, with Asian and Native American guests combined notching 1 percent.[26]

The act of injecting new ideas into the national dialogue can be jarring, no doubt. It can be odd to see journalists and pundits take their empathy to greater levels, wearing hooded sweatshirts on camera to highlight Trayvon Martin's shooting death in Florida or leading protest rallies, as MSNBC anchor Al Sharpton has done.

Fox News contributor Liz Trotta criticized, in particular, a segment on NBC's *Rock Center* newsmagazine in which an array of black journalists from across NBC News platforms reflected on personal stories of dealing with racial profiling or schooling their children on handling race prejudice from others, inspired by news coverage of the Florida teen's death.[27]

Trotta—who once said of the dramatic increase in sexual assaults against women in the military, "What did they [female soldiers] expect?"—concluded the *Rock Center* story was a "sorry show" that "can only hurt their [black journalists'] credibility."[28]

"That's a wonderful term from the far left: 'unique perspective,'" she said, dismissively. "That means they're reaching really far to make their case without any facts to back it up." I guess that was Trotta's "unique perspective."[29]

Anchor Greg Jarrett went on to point out that black people are far more likely to be killed by another black person, and wondered why Al Sharpton and Jesse Jackson were focusing on the "statistically rare" case of a black teen killed by a non-black man. I was thinking it might have something to do with the fact that the shooter, George Zimmerman, wasn't arrested by police until international attention and protests pushed authorities to bring in a prosecutor from another town.

I do think the *Rock Center* piece was premature—given that key facts about the shooting were still in dispute.

But I also felt that NBC's bigger gaffe was including only black journalists to share their stories about race. As the nation grows more diverse, it is obvious that race issues affect us all—regardless of what pundits such as Trotta and Jarrett may think—and the discussions should include us all.

Racial prejudice—and concern over its impact—isn't just a "black thing" anymore.

White pundits have pretended for many years that their cultural background hasn't affected their news judgment or perceptions, when it has. And while things can get a bit unmoored when huge, race-centered stories such as the Martin case break out, it's also the inevitable consequence when new voices have a seat at the table.

This is what happens when more varied perspectives get to define what is news and what is not.

"Context is everything," Lemon said, recalling his 2010 interview with former USDA employee Shirley Sherrod, a black woman unfairly depicted as an anti-white racist in a selectively edited video released by blogger Andrew Breitbart. "You realize there is a certain time when people of different ethnicities and culture see things differently, even when they live in the same place. Sometimes, people see things the way they want to see things."[30]

SHE'S BEEN AN ADVOCATE FOR DIVERSITY in media for many years. But Lyne Pitts didn't really figure out the best way to make her case until, as NBC's vice president of strategic initiatives, she was sitting at a corporate seminar held by General Electric.

"Somebody said diversity was one of GE's five guiding principles," she recalled. "It's not just the right thing to do, it's good business."[31]

Pitts, who already had worked in TV news for 30 years serving as executive producer for the weekend edition of NBC's *Today* show, senior producer for the *CBS Evening News with Dan Rather,* and executive producer of the *Early Show* at CBS, felt a lightbulb go off.

"I realized I had been trying to beat my head against the wall to say 'Why doesn't the broadcast medium that I work in, look like the world that I live in?'" Pitts said. "And I said, you know, 'I am tired of trying to tell people what they ought to do.' The nation's changing. The population's changing. I have to convince people there's a way to make money by doing the right thing."

As a battle-scarred veteran of media diversity struggles, Pitts has her stories. Like the executive at one cable channel who didn't understand there was a black middle class living somewhere between the worlds of the *Cosby Show* and *Good Times,* watching as much or more television than its white counterpart and ready for news and commercial messages that spoke to it.

So Pitts commissioned a marketing study to learn what might move the needle with black audiences. Her discovery: Influencers—people in their lives whose recommendations and opinions they respect—count for a lot.

"They're more likely to do something if their pastor tells them to do it or if [popular African American radio personality] Tom Joyner recommends it . . . much more than an advertisement in the *New York Times*," she said. "You put a four-column ad in the New York Times for MSNBC's Joe [Scarborough] and Mika [Brzezinsky] on *Morning Joe* on the back page of the *New York Times* and that doesn't do anything for the African American audience."

Instead, Pitts developed a 2008 meeting where five black pastors came to NBC News's Manhattan headquarters for a "Day of Dialogue," featuring bishops Charles Blake, Sedgwick Daniels, and T. D. Jakes, along with pastors A. R. Bernard and John Borders III, to speak with NBC News executives and top anchor Brian Williams about issues facing their congregations and possible stories worth covering.

"It was really just a way for us to hear what was on the mind of the African American community, because these are the kinds of people who have their hands on regular folks," said Pitts, who is black. "It was also a way for them to take back the message that NBC is a good place."

Savvy marketing, meet the Right Thing to Do.

Pitts also recalled championing an MSNBC documentary, *Meeting David Wilson*, about a young black man who tracked down the descendants of the white family that owned his ancestors as slaves; hiring a black-centered media firm outside NBC to sell ads in the show; and helping launch NBC's black-focused website TheGrio.com.

But in more recent years—she left NBC in 2009—Pitts has seen less progress than she expected.

"I feel like what I'm seeing on TV is a bit of retrenchment, and no concern about it," she said. "Why is nobody worried that their [prime time] lineup is all white? Why is CNN not worried that they just have white people on from 5 P.M. on or whatever?"

True enough, CNN has had several chances to diversify its prime time host lineup in recent years, thanks to key staff changes: Campbell Brown's departure from the 8 P.M. slot in 2010, onetime star Larry King's departure from the 9 P.M. slot later that year, and the eventual departure of Brown's replacements—ex–New York governor Eliot Spitzer and newspaper columnist Kathleen Parker—in 2011.

But those jobs went to white anchors Anderson Cooper and Piers Morgan, with former CNBC star Erin Burnett, who is also white, hired for a 7 P.M. show that debuted in October 2011. In early 2012, no person of color regularly anchored a show on CNN from 1 P.M. to 11 P.M. weekdays (and before Burnett, CNN also featured a long string of women who failed in prime time, including Parker, Brown, Paula Zahn, and Connie Chung).

The diversity news isn't much better over at the competition. At top-rated cable news channel Fox News, other than Juan Williams popping up among a roster of eight rotating co-hosts on *The Five* and African American anchor Harris Faulkner's contributions to the midday news show *Happening Now,* there were no anchors of color listed as regular hosts of shows from 6 A.M. to 11 P.M. weekdays on the channel's website in early 2012.

MSNBC offered much more diversity before 7 P.M., with non-white anchors Alex Wagner, Tamron Hall, Richard Lui, and Martin Bashir on shows before Sharpton's 6 P.M. *PoliticsNation.* Still, the channel had no anchors of color from 7 P.M. to 11 P.M.

And bad as the numbers looked for African Americans, tallies were even worse for Hispanic and Asian anchors.

The sense is that prime time remains the last glass ceiling for anchors of color. But Mark Whitaker, executive vice president and managing editor of CNN Worldwide, resisted such a focus.

"I feel like sometimes in these discussions, nothing but primetime counts, as though all of these great journalists who have gotten to the point where they get to anchor a show on the weekend or in the morning, somehow that doesn't count for anything," said Whitaker. "It counts for a lot."[32]

Whitaker, who is African American, cited diversity issues as one of the areas he planned to address when coming to CNN from NBC News, where he was the network's Washington bureau chief (he also once served as editor of *Newsweek* magazine).

For CNN, the channel's weekday diversity surfaces in the morning, where non-white anchors Zoraida Sambolin, Soledad O'Brien, and Suzanne Malveaux anchor or co-anchor shows from 5 A.M. to noon. And O'Brien reclaimed her morning spot—she had been removed from CNN's 7 A.M. broadcast back in 2007—in part by building up her image helming the channel's *Black in America* and *Latino in America* documentary series.

But African American anchor Tony Harris left CNN in 2010, later surfacing as an anchor at Al Jazeera English; Cuban American journalist Rick Sanchez was fired in 2010 after making controversial comments on a radio show; black anchor T. J. Holmes left CNN for a job at the Black Entertainment Network channel in December 2011; and analyst Roland Martin only had the briefest of tryouts guest hosting at 8 P.M. back when Zahn was still at the channel.

So does CNN have a problem showcasing minority males?

"Not at all," said Whitaker, noting that CNN's challenge is finding journalists who can deliver a point of view and personality on news stories without being partisan or overly political. "A lot of training that journalists of all colors get, say in local news or a certain kind of news, doesn't really translate that well anymore into being host of a primetime show. You have to have a point of view, you have to have personality, conduct a lot of interviews and be spontaneous . . . that's a very, very high bar for any anchor, no matter what their color."[33]

CNN also faced criticism for how it handled the suspension of Martin, who was taken off the channel for about a month after posting messages on Twitter during that year's Super Bowl broadcast that many judged to be insensitive to gay people. (One read: "If a dude at your Super Bowl party is hyped about David Beckham's H&M underwear ad, smack the ish out of him!")[34]

Some gay activists advocated firing Martin, who apologized and eventually met with officials from the Gay and Lesbian Alliance Against Defamation (GLAAD). Others noted that another analyst, conservative tea party favorite Dana Loesch, suffered few repercussions for saying on CNN, after video surfaced of U.S. soldiers urinating on the corpses of dead Taliban fighters in Afghanistan, "I'd drop trou and do it, too."[35]

"In Dana Loesch's case, she was effectively suspended," said Whitaker. (*Politico*'s Dylan Byers reported that a database search showed she did not appear on CNN from January 12 to January 30, 2012.[36]) "We didn't make it public and she accepted it without making it public on her end, either. But we took her off the air for several weeks and it was directly related to the things she said . . . In general, we're not looking to embarrass our people. If we can handle these situations without doing that, we will. In Roland's case, there was so much attention paid to it . . . that was one where we made the decision it would be hard to just do it privately."[37]

While noting CNN also has Indian American anchor Fareed Zakaria hosting a sharp international politics show on Sundays, Whitaker added they had just hired a key talent development executive to help build a diverse slate of anchors.

"We want shows and anchors who have a broad appeal," he added. "We want part of our audiences to be diverse [but] we're not going to create a show for one population or another. It's about finding that mix . . . that would appeal to a number of different audiences."

Going by the ratings, MSNBC has benefited by drafting Sharpton, who already had the "influencer" status with some African Americans that Pitts spoke about.

According to Nielsen, MSNBC drew an average 67,000 black viewers from 5 P.M. to 11 P.M. in 2011, while CNN attracted 51,000 and Fox News drew 15,000.[35] (Overall in 2011, Fox News was by far the most-watched cable news channel, drawing 1.9 million viewers in prime time, compared to 773,000 for MSNBC and 655,000 for CNN, according to the Project for Excellence in Journalism.[39])

Sharpton's *PoliticsNation* also beat 6 P.M. competitor John King on CNN, drawing 776,000 viewers in the first quarter of 2012, compared to King's 459,000, according to the TVNewser website. Fox News anchor Bret Baier was the overall winner in this timeslot, with 1.8 million viewers.[40]

At a time when CNN and MSNBC are fighting hard for second place in prime time, black viewers and those sympathetic to Sharpton's perspective might be an important component of that success.

Which also might help explain what happened to one of MSNBC's best-known analysts: Patrick J. Buchanan.

I WAS ENJOYING A DRINK with MSNBC president Phil Griffin at a crowded press party back in 2010, when I brought up a delicate subject:

The continuing employment of Pat Buchanan on his channel.

By then, Buchanan had already received the NABJ's Thumbs Down award twice—most recently in 2008 for a column called "A Brief for Whitey," in which he asserted, "America has been the best country on earth for black folks. It was here that 600,000 black people, brought from Africa in slave ships, grew into a community of 40 million, were introduced to Christian salvation, and reached the greatest levels of freedom and prosperity blacks have ever known."[41]

As I noted in a later column, that's a bit like saying if you move into a better neighborhood after someone breaks in your house, you should go thank the burglar.

Buchanan, a former aide to Richard Nixon who has flourished as a pundit and author after running for president in 1992, 1996, and 2000, inspired noted conservative William F. Buckley to suggest he was an anti-Semite in a 40,000-word piece for the *National Review* titled "In Search of Anti-Semitism" (a charge Buchanan denied).

In 2009, as Sonia Sotomayor faced confirmation as America's first Hispanic Supreme Court justice, Buchanan—who often insisted immigrants should learn English—ridiculed her for using elementary grammar books to learn better English while at Yale, insisting her acceptance at the *Yale Law Review* was affirmative action at play (she also finished first in her class).[42]

Buchanan summed up his feelings about her in a column dubbed "How to Handle Sonia," in which he suggested GOP senators at her confirmation hearing shouldn't worry about the Hispanic vote or fail to address what he saw as the concerns of white conservatives.

"These are the folks whose jobs have been outsourced to China and Asia, who pay the price of affirmative action when their sons and daughters are pushed aside to make room for the Sonia Sotomayors," he wrote. "These are the folks who want the borders secured and illegals sent back."[43]

The Anti-Defamation League wrote of Buchanan: "Many of the views he holds are identical to those of self-declared 'white nationalists.' Buchanan repeatedly demonizes Jews and minorities and openly affiliates with white supremacists. Among his frequent claims is that the sovereignty of the United States is being undermined by Israeli control and Mexican incursion, a belief which he disseminates on mainstream cable and network television and in his prolific writings. Buchanan has released a book nearly every two years, many of which take the view that non-white immigrants destroy Western culture."[44]

But when I asked Griffin why he continued to employ him as a news analyst, the MSNBC president seemed to shrug off the criticism like one might overlook the comments of a crotchety uncle. "I talk to Pat about a lot of these issues," he said in 2010. "I don't think he crosses the line. I think sometimes he challenges us . . . I think Pat's part of the debate and I want him to bring it."[45]

What a difference a few years can make.

The first sign of trouble came when Buchanan went on a publicity tour to promote his 2011 book *Suicide of a Superpower: Will America Survive to*

2025? It seemed the one cable channel where he didn't talk up the tome was his employer, MSNBC.

Small wonder, since one big theme of the book is how the European and Christian core of America is shrinking, and "socially, culturally, morally, America has taken on the aspect of a decadent society and a declining nation."[46]

Noting that Buchanan appeared on a white nationalist radio show entitled *The Political Cesspool* to promote the book, the group Color of Change announced in November it had collected more than 275,000 signatures demanding the channel release Buchanan.[47]

Months later, on February 16, 2012, MSNBC finally admitted it had done so, issuing a terse statement: "After ten years, we've parted ways with Pat Buchanan. We wish him well."[48] While denying that his channel's political focus led to Buchanan's ouster, Griffin did tell the *New York Times,* "I want MSNBC to reflect America in the 21st century, not the America of the 1940s."[49]

Buchanan complained of being "blacklisted" by advocacy groups such as liberal watchdog Media Matters, the Anti-Defamation League, and Color of Change.

"The modus operandi of these thought police at Color of Change and ADL is to brand as racists and anti-Semites any writer who dares to venture outside the narrow corral in which they seek to confine debate," he wrote in "The New Blacklist," a column on his own website.

At the column's end, Buchanan wrote: "I know these blacklisters. They operate behind closed doors, with phone calls, mailed threats, and off-the-record meetings. They work in the dark because, as Al Smith said, nothing un-American can live in the sunlight."[50]

Perhaps what couldn't live in the sunlight was Buchanan's often-repeated notion that the rising number of non-white people in America leads to what his book called "social disintegration" and an "end to moral community"—a notion he conveniently left out of the "Blacklist" column.[51]

But what surprised next was the reaction among other pundits.

Andrew Sullivan, Chris Matthews, Juan Williams, Joe Scarborough, and Mika Brzezinski all publicly expressed admiration for Buchanan and sorrow that he lost his job—despite the fact that several of them have often criticized other public figures for racially insensitive statements.

Matthews, in an on-air tribute to Buchanan after his departure was announced, almost seemed to soft-pedal the prejudice Buchanan had mainstreamed over the years: "To Pat, the world can never be better than the one he grew up in as a young boy. Blessed Sacrament Church and Grade School, Gonzaga High School, Georgetown University. No country will ever be better than the United States of America of the early 1950s. It's his deep loyalty to preserving that reality and all its cultural and ethnic aspects that has been his primal purpose and is what has gotten him into trouble."[52]

Not exactly. What got Buchanan in trouble was calling America a "country built, basically, by white folks," forgetting the black slaves, Hispanic immigrants, and Asian conscripts who forged the nation's infrastructure in their blood and sweat.[53] He also wrote admiringly in his biography of the 1940s and 1950s, when the nation was segregated by race, saying, "There were no politics to polarize us then, to magnify every slight. The 'Negroes' of Washington had their public schools, restaurants, movie houses, playgrounds and churches; and we had ours."[54]

When a coalition of groups representing minority journalists demanded the news industry hire enough journalists of color to approach the community's diversity levels, Buchanan noted, "Is there any evidence major news organizations in this country have engaged in systematic discrimination to keep out men or women of color this last half century?"[55]

For Buchanan, too many advances for people of color seemed to come at the expense of white people. And few prominent political people of color—including President Barack Obama or Supreme Court Justice Sonia Sotomayor—seemed to get credit from him for earning their positions through talent and hard work.

These notions—that white Christians are the repository of America's morality and achievement, while the country's growing diversity spells the nation's doom—are the core tenets of prejudice and racism.

Yet Buchanan seemed to articulate them skillfully enough that many pundits, who would condemn those words in a blunter form, felt sorrow when he lost his perch at MSNBC.

Including, surprisingly, Fox News analyst Williams, who commiserated with Buchanan during an interview for Fox News Latino about his own firing from NPR for saying he gets nervous around people in "Muslim garb" at airports during a 2010 appearance on *The O'Reilly Factor*.

Williams's ouster also had a racial dimension, as he was one of the few black males who regularly appeared on NPR. Indeed, some critics theorized that the reason NPR officials endured a growing tension between Williams's statements on Fox News and his role at their network for so long was because he was the outlet's best-known male commentator of color.

But with Buchanan, Williams seemed to be sounding a different note. Was this the same pundit who criticized GOP candidate Newt Gingrich for echoing "segregationist politicians of the past" in his words on the stump about black people and food stamps?[56]

"One is, I think, making purely racial appeals in order to win votes in an election . . . we know the history of that, but Buchanan is not running for any office," Williams told me. "He is speaking as an older white American who wants to make the case that his country is not the same. I think it's important that you not dismiss people out of hand and force those arguments into the dark corners of life."[57]

Yet, media outlets decided a long time ago that some ideas don't deserve to be part of the wider discourse. Journalists don't go asking the Ku Klux Klan for alternate points of view when writing about racial issues anymore.

GLAAD even created a database documenting the most extreme statements of some experts used as opposing voices in stories on gay rights issues, to demonstrate how some pundits offer homophobic speech in friendlier settings and tone down their rhetoric for more mainstream media environments.[58]

Some included on the roster complained it would be used as a blacklist. But Aaron McQuade, GLAAD's director of news and field media, wrote that "if a reporter is interviewing someone who insinuates that his or her political opponent is controlled by the devil, it's the reporter's journalistic responsibility to put that person's opinion in perspective."[59]

This, too, is what happens when more perspectives get to fight in the public space to define what is news—and ethical commentary—and what is not.

SEVEN

HATE RADIO

*Why Talk Radio May Not Be a Haven
for Angry White Guys Much Longer*

You put your kids on a school bus, you expect safety but in Obama's America
the white kids now get beat up with the black kids cheering, "Yay, right on,
right on, right on, right on," and, of course, everybody says the white kid
deserved it, he was born a racist, he's white.

> —*Rush Limbaugh, on an incident where a white student was beaten
> by two black youths on an Illinois school bus, September 15, 2009*[1]

IT WAS, FOR RADIO STAR RUSH LIMBAUGH, LIKELY A TYPICAL
Wednesday afternoon.

But Feb. 29, 2012, would prove a landmark day for Sandra Fluke, an
unknown Georgetown University Law School student who had spoken at
a U.S. House of Representatives committee hearing a week earlier, insisting that her Jesuit and Catholic school's student health plan should include
contraception.

That speech would inspire the most powerful talk radio host in America
to make her a household name, as another demeaning example of All That's
Wrong with Liberals.

Fluke had testified that the annual student cost for contraception outside their health plan could reach $3,000, giving Limbaugh just the opening
he needed. He even mangled Fluke's first name in the process.

"What does it say about the college co-ed Susan [*sic*] Fluke, who goes
before a congressional committee and essentially says that she must be paid

to have sex, what does that make her?" Limbaugh thundered. "It makes her a slut, right? It makes her a prostitute. She wants to be paid to have sex. She's having so much sex she can't afford the contraception. She wants you and me and the taxpayers to pay her to have sex. What does that make us? We're the pimps . . . The johns? We would be the johns? No! We're not the johns . . . Yeah, that's right. Pimp's not the right word. Okay, so she's not a slut. She's 'round heeled.' I take it back."[2]

The next day, as controversy built over his insults, Limbaugh doubled down: "If we are going to pay for your contraceptives, and thus pay for you to have sex, we want something for it . . . We want you to post the videos online, so we can all watch."[3]

Of course, Fluke advocated having her health insurance cover contraception, so neither Limbaugh nor any of his listeners would have to pay anything, unless they also got student health insurance through Georgetown University.

And, though Limbaugh eventually played audio clips of Fluke's congressional testimony on his show, his original criticisms left out many of her actual arguments—including that some women who needed birth control pills for health problems were often forced to fight skeptical health plan administrators. She also described a rape victim who didn't go to the hospital, assuming treatment wouldn't be covered.

"When you let university administrators or other employees rather than women and their doctors dictate whose medical needs are legitimate and whose are not, women's health takes a back seat to a bureaucracy focused on policing her body," Fluke told the committee.[4]

There were plenty of ideas in Fluke's testimony worthy of debate, including whether her $3,000 cost estimate was inflated or how many women might actually have an illness requiring regular intake of birth control pills for treatment.

But Limbaugh instead turned Fluke into an empty caricature for his listeners, painting her as a young "slut" who was pushing "welfare disguised as women's health." At a time when House Republicans already faced criticism for holding a hearing on the contraception requirements in Obama's health care plan—a gathering at which few woman spoke, and from which Fluke herself was barred—Limbaugh's antics conveniently reframed the debate in terms his audience would accept.

For anyone who has spent any time listening to Limbaugh, this was no surprise.

This is the host who routinely calls females who speak up on women's issues "feminazis."

This is the pundit who told Fox News, "I love the women's movement; especially when walking behind it."[5]

This is, in short, what Limbaugh lives for: tweaking the sensibilities of political foes with a mix of brash bluster and a finely tuned talent for obscuring the truth.

The result: At least some of the stories filling news outlets in the days immediately following his remarks focused on the words Limbaugh chose to describe Fluke, rather than the issues she raised. Questions at hand shifted from whether Republicans were unfairly excluding women from the contraception debate to how Fluke felt about having her own sexual history lampooned before 15 million weekly radio listeners.

For a host whose show airs in the wilds of AM radio, the Fluke controversy once again put him at the center of every network newscast, discussed in detail by Fox News's Bill O'Reilly and MSNBC's Ed Schultz, written up in all the major newspapers in ways his fans would love.

And Limbaugh seemed to be loving it. At least, at first.

"People like Limbaugh's listeners are people who are always condescended to in American culture," said Zev Chafets, a former columnist for the *New York Daily News* who got unprecedented access to Limbaugh for a largely complimentary 2010 book on the host, *Rush Limbaugh: An Army of One*. "Rush came along . . . he was the guy, for them, the badass who came along and he didn't take a step back. You want to say we're homophobes, you know what, I'm proud to be a homophobe, if that's what a homophobe is . . . Women [get upset], okay you're a feminazi . . . when people said 'You can't say Nazi.' His response was . . . 'Hell I can't. If you don't like it, fuck you.' That's his standard attitude."[6]

But there was a new twist to this particular incident that even Limbaugh may not have anticipated. Amid growing controversy, the expected calls for advertisers to drop his show had an unusual result.

They worked.

Three days after his first comments aired, five advertisers announced via Twitter and Facebook that they would be dropping commercials on

Limbaugh's program. Within a week the tally had swelled closer to 50, with companies either pulling their ads or insisting publicly that they never intended for their commercials to air on his show.[7]

The progressive rock band Rush and art rocker Peter Gabriel both demanded Limbaugh stop playing their songs on his show (strains of Gabriel's song "Sledgehammer" played in the background when Limbaugh first used the s-word on Fluke). Even President Obama got involved, calling Fluke to offer support because, as he said in a press conference days later, "I thought about [my daughters] Malia and Sasha . . . I want them to be able to speak their mind in a civil and thoughtful way. I don't want them attacked and called horrible names because they are being good citizens."[8]

Limbaugh tried to shrug off the sponsorship mess as comparable to "losing a couple of French fries" from a container, but there was a more troubling sign amid the ad suspensions and online protests, noted by those already worried about the prospects for aggressively provocative, often-conservative commercial talk radio.[9]

Rumblings that advertisers might be fed up with the genre for good.

"Limbaugh's remarks have us rethinking our future use of talk radio," wrote David Friend, CEO of the online computer backup company Carbonite, on the firm's Facebook page three days after Limbaugh's tirade.

"We use more than 40 talk show hosts to help get the Carbonite message out to the public," explained the executive, noting that customers have demanded in the past that they also pull ads from liberal talkers such as Stephanie Miller and Ed Schultz, along with National Public Radio. "However, the outcry over Limbaugh is the worst we've ever seen."

One day after posting that message, Friend pulled all of Carbonite's advertising from Limbaugh's show.

"It was a three day attack on someone who is powerless, who is not a public figure . . . I think there's a line, and Rush Limbaugh appears to have crossed it," said radio host Stephanie Miller, a liberal who nevertheless feared that left-wing groups pressing for a boycott of Limbaugh just might catch her show in the crossfire.

"We've been saying be careful about this boycott thing from the beginning," she added. "It would be a lot easier for a right wing organization to crush our little show . . . It's a slippery slope. Some of those companies may decide we're not going to do talk radio at all because it's too risky and controversial and they don't want to offend anybody. And that hurts all of us."[10]

But Limbaugh has faced calls for boycott before. The big difference this time?

The impact of social media.

From the moment he uttered his remarks, Twitter feeds and Facebook pages of companies sponsoring Limbaugh filled with complaints from the public and harsh words for his advertisers.

Thanks to YouTube, Facebook, Twitter, and other social media platforms, clips featuring webcam video of Limbaugh's comments from his own studio were instantly available, allowing viewers to decide for themselves what he said and how he meant it.

Much as companies exploit online channels and communities to bond with customers, those conduits can become a two-way street, allowing disgruntled people from the general public to post messages where other prospects may congregate. Advertisers couldn't have been happy seeing their company Facebook pages turned into worldwide signposts for angry strangers to argue over Limbaugh's use of the word "slut."

As someone who tracks Limbaugh's more egregious bouts with sexism and race-baiting, even I was surprised the host was so direct with Fluke.

Back in 2007, I wrote a column about how Limbaugh was much more sophisticated in his race-baiting tactics than Imus, creating a parody song, "Barack the Magic Negro," that he used to needle Democratic supporters throughout much of the 2008 election season.[11]

Set to the tune of "Puff, the Magic Dragon" and sung by an awful Al Sharpton impersonator, Limbaugh's song highlighted then-percolating talk that the biracial Obama wasn't "black enough" to woo African American voters. It skirted the edge of racial stereotypes enough to spark protests from liberals, while allowing Limbaugh to claim he was just joking.

A sample: "*Barack the Magic Negro lives in D.C./ The L.A. Times, they called him that / 'Cause he's not authentic like me.*"[12]

Here's a few reasons why the song avoided Fluke-level backlash:

Limbaugh didn't create the parody. Instead, he enlisted conservative "humorist" Paul Shanklin, who had also parodied Bill Clinton and Joe Lieberman. Limbaugh also often uses his longtime call screener James Golden, who is black, in a similar way under the stage name Bo Snerdly. During the 2008 election, Snerdly became the "Official Obama Criticizer," launching critical jabs in dialect, pronouncing himself an

"African-American-in-good-standing-and-certified-black-enough-to-criticize-Obama-guy."[13]

The most incendiary term in the parody came from someone else. The title of the song came from a March 2007 *Los Angeles Times* column, "Obama the Magic Negro," in which the writer explains the Democratic politician's appeal by using a term from academic film criticism and sociology. As we discussed in Chapter Five, the "Magic Negro" is a black character who appears in a film or TV show to help the white star with a mystical insight into life or actual supernatural powers.

Magic Negro characters replace the negative stereotypes of dangerous black people with a more benign but still subordinate stereotype. The author of the original column, biracial critic David Ehrenstein, suggested that Obama's rise to fame and sidestepping of harsh criticism occurred, in part, because his supporters projected "fantasies of curative black benevolence" onto him—just the kind of lofty, intellectual talk Limbaugh lives to skewer.[14]

Limbaugh made fun of someone even some liberals don't like. Uncomfortable about Sharpton's role in the Tawana Brawley scandal and his actions during subsequent protests, even some liberals don't have the warmest feeling for the civil rights activist, who is lampooned as much or more than Obama in the song.

He used humor. Some of Limbaugh's most ardent defenders insist that his critics are just poor sports or ideologues looking to turn a good joke into something more. Limbaugh used this defense on NBC's *Today* show, insisting, "I love parodying the left . . . The *L.A. Times* called him that, I'm just repeating it."[15] Of course, this is when stereotypes can be most seductive; cloaked as humor or entertainment, they are often more palatable.

Look over the list above, and you see that Limbaugh's actions in the Fluke controversy were the exact opposite of his tactics in the "Magic Negro" parody, which may explain why he landed in such hot water this time.

And the roiling controversy also explains why Limbaugh took another unheard-of step, days after joking that Georgetown University should establish a "Wilt Chamberlain scholarship exclusively for women" (referencing the professional basketball star who boasted of sleeping with 20,000 women).

Limbaugh apologized.

"For over 20 years, I have illustrated the absurd with absurdity, three hours a day, five days a week," the host said in a statement posted on his website the Saturday after his original tirade, which he reiterated on radio the following Monday. "In this instance, I chose the wrong words in my analogy of the situation. I did not mean a personal attack on Ms. Fluke . . . I think it is absolutely absurd that during these very serious political times, we are discussing personal sexual recreational activities before members of Congress. I personally do not agree that American citizens should pay for these social activities . . . [But] my choice of words was not the best, and in the attempt to be humorous, I created a national stir. I sincerely apologize to Ms. Fluke for the insulting word choices."[16]

Though his apology hardly addressed the inaccuracies or sexism embedded in his three days of tirades, Limbaugh was right about one thing: It is truly absurd to suggest that calling a woman a slut and prostitute is not a "personal attack."

Still, Limbaugh's deepening public relations disaster can be understood through an analysis by New York University journalism professor Jay Rosen, who has looked at how certain topics and terms move in and out of the sphere of acceptable public debate. Rosen's analysis used a diagram developed by press scholar Daniel C. Hallin: a simple figure, drawn by tracing one circle, then placing a larger circle around it.[17]

The innermost circle is dubbed the "sphere of consensus"; that's where ideas lie that are so universally accepted that no one in media spends much time debating them. Watch TV news anchors, especially on local broadcasts, and these are the opinions they will echo without fear of criticism; for instance, expressing sorrow over a tragic accident or touting the success of a local sports team.

(It's heartening to note that condemnation of obvious, open racial discrimination seems to lie inside that first sphere, perhaps one of the greatest victories of the civil rights movement.)

The area between the first circle and the boundary of the second is the "sphere of legitimate debate." Here are the notions journalists and pundits accept as contested ideas, often defined by big institutions such as political parties or presidential administrations. It's where the fights over tax cuts or stimulus spending are fought, along with the contraception battle Fluke represented.

Outside the two circles, however, is the "sphere of deviance." This is the place for ideas that, Hallin wrote, "journalists and the political mainstream of society reject as unworthy of being heard."[18] One idea might be the notion that Communism should be an acceptable political alternative in America. Another might be the concept that the racist Ku Klux Klan deserves a voice in debates over race and prejudice in the Unites States.

Building on Hallin's analysis, Rosen said online media is changing the rules of the game, giving the general public greater power to decide what lies inside the sphere of legitimate debate and what gets pushed into the sphere of deviance.

"The authority of the press to assume consensus, define consensus and set the terms for legitimate debate is weaker when people can connect horizontally around and about the news," Rosen wrote, noting that those who don't accept the press' definition of these boundaries can now gather and express themselves online.[19]

Back in 2007, enough people objected to radio host Don Imus's description of Rutgers University's female basketball players as "nappy-headed hos" that he lost his jobs at MSNBC and CBS Radio.

The public decided that his awful words, which they saw via video clips circulated online, fell squarely inside the sphere of deviance. Advertisers began to balk. Executives worried about their corporate brands. Bye-bye Imus.

A decade ago, radio hosts who trafficked in prejudice, sexism, and anger were speaking mostly to sympathetic audiences. When called on a particular statement or action, they could deny it or spin it as satire, but today's social media structure takes all those words and makes them instantly available for wide review.

And there's also well-funded advocacy organizations monitoring media for such messages, from liberal watchdogs such as Media Matters to conservative press monitors NewsBusters. There's also the Women's Media Center, the Gay and Lesbian Alliance Against Defamation, and the National Association of Black Journalists. These alliances often highlight speech that flirts with prejudice, stereotypes, sexism, or racism, garnering media coverage and helping organize protests.

With the Fluke controversy, talk radio's biggest star stumbled into the same crosshairs. In perhaps the greatest sign of Limbaugh's post-Fluke vulnerability, rival Cumulus Media launched a radio show on April 9, 2012, featuring former Arkansas Gov. Mike Huckabee, competing directly against him with a format dubbed "more conversation, less confrontation."[20]

Which only further presses the question: What if the wider world has finally decided that it will no longer tolerate how these more extreme radio hosts talk about women, people of color, and social issues?

What if they *all* get stuck in the sphere of deviance?

> One out of every six Americans is now Latino. Most of them illegal, by the way.
>
> —*Michael Savage, on America's growing ethnic diversity, June 21, 2011*[21]

ASK IF AMERICA'S COMMERCIAL TALK RADIO INDUSTRY is dominated by angry conservative voices, and Michael Harrison balks with immediate exasperation.

As founder and publisher of the trade magazine *Talkers,* he is often both reporter on and guardian of the talk radio industry's reputation. And he resists the notion that the genre is ruled by "angry white guys" speaking to listeners just like them.

"I see them as big stars that get a lot of attention," Harrison said, speaking of the biggest names that fit the "angry white guy" category: Limbaugh, Savage, Sean Hannity, and Glenn Beck, among others. "Collectively, they are still a niche, though they're a niche which has captured a tremendous amount of attention."[22]

Talkers's own host rankings show Harrison may be understating the case.

According to the publication's 2011 figures—which even the magazine calls "rough projections"—six hosts averaged more than 6 million listeners per week; all were white, middle-aged men. Other than financial guru Dave Ramsey, they were all conservative political talkers too: Limbaugh (15 million listeners), Sean Hannity (14 million), Michael Savage (9 million), and Ramsey, Glenn Beck, and Mark Levin (all at 8.5 million).[23]

Some have scoffed at those figures; Current TV host Cenk Uygur offered Limbaugh $10,000 if he could prove his show still reaches 20 million listeners each day, as one of his employees told *Billboard* magazine back in 1993.[24]

But one has to look ten names further down *Talkers*'s list—past conservative hosts such as Laura Ingraham (6 million) and Bill Bennett (3.5 million)—before you see the first overtly liberal broadcasters: Alan Colmes,

Thom Hartmann, Stephanie Miller, and Ed Schultz all pegged at about 3 million listeners per week.

Among the magazine's 2011 "Heavy Hundred" list of most important talk show hosts in America, just 16 were women (two of whom co-hosted shows with men) and seven were African American, the only non-white ethnicity to even make the list.

These numbers are important; among America's biggest radio markets, where Arbitron uses pager-sized electronic devices to measure what shows listeners frequent, news/talk was the top format in fall 2010. At the end of 2010, nearly 1,922 AM and FM stations featured the format (including 376 public radio stations); more than any other genre.[25]

Its listeners are among the most educated and affluent in radio; 40 percent live in homes with an income above $75,000, and more than 75 percent attended college or earned a degree.[26]

But only 10 percent of them are black or Hispanic; 59 percent are male and 77 percent are age 45 or older. And they are more likely to identify as Republican or independent than as Democrat.[27]

At a time when the nation's population is growing more diverse—and the young people sought after by advertisers are especially so—political commercial talk radio seems to have locked itself into an aging, politically polarized demographic at odds with the nation's multicultural future.

"You start to look at Rush [Limbaugh], you're looking at [hosts] moving into their 60s," said Bob Neil, former president and CEO of Cox Radio, which owns 86 radio stations across the country.

"Rush was fresh when he started in 1989, but he's still playing the same songs [from his show's early years] in 2012 and guess what—that doesn't appeal to 35 year old men anymore," said Neil, who retired from Cox in mid-2011 to start his own consulting firm. "If you don't get some new, young talent in there that will bring a group of younger [listeners], Rush will die and this won't be around anymore. This is something under discussion in the management councils of a lot of big radio [companies]."[28]

Which leads to a natural question: How did this happen?

Turns out, the story of how commercial talk radio became dominated by the Limbaughs, Becks, and Hannitys of the world is a tale of ambition, corporate muscle, government deregulation, and a chase for profits, mixed in with a healthy dose of dumb luck.

Pugnacious, politicized talk has been a part of America's airwaves for more than a half-century, reaching back to the days of Joe Pyne—a '50s- and '60s-era radio and TV talk show host known for his aggressive, socially conservative opinions and confrontational style.

Pyne hosted radio and TV shows from Los Angeles in the 1960s featuring controversial guests such as Satanists, transsexuals, feminists, and black militants. Often, Pyne would get into arguments with them—a favorite insult was "jerk" or "dingbat"—threatening to throw them off his show.[29]

His empire, which included syndicated radio and TV shows along with a television game show, inspired later efforts by everyone from schlock talk show king Morton Downey Jr. to syndicated radio star Michael Savage. Pyne's Los Angeles talk show was inherited by Bob Grant, another opinionated broadcaster who would move to New York in 1970 and become legendary for his own conservative, incendiary, race-based talk.

Despite denying any bigotry, Grant gained notoriety for calling Martin Luther King Jr. a "scumbag," dismissing black New York Mayor David Dinkins as a "men's room attendant," and shrugging off black people advocating a national holiday for King's birthday as "savages."[30]

"Minorities are the Big Apple's majority, you don't need the papers to tell you that; walk around and you know it," said Grant, in one diatribe published by *Newsday* in 1992. "To me, that's a bad thing. I'm a white person." An analysis by the group Fairness and Accuracy in Reporting noted that Grant often touted the notion that people of color were genetically inferior to white people, a pseudo-science known as eugenics, promoting the "Bob Grant Mandatory Sterilization Program."[31]

But Grant's reign as the king of New York talk radio hit a speed bump in 1994 when *New York* magazine published a scathing feature on him subtitled "Why He Hates Blacks." Sixteen years later, Grant would blame that story for his inability to land a syndicated show or a spot on the conservative cable news channel Fox News. ("The writer never asked me if I hated blacks," the host complained online in November 2010, one month before putting up another blog post saying the changing of immigration standards in 1965 "signed our nation's death warrant." [32])

Still, like Pyne, his work inspired a range of younger hosts to aggressively push the boundaries of talk on race, gender, and social issues, including shock jock Howard Stern, Glenn Beck (who uses Grant's signature phrases "get off my phone!" and "sick twisted freak"), and Grant's eventual successor on WABC-AM, Sean Hannity.[33]

Grant was fired from WABC in 1996 after noting wryly on air that he was a "pessimist" for believing then-commerce secretary Ron Brown, who was black, had survived a plane crash in Croatia. Eventually, the public learned Brown had died.[34]

By the 1980s, a number of forces were coming together to produce the first big national boost to conservative talk. Ronald Reagan's election had sparked a resurgence in conservative politics, aided by and dovetailing with a rise in political power among religious groups such as the Moral Majority and Focus on the Family—some of which had their own broadcast shows to advance a religiously conservative perspective.

Even then, broadcasters were limited by the Fairness Doctrine, a rule adopted by the Federal Communications Commission in 1949 that required TV and radio outlets to air material on issues of public interest and ensure there were contrasting views available. It wasn't the same as equal time provisions for political candidates, but citizens could use the rule to challenge a radio or TV station's license if it didn't show a track record of featuring opposing viewpoints across its broadcasts.[35]

That rule wouldn't survive the Reagan era. An FCC filled with his appointees stopped enforcing the doctrine and later repealed it altogether in 1987, just as technology, the radio industry, and the ascendance of conservative politics were coming together to fuel the rise of one guy.

Rush Limbaugh.

According to author Zev Chafets, by this time Limbaugh had already been honing his craft for more than two decades. A former Top 40 disc jockey and onetime staffer in the marketing department of the Kansas City Royals baseball team, he had bounced around various jobs in radio until he learned how to channel his father's conservative attitudes into his now-legendary "El Rushbo" persona in Sacramento, California.

Hired to replace Morton Downey, 1980s-era Limbaugh came off as less caustic and more fun-loving, coining the phrase "feminazis" and declaring he was blessed with "talent on loan from God" spread along the then-fictional "Excellence in Broadcasting" network.[36] As long as listeners were laughing, they could overlook the sexism and prejudice embedded in some of his routines.

And with no Fairness Doctrine to rein in the station, Limbaugh could rail about the supremacy of conservative politics for hours, no rebuttal required.

"Rush's opinions are really a reflection of the attitudes of his father," said Chafets, referring to Rush Limbaugh Jr., an attorney and former World War II pilot known as a passionate patriot and conservative. "He was the kind of guy who would holler at the television; scream at Dan Rather every night for being too liberal. And when [Limbaugh] became political, he adopted his father's rap entirely."[37]

Introduced to former ABC Radio head Ed McLaughlin, Limbaugh seemed ripe for a concept that was frowned upon in talk radio circles back then: a nationally syndicated talk show based out of New York and offered to radio stations for free in exchange for the right to sell their own advertising inside the show.

Conventional wisdom in those days held that talk radio shows had to be local to work. But technology was making live satellite transmissions easy and cheap; a show with zero costs could look pretty attractive to radio station owners (these days, of course, Limbaugh gets a fee from station owners *and* commercial spots to sell inside his show).

By 1988, McLaughlin had gotten him a job at WABC and a syndication deal; by 1990, Limbaugh had 5 million listeners a week nationwide, according to the *New York Times*.[38]

The gold rush of conservative talk radio had begun.

"[Back then] AM radio, people had written it off; you couldn't give away AM radio stations," said Dan DiLoreto, who retired in 2010 as market manager in Tampa, Florida, for Clear Channel Radio after 23 years in the job. DiLoreto, who managed Clear Channel's eight stations in the Tampa Bay market, recalled that just before Limbaugh hit the national scene, a lot of music programming had moved to the FM band.[39]

"All of a sudden, that middle aged white guy who was afraid of change and needed a spokesman, a platform to share his views, well, Rush was there," DiLoreto added. "It just clicked. That conservative audience was consuming more radio than the liberal audience ... [and] we were following the money."

Beginning each show with a blast of classic rock, Limbaugh was a well-fed, confident guy who boasted of beating opponents with "half my brain tied behind my back to make it fair."

Limbaugh didn't just articulate a conservative point of view; he was a compelling broadcaster—even to listeners who didn't share his views. He made fans feel they were on the edge of a fresh revolution, the embodiment of the success and good times he insisted spring from conservative values.

"Limbaugh doesn't so much discuss the issues of the day with his listeners as hold forth on them," read one 1990 profile in New York's *Newsday* newspaper, which estimated his earnings that year at $750,000. "Like everyone's favorite blowhard uncle after a long meal, Limbaugh simultaneously offends and entertains while tossing off stern anti-liberal epigrams to his audience of devoted 'dittoheads.'"[40]

So what if he joked about creating a special military battalion of women who could take out any fighting force under the effects of premenstrual syndrome?[41] Or if he often cited a newspaper column he wrote in 1988, saying one of life's "undeniable truths" is that "feminism was established so as to allow unattractive women easier access to the mainstream of society"?[42]

Moving to New York two years before the city would elect its first black mayor, Limbaugh then asked callers if they ever noticed "how all newspaper composite pictures of wanted criminals resemble [black civil rights leader] Jesse Jackson?"[43]

"Virtually no one else—in radio or television—gets three hours, five days a week to launch unfettered, virtually unopposed political opinionizing to a big national audience," wrote the *New York Times* in 1990.[44]

"Much has been made of this 'angry white male' line; [Limbaugh] was really appealing to 35 to 45 year old men," said ex-Cox Radio executive Neil, noting that, for AM radio, those were young demographics who had previously fled the platform. "Some advertisers were nervous about the content, and didn't want to be on it. But his show was bringing in younger men, which was something different up to that point."[45]

But there was a dark side to this success, as noted by University of Michigan professor Susan J. Douglas in an essay on '90s-era talk radio for the *El Dorado Sun* titled "Letting Boys be Boys."

"Talk radio is as much, maybe even more, about gender politics than it is about party politics," wrote Douglas, calling Limbaugh-style radio hosts "decidedly macho and loud" in their presentation. "There were different masculinities enacted on radio, from [FM-based shock jock] Howard Stern to Rush Limbaugh, but they were all about challenging and overthrowing, if possible, that most revolutionary of social movements, feminism."[46]

Longtime radio personality Michael William Lebron, better known as Lionel, remembered what it was like when Limbaugh reordered the talk radio universe. At that time, he was a practicing attorney moonlighting as a radio guy in Tampa, Florida, just a few years after getting his start making prank calls to the city's talk hosts while in law school.[47]

In the early 90s, his station in Florida, WFLA-AM, had a mix of voices, from his own apolitical comedy-based shows to left-of-center misanthrope Bob Lassiter. But once Limbaugh burst onto the scene, Lionel saw an immediate change in talk radio.

"Destroyed it," Lionel said. "He put [AM talk] on the map. Bad news: Everybody wanted to be Rush. They wanted to out-Rush, Rush. It became 'Oh, you think you're a conservative? I'm more of a conservative than you.' And it kind of ruined it, because they all wanted to be Rush."[48]

And radio executives, seeing a way to make AM stations profitable again, began looking for ways to extend the formula. So, instead of programming a contrary voice at the 3 P.M. end of Limbaugh's show, they would look for another host who would reflect the sensibilities of the audience Limbaugh had gathered.

"The more time an individual spends with a station, the better that station does," said DiLoreto, explaining how companies can charge advertisers more for shows with sustained listening over long periods. "I'm better off having one person listen all day than having 10 people listen for 20 minutes in the morning . . . So you can't have Rush on from noon to 3 P.M. and then come back with a liberal host from 3 P.M. to 7 P.M.; you have to be consistent. So if Rush is going to be conservative, all the shows around him will have to be conservative."[49]

The 1991 conflict in Iraq, when U.S. forces pushed Saddam Hussein's army out of Kuwait after an attempted invasion, also helped. With no Internet for the general public and just one 24-hour cable news channel in CNN, radio stations featuring news and talk became go-to destinations.

It's a pattern that would be repeated again a decade later, in the aftermath of 9/11: National crises that spark a rush of patriotism often benefit conservative-leaning media, which play to the patriotic impulses of Americans seeking to support their country in a time of need.

"Radio has always been kind of a monkey see/monkey do kind of business," said Gabe Hobbs, who served as senior vice president in charge of Clear Channel's talk programs until his layoff in 2009. "What brought the audience over was the news. And all the suits and managers were like, 'Let's get some more of this kind of host.'"[50]

And then came another tidal wave: the Telecommunications Act of 1996.

Signed by Democratic president Bill Clinton, the act overhauled major parts of U.S. telecommunications law for the first time in more than 60 years. But for big corporate radio station owners, the act was a windfall of tremendous proportions, removing national caps on ownership and doubling the amount of stations a company could own in one market, from four to eight.[51]

The first week after the act was made law, about $700 million in station sales and purchases took place. By 2001, the number of station owners had dropped by 25 percent and by 2005, four radio companies controlled 70 percent of the radio audience.[52]

"Everybody was intoxicated; it was knee-deep in dollar bills, man," said Hobbs, noting that the ballooning size of radio companies made them attractive to Wall Street, which turned on the money spigot.[53] In 1999, the Justice Department approved Clear Channel's purchase of Jacor Communications, where Hobbs worked at the time, for $3.8 billion, including 230 stations in 59 markets, along with the Premiere Radio Networks syndication company, which sold Limbaugh's show across the country.[54]

As part of the deal, managers from Jacor such as Hobbs and infamously crude CEO Randy Michaels kept running Clear Channel's radio business, according to a 2001 story in *Salon*. Critics accused the company of importing a sexist style from Jacor that tolerated sophomoric stunts from talent and conducted business with a bullying, ruthless zeal.[55]

Dominant companies such as Clear Channel sold off weaker stations in many markets, ensuring their competitors wouldn't present strong challenges and keeping the most popular conservative lineups on the more powerful stations.

"Now we can find guys like Rush and put them on 100 stations, whether its Glenn Beck or Sean Hannity or whomever and they get good ratings and its incredibly efficient," Hobbs added, noting that companies could save costs by airing the same conservative talkers across many different stations at once. "We had struck a vein of gold in those days and corporate bosses saw no reason to dig a new mine [developing non-conservative talk hosts] when we might not find anything there."[56]

And in 2001, the conservative talk world would get another jolt to prolong its profitability and profile in the form of the worst terrorist attack to strike a domestic American city in history.

> It took me about a year to start hating the 9/11 victims' families . . . I don't hate all of them, I hate probably about 10 of them. But when I see a 9/11 victim family on television, or whatever, I'm just like, "Oh shut up." I'm so sick of them because they're always complaining.
>
> —*Glenn Beck, September 9, 2005*[57]

ALL GABE HOBBS REALLY WANTED was to find someone who could talk about the sky falling in.

At least it felt a little like that, back on Tuesday, September 11, 2001, when Hobbs, then in charge of talk programming for radio giant Clear Channel, stood in the middle of Manhattan not long after two hijacked commercial airliners slammed into the World Trade Center blocks away.

A Kentucky boy, he already felt a bit out of place in New York City, flown into town from Atlanta for a business meeting, when terrorists erased two signature buildings from Manhattan's skyline forever.

But the calamity also created a challenge for Hobbs to meet this national tragedy with 24/7 coverage on talk radio. In their homes and offices, people were scared, angry, and searching for answers—a perfect audience for programming that promises to explain the inexplicable while providing an outlet for their sorrow and fear.

But he had a problem: One of his biggest stars wasn't interested.

"I didn't talk to Dr. Laura, but her husband was sort of helping manage her then," said Hobbs of Dr. Laura Schlessinger, one of Clear Channel's most popular talk hosts—a therapist and physiologist who dispensed advice to callers, often leavened with a healthy dose of her own conservative-leaning personal philosophies.

Word came from her husband—who Hobbs said had an odd habit of handwriting notes he would then fax over—that Dr. Laura didn't think 9/11 talk suited her show.

"On any other day, I'd agree with [him], but—Hello!—there's lots of things she could talk about which would be relevant in this," Hobbs said. "Nope. Not her thing."[58]

So the executive decided instead to create a special, alternate channel featuring hosts in Clear Channel's Premiere Radio Networks syndication company talking about 9/11-related issues and news. Every three hours the roster would change, topped by the company's biggest star, Rush Limbaugh, and every Clear Channel station could tap into the shows whenever they liked.

And Hobbs already knew someone who could plug the hole left by Schlessinger's decision: a onetime Top 40 personality who had moved to Tampa, Florida, and whose foray into talk radio was just taking off, thanks to his acid criticisms of Democrats and liberals during the fight over the state's election results in 2000.

He called Glenn Beck.

On the day of the attacks, Beck went on air in Tampa seven hours after the towers fell, leading his audience in a tear-filled prayer, telling fans to pull over in their cars, "hush your surroundings," and pray to "our father who gave us life." He played a choir-filled, orchestral version of "The Star-Spangled Banner" every hour and followed Hobbs's sage advice: After a major event, just open the telephone lines and let people vent.

"I always say, don't be directive, be reflective," Hobbs noted. "Don't tell people what to feel and think. Reflect what they already feel and think and you'll be much more successful."[59]

That formula would become a mantra for more hosts than Beck, who did well enough in his post 9/11 show that Clear Channel took his program to national syndication in January 2002.

In the same way that Limbaugh found meteoric success amid the hunger for information and commentary during the 1991 Iraq War, Beck and Hannity—whose radio show began national syndication from New York one day before the attacks—saw their fortunes supercharged by the trauma of 9/11.

Beck's success would be a prominent victory for Hobbs, who had met him as a Top 40 disc jockey in New Haven during the fall of 1999, when the host decided he was tired of spinning records and insisted on moving to political talk. Until then, Beck was known as a "morning zoo" kind of radio performer who would pull pranks on rival radio stations and present sophomoric bits on radio.

But Hobbs took Beck to Tampa, Florida, where his political talk career floundered—his first show began with him lamenting leaving his children in

Connecticut and speculating that he may have made "the biggest mistake of my life"—until he took Hobbs's advice and positioned himself as an expert on the 2000 presidential vote recount in Florida.[60]

"For about nine months, it was an unmitigated disaster . . . he was being a little immature and seemed all over the road, scattered," said Hobbs. "Lo and behold, the presidential election of 2000 was upon us, so he started talking about that and . . . he became the expert. The [ratings] numbers came out and he went from 17 to 1st, from the summer to fall . . . Once you get them in the tent, he was very good at keeping them, and so he became successful."[61]

By the mid-2000s, conservative hosts had dominated talk radio for more than a decade. And their particular style ensured that the perspective of conservatives and middle-class men would dominate—even when the hosts themselves weren't necessarily part of that group, like Schlessinger or conservative talker Laura Ingraham.

"To succeed, a talk show host must perpetuate the notion that his or her listeners are victims, and the host is the vehicle by which they can become empowered," wrote Dan Shelley, a former assistant program director at WTMJ-AM in Milwaukee, for *Milwaukee Magazine*. "More often than not, however, the enemy is the 'mainstream media'—local or national, print or broadcast."[62]

Shelley described two strategies: the *you know what would happen if* scenario (example: "You know what would happen if a conservative called Hillary Clinton a boob like Bill Maher did Sarah Palin? The liberal media would kill them") or the *pre-emptive strike,* predicting harsh media coverage of an issue the host knows will embarrass conservatives, like revelations of Rush Limbaugh's prescription drug addiction.

"The key reason talk radio succeeds is because its hosts can exploit the fear and perceived victimization of a large swath of conservative-leaning listeners," Shelley wrote. "And they feel victimized because many liberals and moderates have stereotyped these Americans as uncaring curmudgeons."[63]

But while Shelley's essay insisted such hosts could influence elections and public policy, directing listeners to complain to elected officials or affect the perception of politicians in a community, ex-Clear Channel executive Hobbs doesn't buy it.

"I need only point out [conservative talk radio dominance] didn't seem to stop Bill Clinton in '92 and '96 from getting elected," said Hobbs, adding that Clear Channel's research showed America as a whole falling a shade to the right, politically, but much more right wing in selected markets such as Tampa, Florida.

Still, commercial radio is a multi-billion-dollar business based on a simple idea: Hearing messages urging you to buy something in an advertisement will eventually convince you to purchase it. Otherwise, how could Limbaugh, Hannity, and the giants of talk radio charge so much for advertisers to reach their millions of listeners?

So why wouldn't a steady diet of messages reinforcing stereotypes of minorities, lauding sexist views of women, and stoking fears of liberals motivate listeners as well? (Some critics suggest the niche of listeners influenced by talk radio isn't big enough to swing major national elections anymore.[64])

Still, there was obviously an audience out there unaddressed by conservative radio talkers, and it was possible someone could make a good business out of reaching them.

It's too bad for liberals that the highest-profile company that tried to fill that niche was a scrappy outfit with a funky name: Air America.

> All those clowns over at the liberal radio network, we could incarcerate them immediately . . . Send over the FBI and just put them in chains, because they, you know, they're undermining everything and they don't care.
>
> —*Bill O'Reilly, suggesting the penalty Air America should endure for undermining the war effort, on his radio show, June 20, 2005*[65]

IN THE END, JON SINTON BLAMED THE WHOLE MESS on trusting the wrong guy.

Back in 2002, Atlanta radio executive Jon Sinton was approached by a wealthy couple in Chicago, Sheldon and Anita Drobny, who loved progressive talk host Mike Malloy and wanted to take his Windy City show national.

But Sinton recalled giving them a better idea: Let's raise a ton of money and create a 24/7 liberal-oriented radio network.

"You can't just put a progressive talker in this conservative swamp, it'll violate the expectations of both the audience and the advertisers," he said. "Radio is unlike television, in that radio presents this formatted purity. You sit down in the car and you press a button on the dial and you know what you're gonna get."[66]

But as Sinton, the Drobnys, and others were organizing plans for Air America, they were introduced to Evan Cohen, a charismatic guy who said surviving cancer led him to embrace liberal politics. According to the *Wall Street Journal*, Cohen and another partner eventually bought the concept from the Drobnys, assuring the couple they had $30 million in financing to operate the liberal-oriented talk radio network for a few years.[67]

It debuted on March 31, 2004, as Air America.

"We know that [right-wing radio hosts] are lying, lying without shame, lying with impunity, safe in the knowledge that there is no watchdog with a platform large enough to call them on their willful untruths," quipped Al Franken, star of Air America's first show, *The O'Franken Factor*, during its first moments on air.[68] "Someday, we will find that watchdog. Until then, I will have to do."

But as the 2005 HBO documentary *Left of the Dial* painfully recounts, Air America never had the $30 million Cohen talked about. (Cohen denied misleading investors to the *Wall Street Journal*.) As money ran short, the network bounced checks to stations where it had leased air time, rendering the company unable to meet its payroll within two weeks of its debut.[69]

Eventually, other investors took control of the company, but the early problems proved a scarring experience, Sinton said. Originally conceived as an entertaining showcase for stars such as Franken, comic Janeane Garofalo, and radio host Randi Rhodes, Air America had to be whatever its new investors demanded—becoming ever more strident and fumbling sales efforts, he added.

"At first, we said, 'The right is full of ideologues and the left is fun,'" Sinton said. "We win culturally . . . we win on music, we win on art and why wouldn't we tap into that? But every two weeks, it was a struggle to get somebody to write a check so we could make payroll . . . The investors began to drive the content to the extent that they wanted it to be more ideological. Some of the people they brought along didn't get the joke."[70]

The fledgling network even got help from an unlikely source, when Clear Channel Radio flipped nearly two dozen stations to Air America's format within a year of its debut.[71] Clear Channel's Hobbs signed a one-year contract to serve as a consultant; within six months he asked out of the deal early, because politics seemed to come before entertainment, he said.[72]

"You have to be entertaining and compelling first," Hobbs added. "Then you can sell [listeners] pretty much anything you want."[73]

Lionel, hired in 2007 to host a 9 A.M. show, recalled trying to learn how many stations carried Air America. "I'll give you a hint," he cracked. "It's probably not a good sign when you walk into a sales office [asking,] 'How many affiliates are we on?' And they say, 'I dunno.' That's not so good."[74]

If Air America had pulled together the $30 million or more they originally expected, they could have become a *Daily Show* on the radio, said Sinton, who left the company in 2006.[75] Instead, the network soldiered on for four more years before shutting down, featuring everyone from Rachel Maddow and Thom Hartmann to Jerry Springer and Ron Reagan.

Liberal media was still percolating. Former vice president Al Gore had begun talking up plans for a youth-oriented television network that would become Current TV in 2003; Stephanie Miller and Ed Schultz both started their radio shows outside Air America the same year it debuted. Former CNN and MSNBC host Bill Press began his liberal-focused radio show a year later, in 2005.

What Air America's failure really proved was that a good idea rarely overcomes bad execution.

"There's the fallacy that any chimp can do [radio], but you gotta at least be a talented chimp," cracked Miller. "[Commercial] progressive radio is only a few years old; we're on 50 or 60 stations, mostly lower wattage, so we need time."

Her bottom line: "It's about entertainment. It's not about ideology."[76]

> Black guys use it all the time. Turn on HBO, listen to a black comic, and all you hear is nigger, nigger, nigger.
>
> *—Dr. Laura Schlessinger, who is white, explaining to a black*
> *caller why she shouldn't be upset when her white husband's*
> *friends use the word "nigger" around her, August 10, 2010*[77]

SOME RADIO EXPERTS SAY Rush Limbaugh's more recent problems threw a spotlight on the biggest danger facing conservative talk radio:

Its biggest stars aren't so entertaining anymore.

Dr. Laura Schlessinger moved to satellite radio in 2010 after a shameful episode in which she tried to prove a black caller was "hypersensitive" about language, hurling the epithet "nigger" at her nearly a dozen times.[78]

Glenn Beck, who saw his Fox News TV show targeted for sponsor boycotts after calling President Obama "racist," was dropped from radio stations in New York and Philadelphia in 2011, as his show took a turn toward more religious themes. Even Limbaugh, who defined the genre of entertaining, button-pushing talk, was criticized by some fans in the Fluke incident for just not being particularly funny.

"When [Beck] first started off, he was irreverent and funny," said former Cox Radio president Bob Neil. "I think when people start quoting Bible verses and want to turn it into a religious platform, people don't find it as entertaining."[79]

Some experts predict more FM stations will feature talk programming, as costs to air music rise and online technology spreads to automobiles— creating a prime opportunity for younger-skewing moderate and liberal talk hosts to try speaking to FM's younger audience. In New York, the move by ESPN Radio to lease the 98.7 FM frequency for a sports talk station in April 2012 forced longtime black-focused "urban" station Kiss FM (WRKS) to merge with competitor WBLS-FM (107.5).[80]

But Sinton has a different idea. He's developed an app for iPhones and Android smartphones called Progressive Voices, which aggregates video clips, audio podcasts, and links featuring a host of progressive pundits, including Press, Miller, Malloy, and Rhodes.

With plans to register as a non-profit, Sinton's Progressive Voices seems built as an object lesson from all the failures of Air America: starting small, avoiding dependency on advertisers, and trying to dominate a youth-skewing media space with liberal punditry before conservatives get there en masse.

"There will never be another *M*A*S*H*, there will never be another hit record everyone can sing along to and no one will ever be as big as Rush Limbaugh was," he said. "So why try to duplicate that?

"My big lesson from starting Air America was simple," he added. "Don't bring a knife to a gunfight."[81]

EIGHT

FROM FLAVOR FLAV TO ALL-AMERICAN MUSLIM

Searching Past the Stereotypes in "Reality TV"

FOR FANS OF CBS'S UNSCRIPTED COMPETITION *BIG BROTHER*, it's probably a little like hearing Kim Kardashian complain that people think she's shallow.

But Chima Simone, who made history in 2009 as one of the few contestants removed from the competition by producers, insists on two things.[1] First, that she's not exactly the petulant and occasionally prejudiced diva the show portrayed her as during her time in the competition.

And second, that a major reason she failed on the show was because she is black.

"I've been known for saying I have a better chance of surviving a Klan rally than surviving *Big Brother*," said Simone, who added she often advises people of color not to consider appearing on the show. "This is Red State TV we were [creating] . . . That's the audience producers are trying to appeal to."[2]

This idea might be a tough sell for fans who watched Simone, a contestant on the show's eleventh season. With a flamboyant style and cutting remarks, the freelance journalist developed a reputation for her direct attitude, even calling *herself* a diva at times during the competition.

The game featured 13 contestants (called "houseguests") cooped up inside a space built on a TV soundstage to resemble the interior of a home. The area is filled with cameras and surrounded by two-way mirrors hiding more cameras, subjecting the players to 24-hour observation, with footage edited into episodes for CBS and broadcast continuously on the Internet. One houseguest is ejected weekly during a live event also broadcast on the network.

Nominated for eviction on day five, Simone told viewers during a live show that the other person facing ejection with her, surfer Braden Bacha, had used the racial slur "beaners" against two people of color in the house and called host Julie Chen a "whore." (CBS cut audio during her speech.)

Eventually, Simone was removed by producers after refusing to cooperate with the rules: declining to wear a personal microphone to pick up her conversations; obscuring cameras; and refusing to enter the "diary room," where producers talk to individual contestants shielded from the group.

What inspired her rebellion? A game-changing twist called the "coup d'état," in which producers can give one contestant, chosen by a viewer vote, the power to replace one or both people nominated for eviction.[3] When Simone's nominees were changed at a crucial moment, she felt as if producers had sabotaged her to satisfy the show's fans, who had been filling Internet message boards with racist comments about her.[4]

She also noted the show aired footage of her calling a fellow contestant who is Lebanese a "terrorist," but clipped out audio of Bacha's "beaners" rant. Reality TV expert Andy Dehnart, who runs the website RealityBlurred.com, wrote that the incident followed a pattern on *Big Brother* of eliminating racist and homophobic comments by some participants.[5]

In Bacha's case, Dehnart noted that producers cut out the line "I'm fucking white and American . . . you're all beaners," but left Latina Lydia Tavera's retort that he should "kiss my Latin ass," making it look as if the person of color brought up race first.[6]

Simone suspected the show preserved some white players' images as "all-American" by keeping such exchanges from the broadcast, which fed her suspicions when she faced a sudden reversal during the game.

Once out of the *Big Brother* "house," Simone eventually apologized for her terrorism-related insults, admitting she'd crossed a line. But she couldn't escape the nagging feeling she had already played into a typical reality TV stereotype: the Angry Black Woman.

"I definitely fell into the role . . . when they showed me and I'm pissed off like the Angry Black Woman, at that point, I was," she said. "But I feel like I was set up."[7]

And Simone is not alone.

There is little doubt some reality shows have deliberately cast people who fill limited, stereotypical roles, feasting on the friction along race, gender, culture, and class lines.

"Every person gets a box, even the white people," said Rose Rosen, a Tampa, Florida–based casting agent who has found participants for *Dr. Drew's Lifechangers* and *Bridezillas,* among other shows. "There's the bitchy white girl, or you look at the blonde, and she's stupid. Life is stereotypical. Really, all they try to do is get a cast which is interesting together. And the more offensive they are, the more people tune in."[8]

Never mind that catering to stereotypes also hurts white people, especially white women (we'll discuss that later in the chapter); Rosen's admission raises another point.

When you reduce everyone on a show to a stereotype, aren't people of color—already struggling to fight prejudice and racism in other parts of society—hurt more?

THE TERM "REALITY TV" actually covers a wide range of different programs, from competition shows such as CBS's *Survivor* or NBC's *The Biggest Loser* to lifestyle feature programs like Bravo's *Real Housewives* series, stunt shows such as MTV's *Jackass* and ABC's *Wipeout,* and makeover showcases like MTV's *Made* or ABC's *Extreme Makeover.*

What they mostly have in common is two things: people (usually non-celebrities) placed in unusual situations to capture real reaction and boat-loads of manipulation by editors, producers, and hosts.

Viewers are often encouraged to see participants as empty caricatures—defined with easy labels, even in commercials or opening credits (in one such show, the WB's *High School Reunion,* cast members were labeled right away with their images from high school, such as "The Loner," "The Class Clown," or "The Pregnant Girl").

Casting and environments are crafted for maximum friction and drama, with participants who are uncomfortable around gay people or individuals outside their ethnic group brought into close proximity with exactly that. MTV's *The Real World* is perhaps most notorious for this technique, with its San Diego season in 2011 featuring a bisexual man and lesbian woman living in a group that also included a churchgoing, self-described conservative housemate who was clearly uncomfortable with their sexual orientation.[9]

Considering the already limited images available to people of color in big media, minorities can find themselves in the most constricted strait-jackets. Rapper Flavor Flav (born William Jonathan Drayton Jr.) has head-lined several different reality TV franchises, where he often lived down to the worst images of ignorance, hypersexuality, and pleasure seeking that have defined historic stereotypes about black men.

His odyssey started with the third season of *The Surreal Life,* a series broadcast on the long-gone WB network (and later VH1) that crammed a host of mostly washed-up celebrities into one house. Flav's chemistry with another celebrity trainwreck, onetime Sylvester Stallone squeeze Brigitte Nielsen, led to another series, *Strange Love,* which featured the six-foot-tall European model feuding and dating the 5-foot, 6-inch, Long Island–raised rapper (Nielsen's manager told a reporter the two had more of a "strong friendship" and she married an Italian boyfriend before the show finished airing).[10]

Then he landed on *Flavor of Love,* the minority-centered copy of ABC's hit dating series *The Bachelor.* The show placed the former Public Enemy sideman inside a mansion filled with garish furniture and low-class ladies— including one contestant who relieved herself on the floor while racing to a bathroom. Instead of *The Bachelor's* romance and sentimentality, *Flavor of Love* centered on fights, Flav's own manic personality, and women who the *New York Times* said "look like castoffs from a bad rap video."[11]

Like so many so-called "reality" shows, it was television compelling as a bad traffic accident. It was also successful: *Flavor of Love's* first season finale in 2006 was the highest-rated show on VH1 to that date, spawning a flood of spinoffs. In a flash, a celebrity, born as the "hype man" electrifying the pro-black message of a militant rap group, had become the face of a TV show leveraging a boatload of stereotypes about streetwise black folks.

Flav had gone from Public Enemy to public buffoon in the time it took to cash a residuals check.

Of course, VH1 executives insisted they weren't making any such state-ments in *Flavor of Love* or its spinoffs. "It feels fresh to an audience who got so tired of seeing fake romance shoved down their throats," Jeff Olde, a senior vice president at VH1, told me about the *Flavor of Love* spinoff *I Love New York,* for a 2007 story in the *St. Petersburg Times.* "We didn't set out to make a show about race. We're just putting out a show for entertainment value."[12]

But the entertainment value of the show seems rooted in exploiting stereotypes and the controversy that results.

As we will see later in this chapter, several groups have conducted polls and studies noting that young viewers' attitudes about women may be affected by what they see on reality TV shows. And given the lack of scripted shows featuring people of color, reality series increasingly become an important showcase for images of minorities.

The typical defense—that many people of color also watch such shows (VH1's Olde told me 20 million black viewers watched *Flavor of Love*'s second season)—doesn't make it better.[13] Anyone can be seduced by stereotypes, especially young viewers of color starved for any glimpse of their culture on a television show—even a twisted one.

And it's not just a problem for black and brown people.

Women often find themselves on the losing end of stereotypes in unscripted series, particularly in dating and romance competitions where contestants typecast as "the bitch" or "the good girl" are pitted against each other for the affections of a man they hardly know.

The moments can be fleeting. One *Tampa Bay Times* reader complained to me about a segment from the 2011 finale of Fox's unscripted singing competition *The X Factor* called "The Cry-Off." According to host Steve Jones, this was a collection of clips showing a battle between the "girls" judging the show, pop stars Paula Abdul and Nicole Scherzinger. These women may have headlined major tours and choreographed the biggest videos around, but on *The X Factor* their contest came down to a simple metric: who had the most instances of high-profile crying.

The male judges on the show—former *American Idol* star Simon Cowell and ex–record company executive Antonio "L.A." Reid—got decidedly different treatment in *their* video competition. Formatted like a boxing match and tagged as a heavyweight "smackdown," the guys' clips played out complete with clanging ringside bells and rocking blues guitar in the background. The only way it all could have looked more macho was if Reid and Cowell sauntered onstage in loincloths.[14]

In contrast, Abdul and Scherzinger's segment consisted of a blizzard of clips showing them losing control of their emotions and dissolving into tears, often at key moments of the competition. As strains of the Partridge Family song "Come On, Get Happy" played, a scoreboard tallied up all the moments—crowning Scherzinger the winner after a clip of her emotional reaction to the ejection of 13-year-old singer Rachel Crow sent her into total overdrive. Within a few minutes, producers had created a towering vision of female weakness through emotionalism, a technique echoed in far too many unscripted television shows.[15]

And when the show went through a major retooling after a disappointing first season, guess which judges got their walking papers? Both women were axed, along with host Jones, amid rumors Abdul was struggling to handle the pressure of the show and Scherzinger didn't spend enough time mentoring singers.[16]

At a glitzy presentation to advertisers in mid-May 2012, their replacements were revealed: 30-year-old pop star Britney Spears and 19-year-old actress/singer Demi Lovato were announced as judges to replace Abdul, age 49 and Scherzinger, age 33.

They had literally been traded in for younger models.

The teaser commercials for the early 2012 edition of *The Bachelor* also echoed this retrograde attitude, focusing simply on a beautiful, twentysomething woman crying for 15 seconds. No voiceover interrupted her sniffling, which continued as a graphic flashed across the screen with the words, "It's back."

Indeed, encouraging an audience to find entertainment in the tears of an emotional young woman had returned with a vengeance.

Observations like this rarely surprise author Jennifer L. Pozner, a long-time media critic, journalist, activist, and founder of the analysis and advocacy group Women in Media & News. After years monitoring reality TV—she watched about 1,000 hours of unscripted shows over a decade—Pozner put all her observations into a book, *Reality Bites Back: The Troubling Truth about Guilty Pleasure TV.*

One of her biggest criticisms is that such shows can create and perpetuate horribly stunted views of women. White females often are portrayed as pretty, passive, and pathetic, while white men are the strong providers. Black men often play the buffoon, thug, or sexual athlete, and women of color are unstable, oversexed, ghetto-ized harpies.

"Too often, we see shows that reduce women to glorified 1950s stereotypes," Pozner told me. "These shows are *Mad Men* without the cool clothes and social commentary."[17]

And this stereotyping is frequently disguised as liberation.

Pozner cited supermodel Tyra Banks, a black woman who has become a vocal critic of the fashion industry's sexism and disdain for non-European ethnic features, for creating a show that perpetuates those same ideas: the competition *America's Next Top Model.*

But Pozner saves some of her harshest words for *The Bachelor,* a dating series in which about two dozen women compete for the affections of one man, consenting to be eliminated one by one over a series of competitions and outings until a final woman is chosen. She dismisses the show as executive producer/creator Mike Fleiss's attempt to mask the misogyny of a previous series he produced that drowned in negative press, Fox TV's *Who Wants to Marry a Multi-Millionaire?*[18]

In *Multi-Millionaire,* Fleiss and Fox gave viewers a beauty pageant–style competition in which 50 women competed for the hand of declared multi-millionaire Rick Rockwell—a concept shocking enough back then to spark an avalanche of criticism and widespread concern.

Producers shrugged it off with the typical disdain of reality TV showmen. But this criticism got out of hand, particularly after the program concluded and news emerged that Rockwell had a restraining order filed against him by a former girlfriend alleging he had threatened her and was asked for an annulment by new bride Darva Conger 36 hours into the honeymoon.[19]

Months after the show concluded, Rockwell told me he was a misunderstood man in an interview for the *St. Petersburg Times.* "I can't imagine doing something that would so profoundly affect someone's life as a publicity stunt," said Rockwell, a standup comic known for gimmicks such as riding a bicycle from Los Angeles to Las Vegas to promote a comedy club. "I thought it would be fun. The irony was, I wound up with a woman who didn't feel that way."[20]

But Fox executives came to a different conclusion. Sandy Grushow, then chairman of the Fox Television Entertainment Group, canceled plans to re-run the program or develop any more such exploitative specials—a remarkable move for a network that had once aired *World's Scariest Police Shootouts* and saw 23 million viewers show up for the *Multi-Millionaire* special.[21]

"They're gone; they're over," Grushow told the *New York Times* for a story published ten days after the airing of *Multi-Millionaire,* which earned the National Organization for Women's "network of shame" award for objectifying the prospective brides.[22] (Grushow would later renege on his pledge, greenlighting the sex-drenched, lure-them-into-cheating show *Temptation Island* after CBS hit it big with another widely derided reality TV concept, *Survivor*.[23])

Later, Fleiss would maintain that executives from other networks called him to clone *Multi-Millionaire*. But instead, the producer—who counts infamous "Hollywood madam" Heidi Fleiss as his second cousin—crafted a different show in which women had more time to get to know the man, drenching the process in romance and lots of consensual activity.

In the spring of 2002, *The Bachelor* was born.

"I knew there was tremendous energy in this concept, women competing for someone we certify as a great catch, and I could see there was tremendous audience appeal," Fleiss told *Bloomberg Businessweek* in 2009. "I thought of ways to make it more respectable. With *Who Wants to Marry a Multi-Millionaire?* the contestants didn't see what the man looked like until the end of the show. With *The Bachelor,* they meet the bachelor first and are empowered to leave if they want to."[24]

Bachelor host Chris Harrison defended the show in a 2012 teleconference interview with journalists as a "phenomenal study in human behavior," insisting that the contestants are not encouraged to demean themselves to win over the guy picking a mate.[25]

Harrison was speaking just after the show featured Kacie Boguskie, a 24-year-old administrative assistant from Clarksville, Tennessee, who was dropped from the competition after her father, a strict, non-drinking probation officer, told Bachelor Ben Flajnik he expected they would not live together before marriage.[26]

"In no way, do I feel like any of them have changed who they are," Harrison said. "I feel they haven't compromised any of their virtues, any of their morals . . . Yes, Kacie B. went bikini skiing down a street in San Francisco, which was silly. But did that really compromise her morals? No. She had fun with it, and it was funny. And it was an experience of a lifetime."[27]

But another contestant that season, Jamie Otis, obviously felt pressure to demonstrate her affection for Flajnik in a more physical way than she originally wanted. Otis, who initially said she "wanted to maintain her dignity" during the show and so put off kissing Flajnik, wound up pulling him aside during a cocktail party, straddling him, and conducting a kissing tutorial in an uncomfortable and awkwardly sexual manner.[28]

What did Otis earn for such an embarrassing on camera moment? She was ejected from the contest at the end of that episode.

"This show will force you to question yourself," Harrison insisted. "You know, for Jamie, is it more important to try and win Ben by jumping on his lap and kissing him in a way that you would never do? Or is it more important to not do that? And leave with your morals and your dignity and say, 'You know what? This guy's not for me. It's not working.' And move on . . . I like that this show forces you to make those decisions."[29]

In *Reality Bites Back,* Pozner notes that romance shows such as *The Bachelor* succeed by cloaking their negative messages in a thin yet powerful veneer: the female fantasy of the modern princess/fairytale wedding.[30]

So what if they are pursuing men who they don't know well and who aren't really expending much effort to woo them? Why worry that the competition among the contestants is framed like so many Disney-fied *Cinderella* stories, with each woman facing down her own cadre of "evil stepsisters" only to find liberation by the choice of a man?

"It fits into this paradigm that is so fundamental to the reality TV universe," Pozner said. "Basically, it's the opposite of liberation. This idea that pretty women can accomplish anything they want even if they haven't gotten new skills is so fundamental to reality TV. The only thing that's supposed to be important is male validation."[31]

To hammer home its messages, producers use the most potent tool available to them: selective editing. Or, as the industry (and *Time* magazine) calls it, "frankenbiting."[32]

Frankenbiting is the practice of taking sound bites from one conversation and combining them with another, creating a new "scene" with a different meaning. In this way, reactions to one event can be presented as reactions to a different occurrence and participants can be cast in any light the producer chooses.

The process can be very slick. At times, subjects are speaking in voiceover, narrating footage of something other than what they're actually talking about. In other cases, the audio is massaged so that comments appear to link seamlessly together, even though they may have been said at different times. In an interview with *Time* magazine back in 2006, Tony DiSanto, executive producer of the MTV reality show *Laguna Beach,* said producers might enhance storylines to make better television, but "we never make up something that hasn't happened."[33]

Kirsten Buschbacher, one of the last two finalists on *The Bachelor*'s third season, complained of such editing, saying it turned her into a cartoon villain while trying to woo bachelor Andrew Firestone.

"[Producers] decided early on what character each girl was going to play," Buschbacher told me in an interview for the *St. Petersburg Times*, not long before the show's finale aired in 2003. "I'm kind of [shown as] the girl Andrew really likes, but I don't play nice. I would like people to know who I really am."[34]

There's a side-splitting video on the website Videojug.com titled "How to Spot Reality TV Editing Tricks" that explains a typical technique based on a concept called the Kuleshov Effect. Russian filmmaker Lev Kuleshov found that audiences shown footage of an actor's passive face and then another object assumed the actor was reacting to the object, even when the clips were unrelated.[35]

Modern-day reality TV editors can use that effect, splicing a cast member's reaction to one incident next to footage of a different occurrence, making it seem that the person is reacting to something he or she really isn't.

But even as viewers insist they're aware of the manipulations of reality TV—the term itself may be one of the biggest misnomers in modern television history—the cumulative effect leads fans to believe a lot of what they see, anyway.

"What they see in a reality show is absolutely as crafted as anything they would see in a scripted TV show, and is more insidious because of it," said Pozner. "One of the most damning things I've heard a producer say is, 'It's us being puppeteers.' They use real people as their stock character puppets."[36]

Which leads to the central lie I have always felt hamstrings most so-called "reality TV" programs: Their general unwillingness to acknowledge or display the influence of the show's producers.

Forget about editing; viewers are given little information on how producers set up scenes, film the action, or cast the shows. During an episode of the TLC show *All-American Muslim*, viewers were shown a Muslim couple going to a restaurant outside their neighborhood in Dearborn, Michigan—the American town with the largest percentage of Arabs in its population, at more than 40 percent.[37] When a waitress seemed to avoid seating the couple, the pair was left to wonder why the woman seemed so reticent.

Savvy viewers had to wonder how smart the waitress was; surely she saw the cameras filming the pair and realized her act of bigotry would be captured on video. Did a producer ever ask why the delay occurred in the first place? Was it a minor event hyped by editing? We could only guess, because the information was never provided on camera.

Scenes like this play out all the time on reality TV shows. Participants are often shown telling the camera about their experiences in "confessional" segments, but viewers never see what questions the producers asked to spark their responses. Star Donald Trump fires contestants from *The Apprentice* with little indication of how he reaches his decisions (does he huddle with producers over storylines?).

Los Angeles Times columnist Joel Stein wrote about obtaining the script for a so-called "reality" show, Bravo's *Queer Eye for the Straight Guy,* in which producers painstakingly detailed every scene of the show, even occasionally writing lines for the non-performer participants.[38] The series, which featured a schlubby heterosexual guy who got a makeover from a team of fashion- and food-savvy gay men, outlined the final revelation scene this way, according to Stein:

"[Subject Patrick Mullare] keeps looking down the street; will the girl from the bar come? He sees nothing . . . Over his shoulder a set of car headlights appear and get continuously closer until the car stops. She gets out of the car; Patrick hasn't noticed. She taps him on the shoulder . . . He invites her in to see his new place, she accepts, and they walk off into the proverbial sunset . . . Fade out."[39]

Reality TV shows sustain their power because they tell lies viewers want to believe—particularly in the case of romance shows such as *The Bachelor.*

But this also means that fans cannot fully trust anything they see. Because if producers are willing to lie about anything, they could be lying about everything.

"Reality TV has helped us usher in a fame-hungry culture bigger than we've ever seen before," Pozner said. "They have been misled into seeing [these shows] as their only shot to provide a better life for themselves and their kids. So you see them volunteer for shows where they know they're going to be humiliated."[40]

In a wide-ranging discussion, Pozner and I came up with five distinct lies about reality TV that I outlined in a column for the *St. Petersburg Times.*[41] They are:

Lie #1: Reality TV shows don't have social messages. In fact, as we've discussed earlier in the chapter, these series' power flows from the ways in which they connect to various social messages. Dating shows tell women how to land a man, makeover shows lay blame for life's problems on your appearance.

Lie #2: Reality TV liberates subjects from stereotypes and bigotry. Unfortunately, such shows often *depend* on stereotypes to attract and keep audiences. Seeing the women on Bravo's *Real Housewives of New Jersey* series talk up their Italian roots while slinging profanities and getting in fistfights, it's easy to see how they have been reduced to simple, damaging stereotypes drawn from decades of Mafia movies. A spate of popular shows centered on Southern subjects—from Animal Planet's *Hillbilly Handfishin'* to National Geographic Channel's *Rocket City Rednecks*—indulge stereotypes about people south of the Mason-Dixon line. In this world, even guys with Ph.D.s in aerospace engineering sound like extras in a *Dukes of Hazzard* rerun.

Lie #3: Critical thinking about reality shows means rejecting them. Both Pozner and I actually like some reality TV shows. Her list includes comic Margaret Cho's now-canceled VH1 program *The Cho Show* (because it often subverted stereotypes in funny, entertaining ways) and Lifetime's *Project Runway* (because it glorifies creativity, despite its consumerism). My list featured comic Kathy Griffin's now-shuttered *Life on the D-List* (for its courage in showing Griffin in some really unflattering moments) and Discovery Channel's *Deadliest Catch* (for capturing its crab fisherman subjects as the flawed, fleshed-out, working-class guys they are).

Lie #4: Today's audiences are too sophisticated for manipulation by television shows. As Pozner points out, thinking that you're wise to the game these shows are playing can often make you a bigger patsy. Blanket cynicism keeps viewers from looking at the specific ways their emotions are manipulated, leading fans to insist they are above such influence, even as they fall for it.

"When we think we are above being affected by media messages, that's when those messages have the most power," she said. "Then we're rejecting the notion that we need to be critical media consumers. And that's when the propaganda gets us."[42]

AS A GUY WHOSE JOB CONSISTS OF DECODING the twists and turns of modern media, this is tough to admit.

But when I first heard the concept for the show that would ignite today's reality TV revolution in America, I had an unusual response.

I laughed. Long and hard.

The year was 1999. And Mark Burnett, an energetic former British paratrooper-turned-TV-producer, was selling American media on a program concept he hoped to import from Sweden called *Survivor.*

Burnett saw the program as an aggressive blend of *Robinson Crusoe* and the *Eco-Challenge* endurance races he was already producing for the USA Network. But when some of us critics heard the premise—a group of people stranded on an island, given little food or resources while forced to face cameras 24 hours a day—we thought Burnett was out of his mind.

We shouldn't have been surprised. Also in 1999, I debated a producer on a Tampa Bay–area TV talk show pitching a syndicated program featuring people who suspected their romantic partner of cheating. The idea: Suspicious boyfriends or girlfriends could contact the show to investigate the allegations.

If the cheating was ongoing, the show would bring the person to confront their spouse or significant other *in the act* while cameras taped an emotional scene.

I argued that producers were creating an unstable situation; what if someone pulled a gun or a knife? Other critics suspected some of the scenes might be staged. Regardless, the series eventually got made and has aired for nearly a dozen years; it's called *Cheaters.* (In 2002, the *Houston Press* ran a story quoting several people who said they were paid by an investigator to stage confrontations for the show; producers have subsequently denied these claims.[43])

Back then, conflict-drenched talk shows like *Jerry Springer* were peaking. And MTV's unscripted series *The Real World,* featuring an often-volatile collection of kids living under 24-hour camera surveillance in a common house, was already seven years old.

But who knew that the network known mostly for musty mysteries such as *Murder, She Wrote* and older audiences would snap up a show featuring contestants so hungry and deprived they ate rats in the first season?

It almost didn't happen. As *New York Times* writer Bill Carter detailed in his 2006 book *Desperate Networks,* all the major U.S. networks passed on Burnett's idea for *Survivor* until he lined up an array of sponsors whose product placement on the show would cover costs.[44] It was an economic model that would later be duplicated across an explosion of unscripted shows—from the Coca-Cola cups on Fox's *American Idol* to the trainers touting Brita water filters on NBC's *Biggest Loser*. For an industry watching its traditional ways of making profits wane, Burnett's new funding formula was a godsend.

Survivor mania sparked cover stories in *Time* and *Newsweek* magazines, a flood of fans buzzing over the show online, a new crop of reality TV celebrities led by proudly out gay winner Richard Hatch, and a finale episode that drew more than 51 million viewers in August 2000.[45]

"We all like the idea of an adventure," Burnett said midway through the first season's episodes. "There's one thing that's timeless since Christopher Columbus . . . having an adventure. We all want one, because I can assure you, you won't be finding the meaning of life inside your laptop."[46]

The gold rush–style spirit of the times was captured in a telling 2001 profile on CBS's *60 Minutes* of a young William Morris agent named Ben Silverman. Turns out Silverman, a fast-moving, smooth-talking salesman who was cornering the market on importing reality TV concepts from overseas, was the perfect embodiment of the adrenaline-addicted breed of unscripted television executive.[47]

The *60 Minutes* story was prescient in many ways—the correspondent, Scott Pelley, would eventually become CBS's top anchor, and Silverman would go on to co-chair NBC's entertainment division from 2007 to 2009 (a job he would leave under a cloud after a string of failures).[48]

But at the time, Pelley's piece on Silverman felt like a victory lap for CBS, celebrating its savvy in snapping up *Survivor* and the housebound competition *Big Brother* while documenting the growing hunger for television that shoehorned regular people into bizarre situations. At a time when network TV seemed filled with derivative sitcoms, this new format was thrilling and new.

"By trying something like *Survivor,* people said 'Gee, this isn't my grandmother's CBS,'" Les Moonves, head of television for the network, told Pelley for his *60 Minutes* story. "All of a sudden, there were younger people coming to our network. For the first time, my teen-aged kids came home and said, 'Dad, my friends are talking about a show on CBS.'"[49]

Still, the key to making the shows sizzle—especially for younger audiences—was a cast ready to push society's buttons and create controversy.

And that's where stereotypes often begin.

EARLY IN THE EMERGENCE OF SOME REALITY TV competition shows, I noticed an odd casting trend. They often featured two people of color—usually black—and they had very distinct roles.

One was comfortable with the social norms and practices of white people. And the other wasn't.

It was a dynamic that stood out on the debut season of *Survivor*, where the 16 castaways marooned on the island in Malaysia included Ramona Gray, a then–29-year-old research chemist from New Jersey, and Gervase Peterson, a 30-year-old Philadelphia native. Both Peterson and Gray landed on the same team, called the Pagong tribe, but Gray immediately got sick, making it tough for her to handle the lack of food, sleep, and comfort. Footage in the early episodes made Gray look listless and lazy, but she blamed illness for keeping her down.

She also had another problem. Outside of her job, she had never interacted with white people very much, admitting that teammate Jenna Lewis was her first white friend since high school.

"It was tough living in such close quarters with people different than me [basically whites]," Gray told me in an email back then. "I truly believe that racism is rampant in America today, so that made it even harder. I always wondered if and when I was voted off, would some part of it have to do with the color of my skin?"[50]

The other black person on the show, Peterson, seemed to display some of the classic stereotypes of black men. He was often shown lounging in a hammock or napping while others worked (Peterson said later that it was a deliberate strategy to save his strength for winning challenge competitions).[51]

But Peterson was also more comfortable with his white teammates than Gray and seemed to pay a smaller price for his faults. There was a moment—which happens often on such shows—where the more comfortable Peterson tried to coach Gray through her difficulties, counseling her on how to better fit into the group. But in the end, she was the second person voted off her tribe and fourth voted off overall, undone by her inability to bond with her teammates or talk about her discomfort with the dominant culture.[52]

"It felt like a taboo subject," she wrote to me then. "No one really wanted to talk about it. Gervase and I were on opposite ends of the spectrum, because he'd been around whites all his life and felt totally comfortable."[53]

Mark Burnett, creator and executive producer of *Survivor,* disagreed with this analysis in comments emailed to me through a network official.

"I believe that this angle is wrong, as the percentage of African Americans represented on *Survivor* is reflective of our nation (average 2 out of 16 contestants is [black], approximately 12%–13%)," he wrote. "Over the years, *Survivor* has featured more minority participants and diverse winners on the cast than most other reality shows on television, out of 23 winners; we have had 2 African American Winners, 1 Asian American, 2 Hispanic Winners and 2 Gay winners."

Still, similar dynamics seemed to emerge on the first edition of *Big Brother,* where William "Will Mega" Collins was a militant, pro-black figure who provoked fierce, race-centered discussions with his housemates, while the show's other black contestant, Cassandra Waldon, advised Collins to learn how to relate to the others and avoid "gratuitously seek[ing] to intimidate" them.

That advice also failed, and Will Mega was the first person voted out of the first U.S. version of *Big Brother,* insisting to journalists that "issues . . . brought up through [our] conversations allow people to understand the black man." The sad truth was that Collins had simply allowed discomfort with his housemates to push him into enacting another long-standing stereotype: the Angry Black Man.[54]

On Burnett's *The Apprentice,* villainess supreme Omarosa Manigault-Stallworth was contrasted to Harvard MBA Kwame Jackson, who eventually earned runner-up status in the first season. In the next season, volatile Stacie "Stacie J." Upchurch was fired by Trump after several of her teammates—all white women—suggested she might be schizophrenic.[55] The show's other African American contestant, Wharton-educated Kevin Allen, was fired after being made to sell candy bars at a subway stop, a job some critics derided as stereotypical and demeaning.

"One of the knocks [Trump] had on me when he told me I was fired was that I was overeducated," Allen told the Talking Points Memo blog in 2011, for a story in which the former contestant said the mogul's harsh comments questioning President Obama's educational achievements and birthplace may have been motivated by race. "Racism is not just about racial slurs or what you say outwardly; it's also a mindset and how you feel about folks and how you compartmentalize."[56]

Black contestants who don't fit in are often seen as aggressive, disruptive, arrogant, and confrontational. The males become Angry Black Men, volatile and unreasonable; females are depicted as Crazy Black Women, ready to fight at a moment's notice and nursing a hair-trigger temper. Meanwhile, the more assimilated black people fly under the radar, unable to help their less-assimilated brethren learn the cultural lessons they need to survive in uncharted social waters.

Stacy Blake-Beard, a professor at Simmons College's school of management in Boston, explained to me that both types of characters were showing classic responses to being minorities inside a larger group, similar to the pressures people of color feel in traditionally white-dominated corporate settings.[57]

One strategy is to become "hypervisible," basking in your difference and emphasizing distinction from the crowd. Short term, this can soothe individuals by making them feel they are elevated above any problems, but ultimately, people grow isolated, appearing arrogant and hostile.[58]

Another response is to become "invisible," minimizing difference with the majority so that you fit in. On the surface, this sounds like the easier road, giving individuals the chance to blend in. Unfortunately, this also means the assimilated person may not feel free to be fully him or herself. They also run the risk of being overlooked or taken for granted, getting little credit for their contributions.[59]

Looming over all of these complex social dynamics is another phenomenon called "attributional ambiguity"—basically, the uncertainty a member of a minority group faces in judging how people from the majority culture treat them.

The question always looming: Is my treatment different because of who I am?[60]

Assurances by white people that they "don't see race" may not help these issues much; it sounds too much like dodging the problem by insisting on downplaying and ignoring cultural differences rather than valuing them.

In this way, some reality TV shows become tiny morality plays, suggesting the path to success for people of color lies in assimilation.

Because so much of this stuff happened without on-camera discussion, viewers and contestants were left to wade through these issues of race and culture on their own.

Then *Survivor* decided to tackle race head on.

And stepped in it big time.

AT THE TIME, *Survivor* host Jeff Probst sounded like he had stumbled on a revolutionary idea.

"When you put on a show with a lot of people who are white, and only white people watch, it becomes a self-fulfilling prophecy," Probst said during a 2006 interview previewing one of the more infamous *Survivor* seasons:

The one where they separated teams by race.[61]

"We start looking at these [contestants,] saying, 'Wow, we have fresh points of view again," added the host, who is also an executive producer of the show. "All of a sudden the show, in our minds, rebirthed itself."[62]

But for critics like me who had been writing about the show's lack of diversity and hidden race issues for years, it felt a bit more like watching someone miss the point by a country mile, responding to the series' odd racial dynamics by creating a new and altogether more troubling one.

Heading into its thirteenth cycle, *Survivor* faced the challenge of seeing many major sponsors drop out—including General Motors, Coca Cola, and Home Depot.[63] What the series needed was a new hook to get the public talking and keep viewers engaged with the show. The hook they eventually found—separating contestants into tribes of African Americans, Asian Americans, Latinos, and Caucasians—only highlighted how people of color become symbols on such shows and how little producers had focused on the diversity of their program until it became their major priority.

Describing himself as a "white guy from Wichita," Probst insisted producers casting previous *Survivor* cycles only picked contestants they felt would perform well, regardless of race or ethnicity. So, he suggested, the problems some contestants may have had with assimilation were an unintended consequence.[64]

My question for the host was simpler: Why does *Survivor* so often seem to feature players who reflect typical stereotypes of black people?

"If you have a season where you only have one black guy and everybody else is white . . . if that black guy doesn't perform, or if that black guy can't swim, or if that black guy quits it's like a beacon screaming," said Probst. "If you looked across the board at all of the jackasses we've had on the show who are white—all the people who are white who make the same ridiculous social mistakes—all the white people who are lazy, all of the white people who are bigots. It just so happens, most of the people on the show have been white. So I think the observation you make is correct. I think the conclusion you came to [that stereotyping is deliberate] is not correct."[65]

When *Survivor: Cook Islands* debuted, its segregation strategy was roundly criticized by reviewers—*USA Today* called it "a publicity stunt of the rankest and most obvious kind"—and the feature was dropped as the show's tribes were merged during the game's evolution.[66]

Yul Kwon, the contestant who became the show's first Asian American winner, said he thought the racial segregation would be so controversial that he nearly quit the show when producers revealed the twist just before the competition started. He ultimately decided to stay on the program to increase the representation of Asian Americans on television, but he felt he was unable to speak his mind freely.

"Because of the explosive racial theme, I felt a tremendous amount of pressure to watch my words carefully and not say anything that could be taken out of context," he said. "But it was still a platform to help my community and change stereotypes about Asian Americans."[67]

That cycle also hinted that *Survivor*'s diversity problems might lie in not working hard enough to cast a wider range of competitors—something that could have been easily remedied without turning every contestant's ethnicity into a gimmick. (*Cook Islands* also introduced two other contestants, Parvati Shallow and Ozzy Lusth, who would return again and again for later editions of the series, proving that a better way to keep fans energized was to bring back past stars in new cycles.)

Survivor executive producer Burnett also pushed back against this idea in his email, noting, "The *Survivor: Cook Islands* season wasn't a bad thing and in fact sparked good conversation, did well in the ratings and also increased applications for minority applicants for future seasons . . . Moreover, after we mixed the tribes, the contestants did not stick with their original tribe/race but found commonalities among the other contestants and integrated, which is what I predicted would happen once people were on the island away from their 'normal' lives, and this show resulted in our first Asian American winner, Yul Kwon."

Still, *Survivor*'s experience highlights another way in which race and diversity issues confound assumptions. Because it feels uncomfortable to focus on race, people may assume the best tack for dealing with such subjects is to ignore or overlook them.

Wrong. Because, particularly in the television industry, the environment is already so diversity-challenged, sometimes a special effort is necessary to balance the scales.

According to Probst, when *Survivor* producers got the idea to racially segregate their teams, up to 85 percent of their applicants were white; casting people had to call a Korean beauty pageant in Seattle to find possible applicants.[68] But that kind of effort is sometimes required to overcome the cultural forces at play.

In the same way that the NFL's "Rooney Rule" created more black coaches by requiring professional football teams to seriously consider applicants of color for every coaching position—not *hire*, mind you, but *consider*—the effort to add more diversity in casting can produce better results (a lesson *Survivor* seemed to learn with its casting, which has featured much more ethnic diversity in recent years).

That's why the diversity track record of ABC's *Bachelor* and *Bachelorette* series is so confounding. As I write this chapter in early 2012, the show has never featured a non-white person as the star of either show, despite 23 combined cycles since 2002.

On April 18, 2012, African American Nashville residents Nathaniel Claybrooks and Christopher Johnson filed a lawsuit against the ABC network and the show's producers, saying *The Bachelor* purposefully excluded black auditioners because of their race. Both men said they tried out for the show in August 2011 and were not seriously considered.[69]

ABC declined to comment on pending litigation. But Warner Horizon Television, the studio that produces both *The Bachelor* and *The Bachelorette*, released a statement: "This complaint is baseless and without merit. In fact, we have had various participants of color throughout the series' history, and the producers have been consistently—and publicly—vocal about seeking diverse candidates for both programs. As always, we continue to seek out participants of color for both *The Bachelor* and *The Bachelorette*."[70]

Bachelor executive producer Mike Fleiss shrugged off the show's lack of diversity in 2011, telling *Entertainment Weekly*, "We have to wedge African-American chicks in there" among the women chosen by the Bachelor, and "for whatever reason, they [minorities] don't come forward" to be on the show.[71]

But even another TV producer, Shawn Ryan (*The Shield, The Unit, The Chicago Code, Last Resort*), refused to believe that explanation.

"They blame minorities for not coming forward. What a joke," Ryan wrote on Twitter, calling the casting situation "straight up racism. They just don't think America will watch [a] black bachelor or root for mixed-race marriage. [They] don't have the guts to say that."[72]

In a later interview with me, Ryan was a little more sympathetic—just a little—for the perspective of *The Bachelor*'s producers, who he assumed "had run the numbers" and decided basing a full cycle of their key unscripted romance series on a person of color looking for love would not succeed—or would be too risky to attempt.

"I'm not even saying if I was a producer on that show I would cast it any differently," Ryan said. "But to act as if black people don't want to be on TV in those situations—they've got better stuff to do than to seek fame and fortune—I just bristled at the disingenuous nature of the thing."[73]

Bearing in mind the Rooney Rule, Ryan's got a point. Just because there are fewer people of color in the contestant pool doesn't mean producers can't work harder to find someone to break that color line.

Poll numbers add more weight: according to a survey by Gallup released in September 2011, 86 percent of Americans now approve of interracial marriage, up from about 65 percent when the *Bachelor* debuted in 2002.[74] From 1980 to 2008, the percentage of interracial marriages doubled (from 6.7 percent to 14.6 percent); by 2011, one in seven U.S. marriages were interracial or interethnic, according to data from the Pew Center and CNN.[75]

The Bachelor is an important franchise for ABC; it's the network's second-highest-rated unscripted series with viewers aged 18 to 49 (the audience advertisers care most about) and the network's fourth-highest-rated series overall with that age group, according to Nielsen ratings from the 2010–11 TV season.[76]

Keeping people of color from a starring role feels like an antiquated attitude—that habit of forever progressing just behind America's tastes that TV too often indulges.

The strongest argument for challenging stereotypes in media, however, comes down to a single question: *How are these misguided images affecting us?*

Back in 2001, I once asked Mike Darnell—the man who runs unscripted programming for the Fox network and helped invent or shape every reality TV show there from *Who Wants to Marry A Multi-Millionaire?* to *American Idol*—if he thought the reality TV trend might end if someone were killed on a show such as *Survivor.*

"I think we've got a year or two," Darnell said, standing outside a press conference in Pasadena, California, in a quote that appeared in the *St. Petersburg Times.* "If we can go that long without someone getting killed on a show, then it's much harder to blame the genre. After two years, I don't think anything will stop [these shows]."[77]

Compared to death, what's a little bit of bad behavior?

A 2011 study by the Girl Scout Research Institute asked 1,141 girls age 11 to 17 about reality TV shows they watched and their attitudes about relationships, self-image, and success in life.[78] They found:

- Most of them (75 percent) thought competition shows such as *Survivor* were "mainly real and unscripted"; 50 percent said the same about real-life series such as MTV's *Jersey Shore* and *The Hills.*
- Regular reality TV viewers were more likely to agree that gossiping was a normal part of girls' relationships, girls are naturally catty toward each other, and girls often have to compete for a guy's attention.
- Among the girls who regularly watched reality TV, 72 percent said they spend a lot of time on their appearance (vs. 42 percent of non-viewers) and 38 percent said a girl's value was based on how she looked (compared to 28 percent of non-viewers).[79]

The poll results suggest that girls watching reality TV could be internalizing and reflecting the way such shows traditionally present women—which is often from the point of view of men.

Film critics call it "the male gaze": a set of techniques used by filmmakers to lead audiences into seeing women (or other things) from the perspective of a heterosexual male.[80] It could be as simple as the camera lingering on the curves of a woman or as complex as presenting a story where all the female characters are beautiful, sexy, and romantically available.

Watch too many shows presented from the male gaze, however, and it can start to feel like the only way of viewing the world.

Consider the results of a different study, from the conservative watch-dog group the Parents Television Council, looking at gender portrayals on cable TV's four most popular prime time reality shows for youths aged 12 to 17 in 2011, all airing on MTV: *Jersey Shore, The Real World, Teen Mom 2,* and *16 and Pregnant.*[81]

Logging every descriptor, label, and profanity slung by each primary and secondary character in a season's worth of episodes, they found that the female characters spent more time disparaging themselves and other women than the male characters did. Only 24 percent of what females said about themselves was positive across all the shows.[82]

The study concluded: "There remains an overwhelming message to young girls that their only unique and valued quality is their sexuality. The message to males is that they should lack overt emotion, be uninterested in relationships and be defined by sexual conquests."[83]

Left unanswered: Given the impact of shows such as *The Bachelor, Jersey Shore,* and *America's Next Top Model,* could such attitudes find their way to other corners of American life, too?

NINE

THE KATRINA EFFECT

How Lax Poverty Coverage Helps
Politicians Demonize the Poor

AS THE SAYING GOES, THE DEFINITION OF A GAFFE ISN'T WHEN A
politician says something wrong.

It's when a politician tells the truth.

So consider this line, uttered by then–GOP presidential candidate Mitt
Romney, one day after a landslide primary victory in Florida:

"I'm not concerned about the very poor," he told CNN anchor Soledad
O'Brien on her show, *Starting Point,* on February 1, 2012. "We have a safety
net there. If it needs repair, I will fix it. I'm not concerned about the very rich.
They're doing just fine. I'm concerned about the very heart of America, the
90 percent, 95 percent of Americans who right now are struggling and I'll
continue to take that message across the nation."[1]

Romney's remarks were striking, given the impact of the economic
downturn some experts called the Great Recession. According to a study
released in January 2012 by Indiana University, the amount of people living below the poverty line jumped 27 percent between 2006 and 2010. That
meant almost an additional 10 million people fell into poverty—a total of
more than 46 million people—with poverty defined as a household income
of less than $22,113 for a family of four.[2]

In all, 15 percent of the country's population lived under the poverty
line in 2010, with more Americans among the long-term unemployed than

at any time since recordkeeping started in 1948.[3] More than four million Americans were unemployed at least 12 months or longer. But Romney felt sanguine enough to announce that people who had the least in America wouldn't get his primary focus as president.

To her credit, O'Brien gave Romney a chance to clarify his remarks, asking, "I think there are lots of very poor Americans who are struggling who would say, 'That sounds odd.' Can you explain that?"

Romney just doubled down his statement: "We will hear from the Democrat party [about] the plight of the poor . . . my campaign is focused on middle income Americans. You can choose where to focus; you can focus on the rich—that's not my focus. You can focus on the very poor—that's not my focus. My focus is middle income Americans . . . These are the people who have been most badly hurt during the Obama years."[4]

That's right: A political candidate whose personal worth tops $250 million said people trying to support a family of four on less than $22,000 annually were not hurt the worst during the recent recession and didn't deserve his focus.

Savvy political columnists noted that Romney was just being honest; his campaign probably would focus on people who vote, especially middle-class Republicans and independents hurt by the recession and worried about the economy.

But he also inadvertently revealed one of the biggest problems with poverty today: We rarely talk about it, even in the news media.

The conservative narrative on poverty was on full display during the 2012 GOP nomination fight. Former House Speaker Newt Gingrich turned his repeated criticism of Barack Obama as a "food stamp president" into an advertisement that aired in South Carolina and Florida.

But Gingrich's comments also implied that poor people's biggest problems lie within themselves. If they could only "learn" how to get a job or a better job, their poverty problems would be solved.

Similarly, his words on speaking to the National Association for the Advancement of Colored People—saying he would be "prepared, if the NAACP invites me, I'll go to their convention and talk about why the African American community should demand paychecks and not be satisfied with food stamps"—also implied that black people on food stamps need only "demand" paychecks to get off the program.[5]

That would be news to the more than 12 million unemployed American workers actively seeking jobs in December 2011, totaling four job-seekers for every opening. And though that number was an improvement on the recession's peak—when seven job-seekers lined up for every opening—it leaves little doubt that landing a good position requires more than just "demanding" it.[6]

"In many low-income families, not only do their parents work one job, but many of these families work two jobs and three jobs," said Andrea Levere, president of the Corporation for Enterprise Development in a story aired on NPR December 7, 2011, presented by the network's correspondent covering poverty and philanthropy, Pam Fessler. "So we see extraordinary levels of commitment and hard work in these communities. And so, in my view, it's completely unfair to make a blanket statement like this."[7]

Presenting poverty as the result of choices isn't a new idea for Gingrich, who cast his statements about personal responsibility in fighting poverty as daring "to be politically incorrect" back in 2008, for a column featured on the website for the Washington, D.C.–based advocacy group Spotlight on Poverty and Opportunity.[8]

"The first step is for people to decide the culture that they want," Gingrich wrote. "If they want a culture of prosperity, they must establish the values of that culture. You then have to redesign government so it is rewarding those who follow the culture of prosperity."[9]

Speaking to that idea, the conservative think tank the Heritage Foundation released a report in September 2011 titled "Understanding Poverty in the United States: Surprising Facts about America's Poor," that held that "the Census Bureau's annual poverty report presents a misleading picture of poverty in the United States."[10]

Assembled with data from a host of governmental reports, the Heritage study proclaimed that 80 percent of poor households had air conditioning, 92 percent had a microwave oven, and nearly 75 percent had a car or truck. (Some critics disputed their data, saying that just 40 percent of poor households had central air conditioning, the appliances in many poor homes are provided by the landlord, and those appliances are often more than five years old.)

Still the report was an aggressive argument for the view that U.S. poverty in the modern age isn't necessarily as bad as some might think. "For most

Americans, the word 'poverty' suggests near destitution: an inability to pro-vide nutritious food, clothing, and reasonable shelter for one's family," the study read. "However, only a small number of the 46 million persons classi-fied as 'poor' by the Census Bureau fit that description."

But if people below the poverty line aren't living in squalor and joyless deprivation, couldn't that be a sign anti-poverty programs are helping?

There are lots of reasons why politicians might want the public to be-lieve poverty is a choice. If poor people are deprived because of their own failings, it reduces the obligation for others to help them and avoids thorny discussions on the institutional aspects of poverty. It also makes it easier for politicians across the ideological spectrum to talk about cutting govern-ment-funded anti-poverty programs to save money.

"In politics there are two obvious coalitions; one is when the middle aligns with folks above them and another is when the middle aligns with folks below them," said E. J. Dionne, a columnist for the *Washington Post* and a fellow at the Brookings Institution, speaking during a panel discussion on poverty and electoral politics held by Spotlight on Poverty on January 17, 2012. "Politicians have a habit of only talking about the middle, because that's where the voters are . . . But in being obsessed with the middle class, they often leave out the poor."[11]

Melissa Harris-Perry, a Tulane University professor and MSNBC week-end anchor, said voters may have a compelling psychological reason to be-lieve the rhetoric from politicians such as Gingrich and Romney.

"It's an ego-protecting mechanism," said Harris-Perry. "When you don't have to worry that you might fall below that line because as long as you do the right thing and you're a good person, then don't worry; you won't be punished with poverty."[12]

Greg Kaufmann, who started a weekly blog on poverty hosted by the liberal-focused magazine the *Nation* in January 2012, said he has noticed politicians mostly avoid talking about the details of poverty, noting that Democratic president Barack Obama only mentioned the word once, in passing, during his 2012 State of the Union speech.

"It's that myth that we don't know what to do about poverty or that it's this intractable thing," he said. "We waged a war on poverty from 1964 to 1973, and the poverty rate fell by nearly half [43 percent]. We were doing food stamps, expanding Medicaid and really focused on eradicating poverty. Now, it seems there's a real animosity towards the poor."[13]

This is how politicians achieve the magical feat, famously described by Thomas Frank in his book *What's the Matter With Kansas?*, of persuading middle-class and working-class voters to support cutting programs that might help them directly.

Because when beneficiaries are misrepresented as largely lazy and lacking in ambition, it is easy to see them as someone other than yourself.

"We talk about, 'Oh, poor people don't work,' but the transaction costs of living as a poor person are extraordinary," said MSNBC's Harris-Perry. "It takes an hour and a half worth of buses to get your kid to school in the morning; the work it takes to get to work, the work it takes to buy groceries in a community where the grocery store is inadequate . . . I feel like people who live in middle class and wealthy communities can't even imagine how much it takes just to manage the most basic aspects of life when you don't have that kind of extra resources."[14]

Of course, one reason why middle-class voters may not be able to imagine such scenarios is because news outlets rarely explore them.

In 2011, stories about poverty, welfare, and homelessness filled about 2 percent of news coverage in the top 50 outlets monitored by the Project for Excellence in Journalism, a Washington, D.C.–based, non-partisan think tank. Over that same year, stories about foreign events occupied 18 percent of total coverage.[15]

Those coverage levels, small as they were, turned out to be a marked improvement over 2007; stories on poverty then were just 1 percent of the total. By 2008, coverage of poverty had dropped so low that the Project for Excellence in Journalism couldn't provide a number—except to say it was just above zero. This was midway through the downturn experts now call the Great Recession, which lasted from December 2007 to June 2009 and saw 8.4 million jobs vanish.[16]

Poverty didn't make it into the top 20 stories of 2011 listed by Andrew Tyndall, a consultant who regularly monitors the network evening newscasts. Indeed, of 5,042 stories Tyndall logged in evening newscasts on ABC, CBS, and NBC during 2011, just 76 fell under the poverty category, or 1.5 percent. The top subject category, nature, got 666 stories, while the Middle East generated 515.[17]

Even Fessler, NPR's poverty reporter, turned in just five stories on the subject from October 2011 to January 2012—one-third of the 15 stories she produced during that time, with the rest focused on voting rights issues, election news, and one story on the Susan G. Komen Foundation. A near–20-year employee of the service, she's covered everything from the White House to the 9/11 Commission in her years there.

Fessler explained that because she has a background in covering voting rights issues, she spent much of the election season in 2011 and 2012 looking at election issues, where voting access can also connect to poverty.

"Sometimes, I had been finding it more difficult to get pieces on the air, because poverty isn't really breaking news," said Fessler, who covered homeland security before moving into the poverty beat about three years ago. "If you have a news organization which only has a certain amount of airtime, when you do a poverty story, it's a little bit more difficult to get it on the air. And this is at a news organization which is very committed to these stories. But I felt like [poverty stories] are just as important as covering the day to day changes on Capitol Hill. Whatever you say about Occupy Wall Street or Newt Gingrich . . . they have made this news."[18]

But if the journalism is focused on situations in which poor people are mostly just talked about—defined by others—does that really advance understanding?

"I was shocked when I first started doing [cable news shows], about how quickly you have to make choices and how easy it is to fall into, you know, using your Rolodex to call people who you know will be compelling voices to speak on poverty," said Harris-Perry, speaking a few weeks before starting her MSNBC show.[19]

"The easy way to say it would be, 'Oh, [the lack of poverty coverage] is because nobody cares and we're all the great oppressors' and maybe that's true," she added. "But I think the other possibility is we're just not very good at it and we're trying to figure out how . . . at least some people are trying to figure out how to be better at it."

Some experts say the lack of poverty coverage is just how the news media works.

"The needs of [the] poor and working class are largely left out of the news because journalists see . . . journalism in middle class terms and treat the poor as objects of reporting rather than as citizens," wrote Andrew Cline, an associate professor of journalism at Missouri State University, in a 2011 research paper titled "Citizens or Objects: A Case Study in News Coverage of Poverty."[20]

Cline's paper looked at a specific newspaper, the *Springfield News Leader* in Missouri, and asked what opportunities might exist for the publication to serve the poor and working class in typical news coverage.

But along the way, he also echoed what many other media analysts have said about how journalists handle covering poverty: that news reports are prepared from a middle-class perspective, covering poverty as the occasional feature story or when the poor are at the center of big breaking news stories.

"There's an old saying journalism students learn: journalism should afflict the comfortable and comfort the afflicted," the professor wrote. "What journalism actually does is serve the middle and upper classes because newspapers and corporate news chains are in the business of making money [by] selling advertising to businesses that wish to influence consumers who have disposable income."

Cline suggested a simple solution: Journalists should add "actionable" information for poor and working-class readers to stories, such as news on which businesses might hire working-class people; shops where those below the poverty line can find affordable, quality merchandise; or agencies where they can receive assistance.

The goal: to change the perspective from which stories are told, so that the very DNA of news pieces shifts a bit, landing somewhere closer to the sensibilities of poor citizens.

But to manage that, journalists must also fight another habit of news coverage regarding poverty: the tendency to associate it with people of color.

In their 2000 book *The Black Image in the White Mind,* authors and university professors Robert Entman and Andrew Rojecki examined how, even though TV news rarely centered stories on poverty, ideas about the poor were transmitted by visual images of poverty's symptoms.[21]

Looking at a selection of local and national news broadcasts, they discovered that TV so often illustrated stories on poverty with images of black people that the two had become synonymous for news consumers—especially white viewers.

"The imagery of television news also suggests poverty is concentrated among blacks, so much so that merely showing a black person on the screen appears to be a code for the involvement of poor people," the authors wrote. "Television helps to construct a widespread sense of the prototypical Black as a poor person (and, quite likely, a criminal one)."[22]

Researchers also found that this connection reduced the audience's sympathy for subjects of poverty stories.

"To the extent that poverty becomes overly racialized, it becomes a minority issue and of less interest to non-minority readers and viewers," said Martin Gilens, a professor at Princeton University and author of the 1999 book *Why Americans Hate Welfare: Race, Media and the Politics of Antipoverty Policy.* "We have a very racially stratified society, and while there's been progress over the long term of decades, I don't think much has changed since the era I was looking at."[23]

Gilens's book held that, although opinion polls revealed that Americans approved of many specific anti-poverty programs when asked about them, they had negative reactions to increasing spending on welfare or support for people on welfare. After examining more polls, he concluded that racial attitudes and the idea that welfare recipients don't deserve help fueled much of the reaction.[24]

He also looked at reporting in major newsmagazines such as *Time, Newsweek,* and *U.S. News & World Report,* discovering that from 1967 to 1992, black people were 57 percent of the poor depicted (where race could be determined), nearly double the actual ratio of black people in poverty back then.[25] From 1972 to 1973, he found black people shown in 70 percent of poverty stories and 75 percent of welfare stories.[26]

Before that time, it was a different story—quite literally. According to Gilens's research, from 1950 to 1959, just 18 percent of poor people in those newsmagazines' stories about poverty were African American.[27] Black people have always proportionally struggled more with poverty, but before the 1960s—when the migration of African Americans from the South combined with the civil rights movement's focus on economics and riots in ghettos focused media coverage on poor black people—the face of poverty in much news coverage was white.

When that media focus changed to black people, Gilens noted, white America began to see welfare programs as a means to unfairly hand black people financial support they had not earned.

"In large measure, Americans hate welfare because they view it as a program that rewards the undeserving poor," Gilens wrote in *Why Americans Hate Welfare.* "First, the American public thinks most people who receive welfare are black, and second, the public thinks that blacks are less committed to the work ethic than are other Americans . . . Whites oppose welfare not because they think it primarily benefits blacks, but because they think it benefits blacks who prefer to live off the government rather than work."[28]

So when Newt Gingrich called President Obama "the most successful food stamp president in history," he didn't have to explicitly draw the connection between race and public assistance (in fact, it seemed a surprising rhetorical slip when he brought up the NAACP).

Thanks to decades of media coverage, that association is automatic—especially for the white conservative voters Gingrich was courting.

"Racialization of poverty kind of goes up and down, depending on the nature of the economy," Gilens said. "Generally, during hard times, coverage of poverty becomes more sympathetic and the imagery is much wider. It may be this is not the best time for Republican candidates to trade on the racial connections with poverty, given that such a wide segment of people who are struggling don't fit that frame."[29]

And while there is no doubt people of color are disproportionally poor, they are not necessarily the biggest recipients of such aid programs. Back in 2010, 34 percent of food stamp recipients identified themselves as white people, compared to 22 percent who were black and 16 percent who were Hispanic, according to statistics from the U.S. Department of Agriculture reported by the *Chicago Tribune*.[30]

NPR's Fessler often finds herself trying to cut through such misconceptions about poverty, while also pushing back against anti-poverty activists who may massage statistics to make the plight of the poor look even more dramatic and attention-getting.

"I don't think many people know about the poor, except people who are poor," she said. "Even when I'm doing these sorts of stories, I sort of feel like I'm going into another world . . . I've been amazed by the resilience of the people I've met who are poor."[31]

The program most identified with the term "welfare," Temporary Assistance for Needy Families, implemented work requirements and a lifetime limit of five years in 1996. According to figures from 2009, 33 percent of those recipients were black people, 31 percent were white, and 29 percent were Hispanic.[32] An analysis of a collection of so-called "entitlement" programs offered by the government—including Social Security, Medicare, Medicaid, unemployment insurance, TANF, food stamps, the Children's Health Insurance Program, and others—found that 91 percent of benefits went to people who were age 65 and older, non-elderly disabled people, or households with an individual who worked at least 1,000 hours a year.[33]

As an example of how stereotypes linking poverty, race, and criminality can distort media coverage, consider a story that aired the morning of June 30, 2011, on Chicago's CBS affiliate WBBM-TV. The piece featured a four-year-old African American boy interviewed by a freelance reporter the night before, in the aftermath of a shooting in the city's tough, low-income Park Manor neighborhood.[34]

In the story, the child is asked by the reporter: "When you get older are you going to stay away from all these guns?"

CHILD: No.

REPORTER: No? What are you going to do when you get older?

CHILD: I'm going to have me a gun!

After the story ended, the station's anchors expressed surprise and shock that the young people in a troubled neighborhood were being shaped by exposure to violence.

Unfortunately, the reporter left out a telling comment.

After the story aired, an anonymous emailer sent an unedited copy of the interview to Bob Butler, a columnist for the Maynard Institute for Journalism Education, a California-based non-profit dedicated to improving diversity in journalism and media. Butler found the following key exchange left on the cutting room floor:

CHILD: I'm going to have me a gun!

REPORTER: You are! Why do you want to do that?

CHILD: I'm going to be the police!

WBBM eventually apologized, saying the video should not have aired. But the station never explained why the story was edited so clumsily or whether it was sensitive to the cultural and social implications of such changes.

Viewers were left to wonder why the story presented the false implication of a young black child pushed by violence into wanting a gun, rather than the true story of a kid who hoped to join the police force and stop crime in his neighborhood.

Critics suspected the TV station was looking for a simple, shocking example of how crime in poor black neighborhoods can be passed from generation to generation.

Butler noted that the mistake put WBBM in a controversial spot. "In order to renew your broadcast license, you have to fill out a five-page application in which you state how your broadcasts serve the community interest," said the columnist, a 30-year broadcasting veteran who also serves as an officer with the National Association of Black Journalists. "One could argue that deliberately editing the video the way it was—if that's what they did—could be construed as a violation of FCC policy and a condition to challenge their license."

In one of Butler's stories on the issue, NAACP president Benjamin Jealous said there was a simple reason to avoid such misleading reports: "As somebody who's a former journalist, like many past presidents of the NAACP, it's important to tell the whole truth, because when you tell half a truth you're, in effect, lying."[35]

IT WASN'T THE QUESTION SCOTT PELLEY EXPECTED to cause a problem.

But when he asked a roomful of children in free and reduced school lunch programs how many of them had seen the lights turned off in their homes due to non-payment of the electric bill—and almost every hand went up—CBS News's top anchor couldn't help pausing a bit, water gathering in his eyes.

"You're looking at these lovely little kids, who are the kids in your school; these are the kids who sit next to your kids at school," said Pelley, speaking for a behind-the-scenes video on CBSNews.com documenting his March 2011 story on child poverty in central Florida. "When you talk to them over time, you really get a sense of the struggle—the daily struggle they're under."[36]

Pelley has brought stories on America's poverty problems to the largest newsmagazine audience on television, developing reports for *60 Minutes* on kids who live in their family van, washing up for school in Wal-Mart bathrooms before the start of each day.

Pelley's two reports on poor children in Florida, dubbed "Hard Times Generation," sparked tremendous interest. His first story aired in March 2011, citing predictions that 25 percent of America's children would soon be raised in poverty. He focused on 500 kids housed in cheap motels arrayed around the posh grounds of Walt Disney World.

The same children who raised their hands to Pelley's question about the electric bill shared stories on how it felt to go to bed hungry, get food from churches, or even borrow from better-off classmates, as tears streamed down their faces. One girl spoke of feeling as if her family's poverty were her own fault, because her parents had to pay for her food and clothes as well as their own.

Social worker Beth Davalos, who heads the program helping homeless families at the Seminole County School System in central Florida, was featured in Pelley's reports and said she helped convince her employer to cooperate with the show's producers after two other local school districts turned *60 Minutes* down, fearing the story would make their community look bad.[37]

Davalos knew better. Media savvy after years of working with journalists to publicize her programs, the social worker understood that the district and the show's producers had common interests.

Producers at *60 Minutes* wanted a compelling, emotional story. She wanted to reach the show's massive audience with a message that would cut through all their assumptions about the poor in America.

"One reason there's not enough stories is because recession homelessness is new to our country," said Davalos, a nine-year veteran of Seminole County schools. "In the 1990s, when I was in graduate school, 90 percent of homeless people were that single man, a veteran maybe, with drug issues or chronic problems. But now there's whole families who are homeless, and it's hard to get people to work with [journalists], although it's happening everywhere. People are very fearful about sharing that story."

A second Pelley report in November featured Austin and Arielle Metzger, two attractive, articulate kids living in a truck with their father, an unemployed carpenter. "It's not that much of an embarrassment," said Arielle, a pretty blonde with penetrating blue eyes and an easy smile. "You do what you have to do, right?"

What many viewers felt they had to do, after watching Pelley's report, was help out.

The first report in March 2011 helped spark $4 million in pledges to central Florida institutions; Davalos said she established more than 40 new food pantries for 60 schools across Seminole County.[38] After the second report in November 2011, Pelley reported that CBS News collected over $1 million in promises of aid, including scholarships for the Metzger children from three colleges and job offers for every family featured in the report.[39]

Davalos said that the two stories also inspired a celebrity couple, who chose to remain anonymous, to fund housing for one family for over a year; another company provided the Metzgers with housing for over two years.

"People need to see it; they need to actually see the situation and they have to feel it," added Davalos, noting that she immediately got calls and emails from as far away as Japan and Afghanistan; a year after the first story aired, people were still phoning every day or so. "People were shocked all throughout the United States. I had people calling me—grown men crying—saying they couldn't believe there were people like that here. To hear a child talk about hunger brings it to another level."[40]

One reason Pelley's reports were so convincing, however, was because they centered on subjects who seemed to be plunged into poverty through no fault of their own.

His *60 Minutes* stories disclosed no problems with substance abuse or other vices among the families he highlighted, who seemed plunged into poverty by job loss. Many featured subjects in his reports were children—telegenic and articulate—and often white. Though poverty rates are higher for households headed by single mothers, just one of the families given significant screen time in Pelley's reports was headed by a woman.

Those images distanced Pelley's stories from the stereotypes of more simplistic poverty reporting, but they also presented the most sympathetic people possible.

And Davalos suggested that was no accident.

"It's about judgment; people are going to judge," she said. "I prefer to have families [on camera] with a gentleness about them, that are really trying hard. You have to think of the viewers' perspective and the emotions it's going to evoke in them. You want them to open their hearts. We're trying to change the way we perceive poverty and the way we react to poverty and close that separation gap."

According to Davalos, there's a simple reason why viewers may judge the subjects of poverty stories so harshly. "People don't want to think it's happening here," she said. "They will use any excuse with their own coping skills. They don't want to imagine it happening in their own child's classrooms."

Renowned linguist and social critic Noam Chomsky might call these kinds of story subjects "worthy victims"—people with whom the public can easily identify.

Journalists turning stories on poverty know that part of the struggle is to keep audiences—and editors—engaged. That often means focusing on people whose plight can't be easily explained away because they struggle with alcohol addiction, mental illness, or the consequences of bad life choices.

But it also means turning away from stories about the very people who form significant portions of the underclass. Once again, the middle-class perspective and ignorance of the poor forces significant coverage decisions.

NPR's Fessler discovered that problem firsthand in 2010, when she profiled a family in Pennsylvania that had once lived in a tent and struggled for food but managed to get support from food stamps by the time she met them.

The couple had an eight-year-old son and two teen daughters, one of whom was pregnant; two other relatives also spent lots of time in the apartment because they were homeless. The mother was overweight and jobless because of asthma and arthritis problems; the father was a high school dropout who supported the family on $18,000 a year working in a machine shop.[41]

Once a month, the family would pool the food stamps they had among them and head to the local food pantry. Finding enough food for two weeks could take six hours, as the mother drove to several discount food stores and a farm stand run by the food pantry, scouting for the best bargains.

And when Fessler's two-part story was posted online, featuring a photo of the mother standing behind her minivan alongside a grocery cart packed with food, it drew hundreds of online comments from people who had no sympathy for the family's struggles.

"Feel sorry for this family? Please," wrote one poster by the name of Kathy Dopel, using the online handle KADI. "An example of a typical food stamp family? This family is a mess and are playing the system. She's driving a nice minivan and shops for over 6 hours for food yet she is incapable of working a real job? She's a shop-a-holic. Another pregnant teenager is just what the family needed for yet another government handout. Why is the daughter not working and contributing to help the family? Why work if you can get $600.00 a month in free food?"

Fessler said NPR received thousands of emails about the story, in which many audience members shrugged off the details of the family's struggle to criticize their looks or explain away their problems as the result of personal choices.

"You talk about the 'worthy victims'; if you don't find somebody [like that], then maybe the point is lost," she said. "This family was clearly in a bad way—they lived in such crummy circumstances, but they also had lots of other issues. Maybe if I would have just focused on the young child, just focused on him instead of the whole family, they would have been a little bit more sympathetic."[42]

Such approaches may sidestep the notion that two things can be true at once: poor people can suffer under an onerous economic system while also dealing with some setbacks resulting from their own choices. Yet that may be the story that poor people most need the rest of us to see—humanizing their struggle in ways that also allow them to be fallible, just like everyone else.

Do journalists demand that other troubled stars of news coverage—reformed drug addicts, celebrities in rehab, criminals out of prison—have perfect personal lives before attempting sympathetic stories on their struggles?

Worse, it may help inculcate news coverage habits that further limit the world of possible stories.

"It's either Barbie saves Sambo, or Ken saves Barbie *from* Sambo," said Byron Pitts, chief national correspondent for CBS News and a contributing correspondent at *60 Minutes*. Pitts was not involved with Pelley's stories but has spent many years covering poverty over a three-decade TV news career.[43]

"Every story, at least on the national level, is about how white people save poor black people," said the reporter, an open-hearted, accomplished professional who admitted some deep disappointments in how network TV covers poverty. "Never does Sambo save himself."

Raised in working-class East Baltimore with a stutter and an inability to read that left some experts convinced he was mentally retarded—his amazing journey is detailed in a 2009 memoir, *Step Out on Nothing*—Pitts takes poverty coverage personally. And as an African American male who has worked hard to succeed in white-dominated settings, he's well aware of how race can also contribute to issues that distort coverage.

He recalled watching a long-ago *CBS Evening News* broadcast from Philadelphia and calling then–executive producer Rick Kaplan to congratulate him on a singular show. "I told him it was amazing he could do a half-hour broadcast in Philadelphia and not have a single black person on the show," Pitts said, laughing. "Ours is a business based on relationship and contact. If folks aren't in your Rolodex, you don't think they exist."

His concern: "Too often, stories about people of color are done from the perspective of the pathology of the black experience," he said. "But there's great church groups out there helping people. There's got to be a story out there about how Sambo saves himself."

But even as journalists such as Pitts, Pelley, and Fessler struggle to find the kind of story subjects who connect with viewers, one researcher has developed evidence suggesting they may be approaching the issue in a way that encourages viewers to blame the individuals in their pieces for their own poverty.

Shanto Iyengar, a professor of political science at Stanford University, has produced several studies looking at how news media frame issues—in other words, how they provide context for an audience to judge the meaning of their information. For example, investigative series on local TV stations are often titled "What's That Costing You?" or "Who's Wasting Your Money?," immediately notifying viewers they are about to witness a story where the intrepid reporter (good guy) will tell them how government officials (bad guys) are squandering funding provided by all taxpayers. Before anyone sees a second of video, heroes and villains are already in place.

Iyengar's studies contend that one of the most important frames for news coverage isn't liberal or conservative, but *episodic* or *thematic*.[44] And each frame has a markedly different effect on how audiences feel about subjects depicted in poverty stories.

In an experiment where he showed subjects different news stories and asked them questions about their perceptions of poverty afterward, Iyengar found that people who saw episodic coverage—focused on personal experiences and stories of specific people—tended to think the poverty described in the story was the result of individual choices and actions. Those who saw thematic coverage with stories outlining general trends tended to blame societal factors such as government programs, the economy, or the political climate.[45]

Curiously, when Iyengar looked at the reaction to the race of story subjects, he didn't find they made much difference in test subjects' beliefs about the causes of poverty. But when asked about how to solve poverty issues, respondents who saw stories with black subjects were more likely to cite individual responsibility in general. When single mothers were depicted in stories, black moms produced twice the number of individual treatment responses.[46]

These results echoed Gilens's findings: acceptance of society intervention to help the poor was much higher when the poor person was white, revealing a resistance to providing public aid to black people.

Further, media coverage offering details of individuals' struggles with poverty might cause the audience to blame the individuals more and shift attention from any politicians, agency leaders, or systemic problems—especially when the subjects of stories are people of color.

"Reporters tend to take for granted that a story with personalized story lines will have greater interest for the audience," Iyengar said in a 2009 interview, noting that people instinctively want to know why something happened and how it can be prevented.

"Putting a face on the problem encourages people to seize upon the face as a relevant guide to understanding the causes and cures for the problem at hand," he said.[47]

In the end, it's another high hurdle for those hoping to tell the story of the nation's poor to an under-informed, sometimes unsympathetic audience.

AS WE SPOKE, BRIAN WILLIAMS SEEMED to be in his element: weighing story ideas, figuring out what might be featured on that night's edition of *NBC Nightly News,* and yelling for gaffer's tape to fix a broken window.

The year was 2005, two weeks after Hurricane Katrina and the flooding in its wake had decimated parts of New Orleans, leaving thousands of people stranded in the city with minimal food and water for days while TV cameras documented their misery.

Williams had waited out the storm in the city's Superdome sports arena and was still in the Crescent City two weeks later, covering what had become his signature story.

Weeks later, in a documentary titled *In His Own Words: Brian Williams on Hurricane Katrina,* the news anchor would describe his feelings on entering the Superdome hours before one of biggest hurricanes in recent memory was expected to impact the city.

"I think about the faces I saw going in that dome," he said in the film. "What really troubled me, these evacuees were arriving, some of them with children, some of them with very few belongings. Most of them were obviously poor. And the National Guard were being quite rough verbally and physically with them. Not all, but some."[48]

Williams continued: "I was disturbed enough to try to look for who-ever the colonel was in charge of this event. I was told, 'Homeland Security's in charge of the event.' It felt bad. The men were being aggressively patted down. I asked why? I was told, 'Well, they're looking for cigarette lighters to enforce the ban on smoking inside the Superdome.' Once you were inside, you were handed a military meal-ready-to-eat. Inside every MRE is a pack of matches. It was that kind of thing that didn't make sense."

The experience convinced Williams, like many other journalists work-ing there, that we needed to take a deeper look at how things had gotten so bad in such a storied city.

Speaking to me in 2005 over a crackling cellphone line, he was sure this was a story he'd be working for years to come.

"If this does not spark a national discussion on class, race, the envi-ronment, oil, Iraq, infrastructure and urban planning, I think we've failed," Williams said, speaking with a near-evangelical passion. "We're going to be talking about this in some way for the rest of my lifetime and yours. I think my children will have children before this issue is over. I think this—like it or not—this will color our debates . . . color our conversations on these larger issues for a long time."[49]

In that moment, he wasn't sure what could be done, only that some-thing must. "I'm going to approach my network to do something in prime time," he said. "I don't know if it's one hour or two, a town hall meeting with smart, professional people. It's often said that we blew our last chance at a national discussion on race when the Lewinsky scandal broke [and dis-tracted President Bill Clinton] . . . But I do know we have our next opportu-nity before us."[50]

Much as Williams tried, however, his special on Katrina that year aired on the Sundance Channel, not NBC. And five years later, touting a Katrina documentary that *would* air on the network, he admitted to me that the na-tional conversation he hoped to start was sidelined by a very powerful and important constituency.

His own audience.

"It's a lot easier to watch *Entourage*," the anchor said in 2010. "Jay Leno is a lot more fun every night . . . Remember how we felt about our govern-ment [during Katrina coverage]? And about each other? There's a shot in our [Katrina] documentary of a water drop—pallets of water dropping off a Black Hawk helicopter. As it happens, a one-armed man is unloading the

Black Hawk. And it's a poignant scene. The last time I saw a scene like that, was in Port-Au-Prince [Haiti]. What keeps getting me angry, and what gets me exercised after living through these tapes again, is that this is *my* country. This wasn't a third world relief mission. And yet, it looked for all the world like one."[51]

The experience left Williams yearning for the days when journalists could set the world's news agenda, almost unilaterally. "This is my life— would you be my therapist, I don't have one?" he joked. "The world you and I grew up in—I'm 51 years old. Three channels on TV. The president spoke, you didn't watch anything else. You wouldn't think about it. Men landed on the moon, a global event. I'd like to see what kind of audience share it would get today. Getting people's attention is hard."[52]

What made telling stories about poverty and social issues post-Katrina especially hard was that policymakers and politicians were also avoiding the discussion. Democrats faced thorny questions about local officials' culpability, while Republicans were recovering from the massive failure of the underfunded and disorganized Federal Emergency Management Agency.

And some national voices returned to a familiar refrain: This was evidence that poor people needed to take more personal responsibility.

Fox News pundit Bill O'Reilly thundered: "Every American kid should be required to watch videotape of the poor in New Orleans and see how they suffered [after Hurricane Katrina], because they couldn't get out of town. And then, every teacher should tell the students, 'If you refuse to learn, if you refuse to work hard, if you become addicted, if you live a gangsta-life, you will be poor and powerless just like many of those in New Orleans.'"[53]

Rush Limbaugh was even more direct, accusing New Orleans of a "welfare state mentality" that kept some residents from earning enough to leave the city before the storm hit.

"The non-black population was just as devastated, but apparently they were able to get out," Limbaugh, who is white, said on his show. "Race, in this circumstance, is a poisonous weapon, and it's why the liberals are now gravitating to it."[54]

Glenn Beck, speaking on his syndicated radio show, simply called the people trapped in New Orleans by Katrina's flooding "scumbags."

Once again, race and poverty were linked, and those who suffered in the post-Katrina flooding were "unworthy victims"—individuals who forsook the public's compassion through their own misdeeds.

"One of the challenges of Katrina versus, say, 9/11 [coverage] is that we got to know the stories and the names of some of the 9/11 victims and survivors, the widows of 9/11, and they had an actual voice in policy-making after 9/11," said MSNBC anchor and academic Harris-Perry, who lives in New Orleans. "But people would be really hard-pressed to tell you the names of people who were survivors of Hurricane Katrina. Who are the heroes of the Katrina moment in the ways, for example, that people on that flights which crashed in Pennsylvania were heroes? It hasn't been part of how we've been able to tell that story."

As 2012 began, some news outlets moved to expand poverty coverage.

The American Public Media radio show *Marketplace* started a Wealth and Poverty desk, while the *Huffington Post* website hired a reporter formerly at the *New York Times* to cover poverty. ABC News in April 2012 launched a series of reports titled "Hidden America," which featured reporting on poverty, documenting the struggles of poor kids to get dental care and survive in Florida, Louisiana, and Texas for programs such as *Nightline* and *World News*.

Even *People* magazine got on the bandwagon, announcing a new charity initiative called People First, in which the publication teams with a charity feeding hungry schoolchildren and features their stories regularly.

But NPR's Fessler wondered if that interest would continue once the 2012 presidential election ended, especially if the economy recovered.

"I think it's only temporary," she said of the increased media interest. "The presidential campaign, the Occupy movement . . . they've given a news peg to the story. When that's over, who knows what will happen?"[55]

TEN

TALKING ACROSS DIFFERENCE

Resisting Propaganda while
Integrating Our Lives and Media

THERE MAY BE NO MORE INSPIRING SIGHT THAN WATCHING DR.
Bernard Lafayette Jr. detail the history of non-violent protest in the civil
rights movement.

He's got the credentials. Born in 1940 in Ybor City, Florida, Lafayette
made crucial contributions to the movement, co-founding the Student
Nonviolent Coordinating Committee in 1960 and serving in top administrative posts at the Southern Christian Leadership Conference and the 1968
Poor People's Campaign, appointed by the Rev. Dr. Martin Luther King Jr.
himself.[1]

King was a friend and mentor, teaching Lafayette the principles of non-
violent protest and cross-racial dialogue he now imparts, fifty years later, in
his own classes at Emory University and the Martin Luther King, Jr. Center
for Nonviolent Social Change in Atlanta.[2]

That's where I met Lafayette in the flesh. I was shadowing part of a trip
in 2011 wherein a crew of handpicked college kids retraced the route of the
original Freedom Riders—a biracial group of 436 activists who rode buses
into the South to challenge segregation 50 years earlier.

Lafayette himself was a Freedom Rider, part of a group of students who
joined the protest after the original 13 riders were attacked in Alabama. Their

goal: prodding federal officials into enforcing federal laws against segregating buses and bus terminals.

While walking past the tattered wooden wagon that bore King's casket during his funeral—standing inside the King Center museum—Lafayette schooled journalists and students alike in the tenets of non-violent civil disobedience. Most importantly, he stressed, non-violent protestors accepted the penalty for breaking a law, even one they felt was unjust.

Dressed in a natty charcoal gray suit and sharp straw hat, Lafayette led the group through the civil rights museum on one end of the King Center's grounds, crossing Jackson Street to stroll through the refurbished Ebenezer Baptist Church—where Dr. King was baptized and gave his last sermon—a space nearly gleaming after an $8 million facelift.[3]

Standing in that church, hearing tape-recordings of King's best-known speeches bounce off the newly restored stained glass windows and richly colored, wooden pews, we all felt about as close to history as we could get—given a window into that world by a man who had seen it all firsthand.

And one of his biggest lessons centered on the power and purpose of segregation.

"The whole purpose of segregation was so black and white folks wouldn't talk to each other and find out they had more in common, okay?" said Lafayette, who often told the story of fetching morning coffee for his parents as a boy in segregated Ybor City, where he eventually decided to sit at the deserted, whites-only counter to wait for his order.[4]

Not until he began sitting down did the man who fixed his order start chatting with him as a friend.

"When people sit down together, it implies social equality; that's why most segregation was horizontal and not vertical," he reminded. "We could stand and watch the parades together. We used to ride elevators together. But sitting in a restaurant or a bus terminal, where you see one another as equals? . . . People forget [segregation] law didn't just say blacks had to sit in the back. The rest of the law said whites had to sit in the front."[5]

Among his passionate words, three ideas stood out.

Racial segregation and segmentation limited white people as well as black people. Such divides were a purposeful tactic to keep like-minded people of different races from finding power in their unity. And the best way to overcome those divides was to spend time sitting in each others' spaces.

So when it comes to breaking down the race-baiting of modern media, more than anything, we have to think about breaking down the segregation.

We have to learn, somehow, to sit together.

In a way, the divides now in place are a consequence of two factors: a nation that has never really learned to talk about race, and an on-demand media culture in which the audience's taste increasingly drives all programming.

I dissected this "on demand attitude" back in 2005 for the *St. Petersburg Times,* noting how the growth of technology, which allows people to fill their media world with material they have specifically chosen, also creates an impatience with stuff that doesn't fit that bill.

Twenty years ago, you might sit through a sitcom you didn't like on television in order to watch one that you did or endure the president's State of the Union speech when all the big TV networks aired it at once.

But today's wealth of time-shifting devices for media changes everything. Spend a few minutes programming your digital video recorder, and it will capture every television show you find interesting. You never have to watch a second of TV programming you don't *choose* to watch—including commercials.

The DVR is likely connected to a satellite or cable TV service packed with more than 250 channel options. Apple TV, Google TV, Roku, or even a mid-level DVD/Blu-ray player can dip into a host of online video archives and services such as Netflix or Amazon on Demand.

And that's just your television. Toss in video-sharing sites such as YouTube and Tout, social media outlets such as Facebook, Foursquare, and Twitter, podcasts available on iTunes or elsewhere, along with good old-fashioned text messaging and emails to create a world where each individual person can create their own media diet, crammed with content customized to fit his or her own tastes.

I like to call it a "media ecology"—the constellation of websites, social media spaces, radio and TV outlets, print publications, and even music platforms that each person regularly consults each day.

One reason so many outlets are now touting their Facebook pages and Twitter handles is that media creators realize that in order to reach consumers these days, you must *break into* their media ecology—have your video embedded on their friends' Facebook pages, get retweeted by one of their Twitter followers, or become a topic of discussion on the morning radio show they hear while commuting into work.

If your media presentation occurs outside a consumer's media ecology, it might as well not exist for them.

"We had this large audience all feeding from the same cultural trough—everyone watching the *M*A*S*H* finale or something—which Rome and the ancient Greeks didn't have; such a complete grip on the culture at large," Robert Thompson, head of the Center for the Study of Popular Television at Syracuse University, told me back in 2005. "Now, all that has changed. I don't think we have come close to understanding the effects of taking away that cultural glue."[6]

In a 2009 study, researchers Shanto Iyengar and Kyu S. Hahn documented what they called the revival of "selective exposure"—or people seeking news outlets they expected to provide information with which they agreed. This dynamic increasingly drives niche outlets such as cable TV news channels and websites to provide more and more ideologically focused material.

They took a selection of news stories from the MSNBC daily news feed and randomly assigned labels to each story, marking them as produced by Fox News, CNN, NPR, or the BBC. After surveying over 1,000 people, they found conservatives much more likely to consume news of any type from Fox. Likewise, liberals avoided Fox News on most subjects but spread their consumption around the other outlets.[7]

As the *Washington Post* noted in a January 2012 piece examining how the polarization of news may have affected the South Carolina GOP primary, the result of this dynamic is "an electorate in which conservatives and liberals often have not only their own opinions, but their own sets of facts, making it harder than ever to approach common ground."[8]

Reporter Marc Fisher noted in the article: "About two-thirds of Fox News viewers are Christian conservatives, but only a quarter of those who watch *The Daily Show* or *The Colbert Report* fit that description, [the Pew Center] found in 2010. Six in 10 CNN viewers call themselves progressives, compared with only a third of *Wall Street Journal* readers and a quarter of radio talk-show host Rush Limbaugh's audience. Over the past decade, Republicans have listened to more talk radio as Democrats have watched more late-night topical comedy TV. Conservatives are more likely than liberals to read a daily newspaper, and liberals are more than twice as likely as conservatives to listen to NPR."

Different media platforms are dominated by different audiences, who push them to feature different political ideas in their material.

And a different study confirmed this sort of "selective exposure" in an even more personal area: online dating sites.

In a year-long study on an unnamed major dating site, a psychology professor from the University of California at Berkeley found that more than 80 percent of the contacts white people established were with other white people. Just 3 percent of such contacts were made with black people, though black people were ten times more likely to start contacts with white people.[9]

"What you've got is basically the reluctance of white Americans to date and to contact members of other ethnicities, particularly African Americans," the researcher Gerald Mendelsohn told the *New York Times.* "We are nowhere near the post-racial age."[10]

Even 2010 U.S. Census data on residential segregation—which some hailed as showing "American cities are now more integrated than they've been since 1910"—danced on that same double-edged sword.

While a 2012 study by the conservative Manhattan Institute noted that "all-white neighborhoods are nearly extinct," with 199 of every 200 neighborhoods containing African American residents, an earlier analysis from researchers at Brown and Florida State universities found that the average white person still lives in a neighborhood where 75 percent of residents also are white people.[11]

"Despite a substantial shift of minorities from cities to suburbs, these groups have often not gained access to largely white neighborhoods," wrote John R. Logan of Brown University and Brian Stults of Florida State University in the 2011 study *The Persistence of Segregation in the Metropolis: New Findings from the 2010 Census.*

"A typical African American lives in a neighborhood that is only 35 percent white (not much different from 1940) and as much as 45 percent black," they wrote. "Diversity is experienced very differently in the daily lives of whites, blacks, Hispanics and Asians."[12]

Which brings us back to an important question: If we're continuing this "horizontal segregation" in our media lives, how will we ever limit the power of outlets that play on those divisions for power and profit?

HERE'S HOW THE CYCLE OFTEN GOES.

Someone significant says something that seems fraught with insulting racial implications. Someone else notices it, and it becomes a huge media story centered on one idea: Is the person who said this awful thing actually racist?

Was it "real" racism?

And that, said Rinku Sen, is a debilitating loop that plays out again and again—from ethnic slurs in reports on Asian American basketball star Jeremy Lin to Newt Gingrich vowing he will talk to the NAACP about preferring paychecks to food stamps—ensuring that any talk across race stays confrontational, explosive, and mostly of limited progress.

"We should move from trying to determine people's intentions," said Sen, president and executive director of the Applied Research Center, a think tank devoted to racial justice issues, and publisher of a website devoted to daily news about race, Colorlines.com.[13]

"There's this gap between many groups of color and white folks," she added. "And right now, those debates are almost always focused on the individual intention of the person at the center of the debate . . . If we're able to move from the question of intention to the impact—not just on individuals targeted, but the community represented by it—sometimes that can lower the heat level of the discussions."

For example, rather than asking Gingrich, "Are you using code words for racism?" (which he has consistently denied), why not ask, "Do you know that some people who hear you use those words assume you are speaking in code about racism?" Or ask, "If you're really interested in teaching people to help themselves, why would you risk insulting them first?"

Sen, author of *The Accidental American: Immigration and Citizenship in the Age of Globalization,* said the biggest challenge in talking across racial lines is drawing a distinction between the biases we all have and the way some people's biases can be enabled by larger institutions in society.

In a nation where black and white people use drugs at about the same rate but black people are nearly 12 times more likely to be jailed on drug charges, the question of how institutions respond to bias takes on an even greater focus.[14]

"People can carry out biases they're not aware they have," Sen added. "Asking people to recognize having an unconscious bias, it's almost impossible to get people to do that. It takes a long period of reflection and dialogue to do that. And that still doesn't lead us to [correct] the institutional arrangements which enable that thinking."[15]

Another problem: So much of our dialogue on these issues has been formed by our experience with the civil rights struggle, where conflict and challenge bring results. We are accustomed to talking about race only when there is a crisis: Someone is dead, someone is unfairly jailed, someone is in need, an injustice looms.

But communication experts say this can be the wrong path to progress, because even open-minded people grow entrenched in their positions when in conflict.

"Talking in conflict just polarizes people," said Iyengar, who serves as professor of political science and director of the Political Communications Laboratory at Stanford University. "But psychologists have demonstrated that when people actually realize their views about people tend to be biased according to things that are inappropriate, they become quite concerned and work overtime to correct it. If they come to the realization on their own, without someone telling them—hey, you're biased!—they're going to try and correct it. That's really the only way we're going to achieve some kind of post-racial society."[16]

It sounds like a bizarrely twisted riddle: You can defuse prejudice and racism by talking about it, but bringing up such issues in the midst of attention-getting crises can have the opposite effect.

Complicating matters further is how differently people from different ethnic and racial backgrounds actually *see* issues of race in America.

In 2006, researchers from Yale and Stanford universities developed a series of studies to look at how white and black people assess racial progress. When you ask a white person how much progress America has made on race issues, how exactly do they divine the answer? And what makes their perceptions so different from black people's assessments?

They theorized that black people made racial equality a bigger personal goal, because it was a "security goal"—an objective directly related to their own safety and basic needs. Which only makes sense; for black people, racial equality can mean achieving equal life expectancies, equal lifetime earning power, equal arrest rates, equal employment opportunities, and equal incarceration rates with white people.

It's only logical that people of color would see balancing those issues as an important personal goal, tantamount to protecting their family or providing for their children.[17]

But for many white people, achieving racial equality was instead a "nurturance goal": something that fit in line with their aspirations and ideals, but something much less urgent than a security goal. After all, raising someone else's earning power doesn't directly help you very much.

When people judge progress on security goals, which are more urgent, they often compare the present to the future, researchers said. For nurturing goals, they compare the present with the past.

In one of their studies, "76 percent of white participants either neglected to mention or only briefly mentioned any discrepancies between present racial conditions and some standard of how things ought to be," wrote Richard P. Eibach of Yale University and Joyce Ehrlinger of Stanford University.[18]

They noted that while conservative commentators such as Shelby Steele and John McWhorter have criticized black people for developing a "Cult of Victimology," their studies showed the perception gap didn't come from black people failing to acknowledge progress—almost every African American they surveyed mentioned progress from the past as a factor in judging progress overall.

"This gap seems to be associated with the failure by some white Americans to consider needs for further progress," they wrote.[19]

Author and longtime educator H. Roy Kaplan also wrote about the role in these diverging attitudes of white people's resistance to accepting personal responsibility for the continuance of racism.

"Whites vehemently deny complicity in the perpetuation of racism and poverty," wrote Kaplan, who is white, in his 2011 book *The Myth of Post-Racial America*. "When a hint of shared responsibility for the vestiges of slavery and racism is apprehended, they invoke standard defense mechanisms to protect their self-concept from being excoriated by the taint of racism and social inequality in our glorious meritocracy."[20]

Now the forces behind the perception gap grow even clearer.

"It's the O.J. Simpson case. It's the Rodney King case . . . We need to pay attention to people's subjective goals, their experiences, how they expect to be received or perceived by other groups," noted Linda Tropp, a psychology researcher at the University of Massachusetts, Amherst, who has conducted similar studies on the racial perception gap. "And we live in such a sound bite culture, there's no time for reflection or dialogue."[21]

In her own research, Tropp found that people of color grew most interested in talking across race when they dealt with white people who seemed to value diversity. So, while one of the primary techniques for encouraging bonding across racial lines involves getting people to work on a common task unrelated to race—say, building a house with Habitat for Humanity or operating a soup kitchen—such bonding may not engage people of color if they are doing it with white people who don't seem to value the cross-cultural connection.

"When we have divergent perspectives on the same situation, it seems like we want to know our way of viewing things is heard, before we might be totally open to hearing someone else's side," Tropp said. "We're accustomed to seeing things the way we do. We're not trained to care about how others see the world."[22]

This conclusion may sound obvious. But for real communication to occur, white people must realize how important racial equality is to people of color personally, while racial minorities must find ways to help white people discover their own connections to the fight for racial equality.

And there's one more wrinkle to consider: the biases we're not even aware we have.

Though somewhat controversial, Harvard University's Project Implicit offers tests anyone can take online to measure unconscious or unacknowledged biases.

The test flashes a series of pictures featuring white and black people and words that are positive and negative; test subjects are first asked to associate white faces with positive words, then black faces with positive words. By measuring how long it takes subjects to connect each racial group with positive words, researchers say they can measure how strong any subject's unconscious bias is toward black or white faces.

Test subjects have noted how tough it is sometimes to connect certain faces to positive words, as if they must struggle to overcome reflexive feelings about people who look a certain way.

After crunching numbers on tens of thousands of tests, they found that 88 percent of white people had a pro-white or anti-black implicit bias, along with 48 percent of black people.[23]

"[The] test measures the imprint of the culture on our minds," Mahzarin Banaji, one of three researchers who developed the test, told the *Washington Post*, explaining why many black people also have trouble associating black faces with positive words. "If Europeans had been carted to Africa as slaves, blacks would have the same belief about whites that whites now have about blacks."[24]

Iyengar, the professor from Stanford University, agreed that unconscious bias is an important issue: "In the egalitarian society that we live in, in the post civil rights area, to say anything negative about minorities is politically incorrect. When you ask [people] these kinds of survey questions that political scientists tend to ask—Are blacks lazy?—no one's going to agree with that. Less than 10 percent of people in these national samples admit using pejorative language to describe minorities. But when you look at nonconscious indicators of prejudice, we see that people would like to think they don't have bias, but in fact, they do."[25]

And when we want to talk about race issues, sometimes it feels as if we don't even have the right words.

The term "racism" itself can be overused. I prefer the word "prejudice" to describe acting on racial bias that doesn't rise to the level of overt discrimination. "Bias" is another good word; along with distinguishing between intentional and unintentional reactions, the term helps focus on the impact of actions, rather than an often unknowable intent.

It's worth noting that people of any ethnicity can act on prejudice without being bigots, meaning that *admitting* you might be influenced by prejudices doesn't mean declaring kinship with David Duke or Archie Bunker.

"One thing that's positive about this situation is that people think it's a negative thing to be called a bigot," Sen said. "But it's a challenge to have an authentic conversation that's not so polarizing conversation stops. Those of us who feel anger and outrage and despair, have to be able to express it in ways that keep the conversation going rather than shut it down. Attaching solutions is really critical."[26]

The other critical idea: Keeping conversations about race going all the time, so we're trading ideas and learning about each other in times when emotions are under control.

In media terms, that means journalists shouldn't shy away from discussing race issues, even when they are not the primary focus of stories. For the audience, that means accepting that discussions about race will become a greater part of stories, broadcasts, and media presentations, without accusing people of race-baiting.

"I encounter a lot of people who say, 'If I talk about race in my economics story, I can't talk about anything else,' but I don't think that's the case," said Sen, who features stories about racial issues on Colorlines.com daily. "One thing we have to remember; there was a concerted effort to de-legitimize race as a lens through which to look at American society. In the '80s, the notion of 'identity politics' was a label slapped on us by the right wing in an effort to put it in a box and dismiss it . . . Conservatives may insist that we never talk about race. That's a framework we have to keep taking apart."[27]

All of these ideas presume that people involved in the conversation are open-minded and honest about finding common ground. In conversations on race, intent counts for a lot; if either side starts out obsessively focused on winning an argument or proving points, people wind up talking past each other, focused on goals that have nothing to do with anything outside their own convictions.

One suggestion: retire the reflex of calling people "race-baiters" for starting conversations about racial issues. As I once wrote in a newspaper column, imagine if we only talked about crime prevention after a string of burglaries?

In fact, if we can somehow manage to have lots of little, consistently progressive conversations about race, perhaps the next time a big problem emerges, the impact won't be so explosive.

UNWINDING RACE-BAITING REQUIRES ONE SKILL ABOVE ALL others: media literacy.

My most pivotal lesson on that score came many years ago, during a class on journalism ethics at Indiana University taught by a professor who had once worked at the liberal newsmagazine *Mother Jones*. Amid the usual lectures on plagiarism and the ethics of interviewing, we took apart a book that remains on my mantelpiece today: *Manufacturing Consent*.

Co-written by famed linguist, philosopher, activist, and social critic Noam Chomsky, 1988's *Manufacturing Consent* was one of the first books I read in journalism school that looked at how media actually worked in the world, specifically how America's moneyed elites use mass media to control the people—a necessary tool in a democracy, where the public has so much political power. Indeed, that notion gave the book its name, from a term coined by journalist and media critic Walter Lippmann: "the manufacturing of consent" by manipulating public opinion.[28]

It was a decidedly left-wing viewpoint, and Chomsky's many ideological opponents have long objected to his bruising analysis. But so many of the book's core truths still ring true that I taught portions of the book during stints as an adjunct professor at Eckerd College and the University of Tampa almost 20 years later.

In particular, the book's five filters for editorial bias made sense to me— from the way big media companies cater to the financial interests of their owners to how bureaucracies like government agencies and think tanks subsidize mass media by collecting information in studies and analysis papers that then fuel news stories.

But the two filters most relevant for this book are advertising's effect on media businesses and what the book calls "flak" or negative feedback.

Advertising reduces the cost of media, as creators sell businesses access to the audiences they create. But it also boosts the impact of advertisers' wishes on the media outlet. That's why groups such as the liberal Color of Change and the conservative Parents Television Council often target advertisers to eliminate or modify media content they find objectionable. If enough advertisers reject a project, it doesn't matter how many fans love it; the profitability vanishes.

That's the hidden factor that may affect everything from diversity in casting on network TV shows to the struggle for ardently left-wing radio shows to find success.

And there's the notion of flak, or negative public responses to a media outlet.

Groups such as Media Matters, Color of Change, NewsBusters, Accuracy in Media, and the Media Research Center have mastered the use of flak to pressure media outlets; a state of affairs *Manufacturing Consent* predicted back in the late 1980s.

"If flak is produced on a large scale, or by individuals or groups with substantial resources, it can be both uncomfortable and costly to the media," Chomsky and his co-author, Edward S. Herman, wrote in the book. "Advertisers are still concerned to avoid offending constituencies which might produce flak, and their demand for suitable programming is a continuing feature of the media environment."[29]

Chomsky, hero to the far left, may have envisioned a system of flak controlled by big corporations and wealthy individuals. And while organizations such as Media Matters and the Media Research Center have their deep-pocketed donors, the one thing the authors couldn't have predicted in 1988 was the way online communication and the Internet allow every citizen to produce flak—loading up a business' Facebook page or Twitter feed with a deluge of complaints.

Key to Herman and Chomsky's work, however, is the notion that modern media is filled with propaganda—persuasive distortions designed to promote certain values, ideas, and habits favored by the ruling class.

And while this notion has been loosened by the democratizing efforts of the Internet and social media, a spin through modern media outlets shows that Herman and Chomsky could not have been more prescient predictors of the propaganda techniques in use today.

The most obvious is the use of codewords or shorthand to short-circuit thinking. Conservative blogger Andrew Breitbart was a master in this regard, turning the name of noted left-wing organizer Saul Alinsky into a verb—accusing political foes of trying to "Alinsky" him, implying some underhanded tactic to gain political advantage (GOP presidential candidate Newt Gingrich also claimed President Obama was a student of Alinsky, known as one of the country's smartest community organizers, about 50 years ago).[30]

But Alisnsky's real expertise—channeling the anger of powerless masses into political achievements, sometimes through attention-getting stunts—sounds more like the work of the tea party movement and Breitbart himself.[31] Still, since the name of the organizer, who died in 1972, has been turned into a pejorative among conservatives, there's no thinking required when it comes up; Alinsky = underhanded liberal organizing trick.

Other propaganda techniques that often surface in media:

An appeal to plain folks/populism. Leaders appeal to ordinary people by appearing to be just like them. In media, for example, Fox News Channel pundit Bill O'Reilly comes across as a down-to-earth man of the people, despite having a master's degree from Harvard University and an income reportedly topping $10 million annually.

The bandwagon approach. Earning support by convincing people that everyone shares the host's point of view. Most every opinionated talk show host uses this technique, particularly Rush Limbaugh, who has labeled his fans "dittoheads" and brags about his many millions of listeners.

Transfer. Using the authority of something widely respected and revered to imply support of a less accepted notion. This happened when Dr. Martin Luther King Jr.'s niece Alveda King, a vocal supporter of conservative causes, appeared in a YouTube video insisting her legendary uncle was a Republican. It was an attempt to convince black people that the greatest civil rights leader in history had endorsed the GOP, a conclusion Dr. King's son and close friends denied.[32]

Projection/flipping. Accusing opponents of initiating an objectionable tactic before they can accuse you of the same action, or reflecting criticism back on the accuser. This is what some media figures do in leveling accusations of "race-baiting" or "race-hustling" as described earlier in the book, particularly in the way Fox News anchor Bill O'Reilly referred to me. Such tactics deflect accusations of racism or prejudice by accusing opponents of unfairly bringing up race in the first place.

The big lie. Telling an untruth so big that people assume it must be true. Accusations that President Obama, a longtime Christian with a long track record of attending Christian churches, must be Muslim, fits in this category. Maintaining that Obama wasn't born in America, despite a birth announcement in the newspaper and documents released by the state of Hawaii proving that he was born there, is a similar tactic.

Name calling. Glenn Beck's insistence that President Obama was a "racist" who hated white people is a prime example. So is O'Reilly's habit of calling people he disagrees with "pinheads."

But one of the most pervasive techniques, particularly in opinion media, is the paranoid style.

Pulitzer Prize–winning author Richard Hofstadter wrote a landmark exploration of this tactic way back in 1964 for *Harper's* magazine, an essay titled "The Paranoid Style in American Politics."[33] Reaching back to the anti-Masonic movements of the 1700s and Jesuit persecution in the 1800s, Hofstadter showed how their past "heated exaggeration, suspiciousness and conspiratorial fantasy" had coalesced similarly in the anti-Communist efforts of Joseph McCarthy and the extremist right-wing supporters of Barry Goldwater.

But anyone reading the piece would recognize ready parallels in the way issues are discussed in today's talk radio, cable TV news shows, and political websites.

Hofstadter described a group of conservatives who felt dispossessed, as if America had largely been taken away from them. These people feared a long-running conspiracy—in his time, Communism; in the modern age, socialism—enacted by agents scattered throughout the country, compromising top government officials.

"The paranoid spokesman sees the fate of conspiracy in apocalyptic terms," Hofstadter wrote. "He is always manning the barricades of civilization. He constantly lives at a turning point . . . He expresses the anxiety of those who are living through the last days and he is sometimes disposed to set a date for the apocalypse."[34]

Listen to a bit of Glenn Beck discoursing on the evils of progressivism or one of Keith Olbermann's old "Special Comment" segments, and the messages sound sadly familiar.

Fortunately in the world of media, knowledge is power.

And knowing the techniques the media use to manipulate emotion and perception is a great first step toward resisting them.

WHAT'S OBVIOUS AT THE END OF THIS JOURNEY through race, prejudice, sexism, and media is that so many of these topics are so much more complex than we initially realize.

Think the Internet pushes us to create cocoons of information, insulated from contact with anything that disturbs our worldview?

Then consider a Pew Center survey that found friends on social media often disagreed with each other on political issues and let the comments pass, because their social networks weren't built on using political ideology as a core organizing principle.[35]

Web-savvy journalist and author Jeff Jarvis said such results make sense, because unlike many media outlets, the online world isn't defined by the content it lets you access. So it can be used to create silos of unchallenging information or it can be used to subvert them, depending on how each consumer chooses to use it.

"The Internet is not a medium—it's a connection machine; it connects us to other people," said Jarvis, whose 2011 book *Public Parts: How Sharing in the Digital Age Improves the Way We Work and Live,* described the benefits of how the Internet has made modern life more public.

"When I interviewed [Facebook creator] Mark Zuckerberg for *Public Parts,* I asked him a question he gets asked all the time: How do people in different cultures and different lands use Facebook differently?" Jarvis said. "The answer is: They don't. There's a remarkable consistency with how people use Facebook. We all have family, we all have friends. Facebook is—it's not meant to be a political football field. It really is about adding elegant organization to your family life and friends . . . And that's often how the Internet works. It connects us with other people. And that connection, to an otherwise sociable and decent person, I think can lead to good things."[36]

Which means that online outlets can, in fact, be a cure for our "horizontal segregation," allowing us to spend time on the Racialicious blog, NBC's black-focused website TheGrio.com, or the Angry Asian Man blog, and then scoot over to peruse the *Daily Caller* site's latest anti–Al Sharpton story or click on the *Huffington Post*'s Black Voices section, and sample a wide range of opinions from many different cultural vantage points.

Clay Shirky, another well-known thought leader on the social impact of the Internet, teaches at New York University and has written several books on the power of online connectivity, including 2008's *Here Comes Everybody: The Power of Organizing without Organizations* and 2010's *Cognitive Surplus: Creativity and Generosity in a Connected Age.*

Shirky noted that some online platforms—say, electronic bulletin boards or website commenting systems—don't help race issues because participants can't really discern the race of people with whom they are communicating. And just as some online destinations can be havens for cross-cultural contact, white supremacist sites such as Stormfront can present the opposite experience.

"If you take the bumpers off your search engine and want to go look for overt racism, you're 30 seconds away," he said. "But, and I think this is the single biggest change for any minority group, everybody can find each other now. And society no longer has the ability to limit their ability to speak out or gather somewhere."[37]

Shirky also took heart in two seemingly depressing events.

When Hollywood debuted *The Hunger Games,* a big-budget movie of a popular young adult book series, some Twitter users posted racist comments while complaining that characters they assumed were white in the book were played by black actors in the film. But the comments also sparked a huge wave of criticism toward the complainers, as websites such as Jezebel and Forbes.com reported on the posts. Before long, most Twitter accounts featured in the stories were either shut down or removed from public view.[38]

"Twitter helped dismantle a deeper, institutionalized racial expectation," Shirky said.

He also took heart in an online column by John Derbyshire called "The Talk: Nonblack Version," in which the author counseled his kids to avoid large groups of black people and noted that the average black stranger wasn't as smart as the average white stranger.

This column, discussed earlier in the book, got Derbyshire fired as a contributor to the *National Review.* But Shirky took heart in what the column said about society.

"Derbyshire was basically saying political correctness worked; if you are white and have children, they will no longer absorb racism from the environment like they used to, you have to teach it to them," he said. "If you can, for a generation, make it publicly unacceptable to traffic in this shit . . . [you] further limit the ability of people to indulge casual racism in public spaces."

In today's super-targeted media environment, it's important for media consumers to take action to stay informed, so each one of us can challenge stereotypes, inaccuracies, and race-baiting in our own corners of the media universe.

"There is a continuous temptation to think of race as an essence, as something fixed, concrete and objective," wrote academics Michael Omi and Howard Winant in a landmark 1986 book on racial identities called *Racial Formation in the United States.*[39] "And there is also an opposite temptation: to see it as mere illusion, which an ideal social order would eliminate. In our view, it is crucial to break with these habits of thought. The effort must be made to understand race as an unstable and 'decentered' complex of social meanings constantly being transformed by political struggle."

And it's a struggle any race-baiter worth their salt will engage right away.

Race issues aren't something to "get over." They're not problems to be solved or ignored, depending on which tactic more easily preserves the status quo. They're not political opportunities to be exploited or excuses to be debunked.

They are the beginning of a cultural conversation that, with any luck, will never end.

Our racial identities are a deep and important part of us. This is something people of color discover as soon as we intersect with a largely white world, when we go to school or leave for college, or when we start our first job.

Whenever that moment comes, we must decide—who are we really? How much of the world's vision of ourselves do we accept? How much of my true cultural self can I reveal to these new people without rejection?

As a journalist, I love meeting different people. The thrill of getting to know someone—learning the shape of their culture enough to retell their story to others—has always been one of my job's most special experiences, whether I was sharing a beer with Jon Bon Jovi around the corner from his New Jersey home or interviewing those who flocked to a high-end bar in Osaka, Japan, just to hear African American musicians play soul music.

So it remains confounding to me that mainstream America sometimes struggles to feel that same thrill for the diversity of cultures within its own borders.

In years past, these problems were solved by assimilation. Immigrants were expected to lose their accents, forget their traditional dishes, learn English, and figure out how Americans do things.

But African Americans were barred from the larger American tradition for so long that we have built our own unique culture here. And we've been joined by a host of ethnicities, eager to join the American melting pot while keeping their own distinctive heritage alive and demanding equal treatment under the law, in media, and everywhere else.

Whenever someone tells me, in a well-meaning voice, that they don't see color, I always respond, "What's wrong with seeing my color?"

The key is that when you do see my skin color, you don't think it's a bad thing.

We've all got to teach that lesson to the media outlets we consume, rejecting the worst messages while supporting the media platforms that get it right. Let's fill Facebook pages, comments sections, and Twitter feeds with praise for outlets doing the right thing and scorn for those who choose another direction. It's not enough, in our hyper-connected world, to reject harmful messages; the best race-baiters tell the world why they've made the media choices they have and encourage others to do the same.

Keep in mind—this isn't just about people of color demanding access to a mainstream, white-dominated cultural and media space.

One of the biggest problems with talk about diversity and inclusion is that white people miss out on an important distinction: Segregation limits *them*, too.

We're hip deep in the most ambitious cultural experiment in the world's history. And a healthy dose of the right kind of race-baiting—practiced in the manner outlined in this book—might be the key to making it all work.

So let's get to it, already.

It's time to save media—and maybe even a divided America—from itself.

NOTES

INTRODUCTION

1. Bill O'Reilly, "The Culture War Rages in the Press," *The O'Reilly Factor,* Fox News Channel, Dec. 21, 2006.
2. Bill O'Reilly, *The Radio Factor,* Fox News Radio, Sept. 19, 2007.
3. Bill O'Reilly, interview with the author, Mar. 13, 2012.
4. Eric Deggans, "Add to Katrina's Toll Race-Tinged Rhetoric," *St. Petersburg Times,* Sept. 14, 2005.
5. Bill O'Reilly, "Talking Points Memo," *The O'Reilly Factor,* Fox News Channel, Sept. 8, 2005.
6. Deggans, "Add to Katrina's Toll."
7. Bill O'Reilly, "Most Ridiculous Item of the Day," *The O'Reilly Factor,* Fox News Channel, Sept. 14, 2005.
8. "Fox News Has Discussed Phony Scandal in At Least 95 Segments," Media Matters, July 16, 2010, http://mediamatters.org/research/201007160038.
9. Megyn Kelly, *America Live,* Fox News Channel, July 13, 2010.
10. Dave Weigel, "Megyn Kelly's Minstrel Show," *Atlantic,* July 14, 2010.
11. Eric Deggans, "Pat Buchanan's Dropped by MSNBC, Which Finally Acknowledges His Bigotry," The Feed (blog), *Tampa Bay Times,* Feb. 17, 2012.
12. Glenn Beck, *Fox and Friends,* Fox News Channel, July 28, 2009.
13. Glenn Beck, *Glenn Beck,* Fox News Channel, Aug. 27, 2009.
14. "Call to Service in Colorado Springs, CO," YouTube video, 26:44, speech by President Barack Obama on July 2, 2008, posted by BarackObamadotcom July 2, 2008, http://www.youtube.com/watch?v=Df2p6867_pw&eurl=http://volokh.com/posts/1216451854.shtml.
15. Glenn Beck, "The Glenn Beck Program," Premiere Radio Networks, Aug. 8, 2011.
16. Chris Ariens, "FNC Responds to Glenn Beck Calling Pres. Obama a 'Racist,'" TVNewser (blog), Mediabistro, July 28, 2009, http://www.mediabistro.com/tvnewser/fnc-responds-to-glenn-beck-calling-pres-obama-a-racist_b27714.
17. Andrew Breitbart, "Video Proof: The NAACP Awards Racism—2010," Big Government.com, July 19, 2010, http://biggovernment.com/abreitbart/2010/07/19/video-proof-the-naacp-awards-racism2010/.
18. "Shirley Sherrod: the FULL Video," YouTube video, 43:15, from a video originally broadcast on DCTV in DeKalb county (GA) in March 2010, posted by naacp videos, July 20, 2010, http://www.youtube.com/watch?v=E9NcCa_KjXk.
19. Ashley Hayes, "Former USDA Employee Sues Conservative Blogger over Video Posting," CNN.com, Feb. 15, 2011, http://www.cnn.com/2011/POLITICS/02/14/sherrod.lawsuit/index.html.

20. Andrew Breitbart, interview with the author, Jan. 28, 2012.
21. Eric Deggans, "NPR's White Noise," *St. Petersburg Times,* Apr. 3, 2005.
22. Ron Rodrigues, *Public Radio Today 2011: How America Listens to Radio* (Columbia, MD: Arbitron, July 2011).
23. John F. Harris and Jim Vandehei, "The Age of Rage," *Politico,* July 23, 2010, http://www.politico.com/news/stories/0710/40146.html.
24. Lacey Rose, "Glenn Beck Inc.," *Forbes,* Apr. 26, 2010.
25. Dorothy Pomerantz, "The Celebrity 100," *Forbes,* May 16, 2012.
26. Howard Kurtz, "Keith Olbermann Quits Countdown," *Daily Beast,* Jan. 21, 2011, http://www.thedailybeast.com/articles/2011/01/21/keith-olbermann-quits-msnbcs-countdown.html.
27. Marisa Guthrie, "The Confessions of Keith Olbermann," *Hollywood Reporter,* June 7, 2011.
28. Paul J. Gough, "Bill O'Reilly Reups at Fox News for $10 Million a Year," *Hollywood Reporter,* Oct. 23, 2008.
29. Fox News Channel, "Bill O'Reilly Re-Signs with Fox News for Multi-Year Deal," press release, Apr. 24, 2012.
30. *Huffington Post,* "AOL Agrees to Acquire the *Huffington Post,*" press release, Feb. 7, 2011, http://www.huffingtonpost.com/2011/02/07/aol-huffington-post_n_819375.html.
31. "3rd Annual TV News Trust Poll," Public Policy Polling, Jan. 18, 2012; Jesse Holcomb, Amy Mitchell, and Tom Rosenstiel, "The State of the News Media 2011," Pew Research Center's Project for Excellence in Journalism, Mar. 14, 2011.
32. David Leonard, interview with the author, Mar. 15, 2012.
33. Krissah Thompson, "Black Leaders Regroup to Address Widening Poverty among Black Children," *Washington Post,* Jan. 17, 2011.
34. Tami Luhby, "Big Drop in Unemployment Rate for Blacks," CNN Money, Feb. 3, 2012.
35. "Very Close Race in Both Alabama and Mississippi," Public Policy Polling, Mar. 12, 2012.
36. David Leonard, interview with the author, Mar. 15, 2012.
37. Charlie Rose, "A Conversation with Comedian Stephen Colbert," *Charlie Rose,* PBS, Dec. 8, 2006.
38. Raphael Canet, Laurent Pech, and Maura Stewart, "France's Burning Issue: Understanding the Urban Riots of 2005," Social Science Research Network, Nov. 18, 2008.
39. Bill O'Reilly, "Talking Points Memo," *The O'Reilly Factor,* Fox News Channel, July 23, 2010.
40. Ibid.

CHAPTER ONE

1. Michael Kruse, "Definitions of Race Cloud Black Teen's Shooting," *Tampa Bay Times,* Mar. 21, 2012; Manuel Roig-Franzia, Tom Jackman, and Darryl Fears, "Who Is George Zimmerman?" *Washington Post,* Mar. 22, 2012.
2. Jeff Weiner, Jon Busdeker, and Martin Comas, "Thousands in Sanford Park Join Rev. Al Sharpton in Calling for Justice," *Orlando Sentinel,* Mar. 22, 2012.
3. *PoliticsNation,* NBC News, Mar. 22, 2012.
4. Ibid.
5. Kyle Hightower, "Rally Sentiment: Justice for Florida Teen's Killing," Associated Press, Mar. 23, 2012.

6. Eric Deggans, *Reliable Sources,* CNN, Mar. 25, 2012.
7. Chris Francescani, "Trayvon Martin Call Was 'Mistake, Not Deliberate': NBC," Reuters, Apr. 8, 2012.
8. Jeremy Gaines, email to the author, Mar. 25, 2012.
9. Ryan Julison, interview with the author, Apr. 14, 2012.
10. Daniel Trotta, "Trayvon Martin: Before the World Heard the Cries," Reuters, Apr. 3, 2012.
11. Frances Robles, "Sanford Police Chief Under Fire Amid Trayvon Martin Case," *Miami Herald,* Mar. 21, 2012.
12. Ryan Julison, interview with the author, Apr. 14, 2012.
13. Jesse Washington, "Trayvon Martin, My Son, and the Black Male Code," Associated Press, Mar. 24, 2012.
14. *The O'Reilly Factor,* Fox News Channel, Mar. 22, 2012.
15. M. J. Lee, "Geraldo Rivera: Trayvon Martin Killed Due to 'Hoodie,'" *Politico,* Mar. 23, 2012, http://www.politico.com/news/stories/0312/74392.html.
16. Roland Martin, "Roland Martin Goes In on Geraldo Rivera Over Hoodie Commentary," *Roland Martin Reports,* Mar. 23, 2012, http://rolandmartin reports.com/blog/2012/03/roland-martin-goes-in-on-geraldo-rivera-over -hoodie-commentary/.
17. Jeff Kunerth and Bianca Prieto, "Outrage Proves Colorblind, but Whites, Blacks Often Diverge on Larger—and More Delicate—Issues Surrounding Trayvon's Death," *Orlando Sentinel,* Mar. 25, 2012.
18. Deborah Charles, "Big Gap Between Races in U.S. on Trayvon Martin Killing," Reuters, Apr. 12, 2012.
19. Frances Robles, "Shooter of Trayvon Martin a Habitual Caller to Cops," *Miami Herald,* Mar. 17, 2012.
20. Ibid.
21. Eric Deggans, "How Do Media Images of Scary Black Males Relate to the Trayvon Martin Case?" The Feed (blog), *Tampa Bay Times,* Mar. 21, 2012.
22. Daniel Trotta, "Trayvon Martin: Before the World Heard the Cries," Reuters, Apr. 3, 2012.
23. Alicia Shepard, "The Iconic Photos of Trayvon Martin & George Zimmerman & Why You May Not See the Others," Poynter.org, Mar. 30, 2012.
24. Alex Alvarez, "Bernie Goldberg: Zimmerman Described as 'White' because Media Needs to Further Storyline," Mediaite, Mar. 27, 2012.
25. Matt Hadro, "Contrary to CNN's First Assumption, Prosecutors Say Zimmerman Didn't Use Racial Slur," NewsBusters.org, Apr. 13, 2012.
26. Matt Gutman, "George Zimmerman: Enhanced Video Shows Injury," ABCNews .com, Apr. 2, 2012.
27. John Derbyshire, "The Talk: Nonblack Version," *Taki's Magazine,* Apr. 5, 2012, http://takimag.com/article/the_talk_nonblack_version_john_derbyshire#axz z1wrs5p9mM.
28. Rich Lowry, "Parting Ways," *National Review,* Apr. 7, 2012.
29. Rich Lowry, "Regarding Robert Weissberg," *National Review,* Apr. 10, 2012.
30. Ryan Julison, interview with the author, Apr. 14, 2012.
31. Eric Deggans, "Activist Al Sharpton Makes the Leap to TV Anchor—Or Does He?" *St. Petersburg Times,* Aug. 29, 2011.
32. Brian Stelter, "Sharpton Appears to Win Anchor Spot on MSNBC," *New York Times,* July 20, 2011.
33. Jonathan Turley, "Report: MSNBC Close to Naming Al Sharpton Host of Prime Time Show," JonathanTurley.org (blog), July 19, 2011, http://jonathan

turley.org/2011/07/19/report-msnbc-close-to-naming-al-sharpton-host-of
-prime-time-show/.

34. Ibid.
35. Richard Prince, "MSNBC Reported Ready to Hire Sharpton," Richard Prince's
    Journal-isms, July 21, 2011, http://mije.org/richardprince/msnbc-reported-ready
    -hire-sharpton.
36. Eric Deggans, *Reliable Sources,* CNN, Aug. 7, 2011.
37. Eric Deggans, "Rev. Al Sharpton on Starting His News MSNBC Anchor Job: I
    Don't Think It Was That Big a Leap," The Feed (blog), *Tampa Bay Times,* Aug. 29,
    2011, http://www.tampabay.com/blogs/media/content/rev-al-sharpton-starting
    -his-new-msnbc-anchor-job-tonight-i-dont-think-it-was-big-leap.
38. "Sharpton Says His New Show Is 'The New Battlefield,'" *Loop 21.com,* Aug. 23, 2011,
    http://www.loop21.com/content/sharptons-says-his-new-show-new-battlefield.
39. Ibid.
40. Chris Matthews, *Hardball,* MSNBC, July 25, 2008.
41. Matea Gold, "Fox News Yanks Sean Hannity from Tea Party Rally He Was Set to
    Star In," *Los Angeles Times,* Apr. 15, 2010.
42. National Action Network, "National Action Network (NAN), Along with Labor
    and Civil Rights Leaders to Attack Joblessness and Voter ID Laws That Are Threat-
    ening People's Voter Rights across the Country on December 9th in 25-City Rally
    for Jobs and Justice," press release, Dec. 7, 2011, http://nationalactionnetwork
    .net/press/national-action-network-nan-rev-al-sharpton-labor-leaders-com
    munity-activists-to-lead-rallies-in-over-25-cities-on-december-9th-for-jobs
    -and-justice/.
43. Rev. Al Sharpton, "From Wall Street to Washington, We March for Jobs and
    Justice," *Huffington Post,* Oct. 11, 2011, http://www.huffingtonpost.com/rev-al
    -sharpton/from-wall-street-to-washi_b_1004455.html.
44. Phil Griffin, interview with the author, Jan. 2012.
45. Eric Deggans, "Activist Al Sharpton Makes the Leap to TV Anchor."
46. "Newsroom Policies Vary on Campaign Donations," MSNBC.com, June 21, 2007,
    http://www.msnbc.msn.com/id/19178161/#.TxssSIH4Jc0.
47. Al Sharpton, interview with the author, Aug. 2011.
48. Pew Research Center, "Press Widely Criticized, but Trusted More Than Other
    Information Sources," Sept. 22, 2011, http://www.people-press.org/2011/09/22
    /press-widely-criticized-but-trusted-more-than-other-institutions/1/.
49. Ibid.
50. Ibid.
51. Ibid.
52. Ibid.
53. Frank Newport, "Record High Anti-Incumbent Sentiment toward Congress,"
    Gallup.com, Dec. 9 2011, http://www.gallup.com/poll/151433/record-high-anti
    -incumbent-sentiment-toward-congress.aspx.
54. Pew Research Center, "Press Widely Criticized."
55. Ibid.
56. David Frum, "When Did the GOP Lose Touch with Reality?" *New York,* Nov. 20,
    2011.
57. David Frum, "Waterloo," FrumForum.com, Mar. 21, 2010, http://www.frum
    forum.com/waterloo.
58. Frum, "When Did the GOP Lose Touch."
59. Ibid.
60. Ibid.

61. David Frum, *Reliable Sources,* CNN, Dec. 11, 2011.

62. Tom Jensen, "Fox Leads for Trust," Public Policy Polling (blog), Jan. 26, 2010.

63. "For Second Straight Year, PBS Most Trusted Name in News," Public Policy Polling, Jan. 17, 2012.

64. "3rd Annual TV News Trust Poll," Public Policy Polling, Jan. 18, 2012.

65. Ibid.

66. Eric Deggans, "An Unlikely Homesteader in Scarborough Country," *St. Petersburg Times,* June 14, 2003.

67. Ibid.

68. Eric Deggans, "Pride and Prejudice," *St. Petersburg Times,* Apr. 25, 2003.

69. Ibid.

70. Ibid.

71. Joe Scarborough, interview with the author, July 2008.

72. Lawrence O'Donnell, interview with the author, July 2010.

73. Bill O'Reilly, "Talking Points Memo," *The O'Reilly Factor,* Fox News Channel, Dec. 6, 2004.

74. Megyn Kelly and Kirsten Powers, *America Live,* Fox News Channel, July 13, 2010.

75. Howard Kurtz, "Roger's Reality Show," *Newsweek,* Sept. 25, 2011.

76. Chris Wallace, "Interview with Jon Stewart," *Fox News Sunday,* June 19, 2011.

77. Ibid.

78. Chris Wallace, *Fox News Sunday,* June 26, 2011.

79. Ibid.

80. Juan Williams, *Muzzled* (New York: Crown, 2011), 28.

81. Juan Williams, interview with the author, Sept. 2011.

82. Ibid.

83. Ibid.

84. Society of Professional Journalists, *SPJ Code of Ethics,* http://www.spj.org/ethics code.asp.

CHAPTER TWO

1. Andrew Breitbart, interview with the author, Jan. 28, 2012.

2. Alyssa Newcomb, "Andrew Breitbart Died of Heart Failure: Coroner," ABC News, Apr. 21, 2012.

3. Jim Yardley, "After a Decade, Brawley Reappears and Repeats Charges," *New York Times,* Dec. 3, 1997.

4. "U.S. Files Hate Crime Charges in Fatal Rundown of Black Man in Miss.," Associated Press, Mar. 22, 2012.

5. Andrew Breitbart, interview with the author, Jan. 28, 2012.

6. Andrew Breitbart, *Righteous Indignation* (New York: Hachette Book Group, 2011), 3.

7. Amelia Arsenault, interview with the author, Apr. 2012.

8. Andrew Breitbart, interview with the author, Jan. 28, 2012.

9. California Department of Justice, "Report of the Attorney General on the Activities of ACORN in California," Apr. 1, 2010.

10. Howard Kurtz, "Discussion of ACORN Story," *Reliable Sources,* Sept. 20, 2009.

11. California Department of Justice, "Report of the Attorney General."

12. Andrew Breitbart, "The Politicized Art behind the ACORN Plan," *Washington Times,* Sept. 21, 2009.

13. Glenn Beck, *Glenn Beck,* Fox News Channel, Sept. 30, 2008.

14. Rush Limbaugh, "ACORN's Aim: Chaos at the Polls," RushLimbaugh.com, Oct. 14, 2008, http://www.rushlimbaugh.com/daily/2008/10/14/acorn_s_aim_chaos _at_the_polls.
15. Jess Henig, "ACORN Accusations," FactCheck.org, Oct. 18, 2008.
16. Ian Urbina, "ACORN on Brink of Bankruptcy, Officials Say," *New York Times*, Mar. 19, 2010.
17. Ibid.
18. Andrew Breitbart, interview with the author, Jan. 28, 2012.
19. "ACORN Closing in Wake of Scandal," Associated Press, Mar. 22, 2010.
20. "Extended Definition: Decision Making," *Webster's Online Dictionary*, http:// www.websters-online-dictionary.org/definitions/Decision%20Making.
21. Breitbart, *Righteous Indignation*, 36, 40, 42, 162.
22. Nadia Naffe, "My Time as an Accomplice to Convicted Criminal James O'Keefe," NadiaNaffe.com, Mar. 14, 2012.
23. Tom Rosenstiel, interview with the author, Mar. 2012.
24. Martha T. Moore, "NPR Sting Raises Questions about Media Ethics, Influence," *USA Today*, Mar. 17, 2011.
25. Chris Harris, "Harassment Complaint against Westwood Muckraker Dismissed," *New Jersey Record*, Dec. 21, 2011.
26. Sean Hannity, interview with guests Ben Shapiro, Joel Pollak, Juan Williams, and Michelle Malkin, *Hannity*, Fox News Channel, Mar. 7, 2012.
27. Ibid.
28. Soledad O'Brien, interview with Joel Pollak, *Starting Point*, CNN, Mar. 8, 2012.
29. Laura S. Abrams and Jene Moio, "Critical Race Theory and the Cultural Competence Dilemma in Social Work Education," *Journal of Social Work Education*, Spring/Summer 2009.
30. Robert Delgado, interview with the author, Mar. 2012.
31. Soledad O'Brien, interview with Dorothy Brown, *Starting Point*, CNN, Mar. 12, 2012.
32. Robert Delgado, interview with the author, Mar. 2012.
33. Carl McClendon, "A Modern Racial Rebel," *St. Petersburg Times*, Sept. 18, 1994.
34. Ibid.
35. Twitchy, "Michelle Malkin Launches Cutting-Edge Twitter Curation Website," press release, Mar. 7, 2012, http://twitchy.com/press-release/.
36. Andrew Golis, "The Story behind the Obama Law School Speech Video," PBS.org, Mar. 7, 2012.
37. David Folkenflik, "A Scoop, Really? BuzzFeed, Breitbart.com Spar for Credit on Obama Video," NPR.org, Mar. 8, 2012.
38. Andrew Breitbart, interview with the author, Jan. 28, 2012.
39. Ari Rabin-Havt, interview with the author, Mar. 2012.
40. Ibid.
41. Brooks Barnes, Emily Steel, and Sarah McBride, "In a Blur, Watchdogs, Blogs, Email Spur Radio Host's Firing," *Wall Street Journal*, Apr. 13, 2007.
42. David Bauder, "Radio Campaign Next Step against Limbaugh," Associated Press, Mar. 22, 2012.
43. Bill Maher, "Please Stop Apologizing," *New York Times*, Mar. 22, 2012.
44. Ari Rabin-Havt, interview with the author, Mar. 2012.
45. Janie Lorber, "American Bridge 21st Century Super PAC Is Hub of Left," *Roll Call*, Feb. 13, 2012.
46. Tucker Carlson, Vince Coglianese, Alex Pappas, and Will Rahn, "Inside Media Matters: Sources, Memos Reveal Erratic Behavior, Close Coordination with White House and News Organizations," *Daily Caller*, Feb. 12, 2012.

47. Jack Shafer, "Media Madders," Reuters, Feb. 14, 2012, http://blogs.reuters.com/jackshafer/2012/02/15/media-madders/.

48. Tucker Carlson, interview with the author, Mar. 2012.

49. Ibid.

50. Pew Research Center's Project for Excellence in Journalism, "How the Press Reported the 2008 General Election," Oct. 22, 2008.

51. Eric Deggans, "In the Absence of Facts, Trayvon Martin Case Becomes a War of Images and Reputations Online," The Feed (blog), *Tampa Bay Times*, Mar. 27, 2012.

52. Dan Linehan, "Was Trayvon Martin a Drug Dealer?" Wagist.com, Mar. 25, 2012.

53. Michael Brendan Dougherty, "Why Lots of People Think the Media Is Wrong about the Trayvon Martin Case," BusinessInsider.com, Mar. 26, 2012.

54. Pew Research Center's Project for Excellence in Journalism, "How Blogs, Twitter and Mainstream Media Handled the Trayvon Martin Case," Mar. 30, 2012.

55. Meenal Vamburkar, "Tucker Carlson Clashes with Alan Colmes over Trayvon Case: 'Professional Race-Baiting' Is 'Foolish,'" Mediaite, Mar. 28, 2012.

56. Byron Tau, "Obama: 'If I Had a Son He'd Look Like Trayvon,'" *Politico*, Mar. 23, 2012.

57. Eric Deggans, "The Joys of Seeing an Anchor Sink," *St. Petersburg Times*, Sept. 26, 2004.

58. Tim Graham, interview with the author, Mar. 2012.

59. Kyle Drennen, "NBC Keeps Up Drumbeat of GOP 'War against Women's Health,'" NewsBusters.org, Mar. 21, 2012.

60. Tim Graham, interview with the author, Mar. 2012.

61. Tucker Carlson, interview with the author, Mar. 2012.

CHAPTER THREE

1. Andrew Breitbart, "Video Proof: The NAACP Awards Racism—2010," Big Government.com, July 19, 2010, http://biggovernment.com/abreitbart/2010/07/19/video-proof-the-naacp-awards-racism2010/.

2. Ibid.

3. Ibid.

4. Bill O'Reilly, "Talking Points Memo," *The O'Reilly Factor,* Fox News Channel, July 20, 2010, http://www.billoreilly.com/show?action=viewTVShow&showID=2649.

5. Jon Morgan, "Old and News Media Both Make News, but the Economy Tops the Agenda," Pew Research Center's Project for Excellence in Journalism, July 2010, http://www.journalism.org/index_report/pej_news_coverage_index_july_1925.

6. "Shirley Sherrod: the FULL Video," YouTube video, 43:15, from a video originally broadcast on DCTV in DeKalb county (GA) in March 2010, posted by naacp videos, July 20, 2010, http://www.youtube.com/watch?v=E9NcCa_KjXk.

7. Ibid.

8. Eric Deggans, "Tired in Private but Feisty Onstage, Ousted USDA Official Shirley Sherrod Vows to Educate President Obama and Sue Andrew Breitbart," The Feed (blog), *Tampa Bay Times,* July 29, 2010, http://www.tampabay.com/blogs/media/2010/07/tired-in-private-but-feisty-onstage-ousted-usda-official-shirley-sherrod-vows-to-educate-president-o.html.

9. Benjamin Todd Jealous, "NAACP Statement on Shirley Sherrod," NAACP.org, July 20, 2010, http://action.naacp.org/page/s/sherrodvid?source=youtube&subsource=sherrodvid_desc&utm_source=youtube&utm_medium=video&utm_campaign=ytubesherrodvid_desc.

10. "Shirley Sherrod to Sue Andrew Breitbart," CNN.com, July 29, 2010, http://cnn.com/video/?/video/politics/2010/07/29/sot.sherrod.suing.nabj.cnn; Jim Kavanagh, "Sherrod's Steadfast Motto: 'Let's Work Together,'" CNN.com, July 22, 2010, http://edition.cnn.com/2010/POLITICS/07/21/sherrod.profile/.

11. Louis Jacobson, "Fox News' Handling of Sherrod Story Defended by 'Weekly Standard's' Stephen Hayes," PolitiFact.com, July 26, 2010, http://www.politifact.com/truth-o-meter/statements/2010/jul/26/stephen-hayes/stephen-hayes-defends-fox-handling-sherrod-story/.

12. Deggans, "Tired in Private but Feisty Onstage."

13. Howard Kurtz, "Ousted Official Shirley Sherrod Blamed Fox, but Other Outlets Ran with Story," *Washington Post,* July 22, 2010.

14. Ibid.

15. Ibid.

16. Michael Calderone, "Fox's Beck: Obama Is a Racist," *Politico,* July 28, 2009, http://www.politico.com/blogs/michaelcalderone/0709/Foxs_Beck_Obama_is_a_racist.html.

17. Scott Wilson and Garance Franke-Ruta, "White House Advisor Van Jones Resigns Amid Controversy over Past Activism," *Washington Post,* Sept. 6, 2009.

18. Bill O'Reilly, "Talking Points Memo," *The O'Reilly Factor,* Fox News Channel, July 20, 2010, http://video.foxnews.com/v/4288013/.

19. Ibid.

20. "Shirley Sherrod to Sue Andrew Breitbart."

21. Bill O'Reilly, "Talking Points Memo," *The O'Reilly Factor,* Fox News Channel, July 21, 2010.

22. "Shirley Sherrod to Sue Andrew Breitbart."

23. Ibid.

24. Andrew Breitbart, interview with the author, Jan. 28, 2012.

25. "Timeline of Breitbart's Sherrod Smear," Media Matters, July 22, 2010, http://mediamatters.org/research/201007220004.

26. Andrew Breitbart, interview with the author, Apr. 2011.

27. Ibid.

28. Ibid.

29. Helen Kennedy, "Tea Party Express Leader Mark Williams Kicked Out Over 'Colored People' Letter," *New York Daily News,* July 18, 2010.

30. Rachel Slajda, "Breitbart on Sherrod's NAACP Speech: 'I Did Not Edit This Thing,'" TPMMuckraker, July 20, 2010.

31. Richard Huff, "Fox News Set to Make Ratings Milestone with Ten Years Atop the Nielsen Charts," *New York Daily News,* Jan. 30, 2012.

32. Mackenzie Carpenter, "Ex-Pirates Minor Leaguer, Eric Bolling, Talks Bucks on Fox," *Pittsburgh Post-Gazette,* July 25, 2010.

33. Paul Farhi, "Don Imus Is Fired by CBS Radio," *Washington Post,* Apr. 13, 2007; "Lou Dobbs to Quit CNN," Media Decoder (blog), *New York Times,* Nov. 11, 2009.

34. Eric Bolling, "Bolling's Bullets," *Follow the Money,* Fox Business News, May 23, 2011.

35. Steve Benen, "Fox's Bolling Frets over Hoodlums in the Hizzouse," Political Animal (blog), *Washington Monthly,* June 12, 2011.

36. Ibid.

37. Aliyah Shahid, "Eric Bolling Fox Business Host Apologizes for Racist Obama in the Hizzouse Comments," *New York Daily News,* June 14, 2011.

38. Glenn Beck, interview, *Fox News Sunday,* Fox New Channel, Aug. 29, 2010.

39. John L. Allen Jr., "Key Principles of Liberation Theology," *National Catholic Reporter,* June 2, 2000.

40. Jeff Brumley, "Black Theologian Talks about Liberation and Religion," *Florida Times-Union,* Feb. 8, 2012.

41. Brian Ross and Rehab El-Buri, "Obama's Pastor: God Damn America, U.S. to Blame for 9/11," ABC News, Mar. 13, 2008; Sean Hannity, "Obama's Pastor: Rev. Jeremiah Wright," *Hannity and Colmes,* Fox News Channel, Mar. 1, 2007.

42. Glenn Beck, "Liberation Theology and the Political Perversion of Christianity," *Glenn Beck,* Fox News Channel, July 13, 2010.

43. Ibid.

44. Howard Kurtz, "Roger's Reality Show," *Newsweek,* Sept. 25, 2011.

45. Pew Research Center, "Press Widely Criticized, but Trusted More than Other Information Sources," Pew Research Center for the People and the Press, Sept. 22, 2011.

46. Brian Stelter, "Fox Business Makes Over Its Prime Time Lineup," *New York Times,* Feb. 9, 2012.

47. Alex Alvarez, "Eric Bolling Tells Maxine Waters: 'Step Away from the Crack Pipe,'" Mediaite, Feb. 16, 2012.

48. Tim Mak, "Fox Host Walks Back 'Crack' Crack," *Politico,* Feb. 16, 2012.

49. James Crugnale, "Brent Bozell: You Might Want to Say President Obama Looks Like a Skinny Ghetto Crackhead," Mediaite, Dec. 23, 2011, http://www.mediaite .com/tv/brent-bozell-you-might-want-to-say-president-obama-looks-like-a -%E2%80%98skinny-ghetto-crackhead%E2%80%99/; Eric Deggans, "Add to Katrina's Toll Race Related Rhetoric," *St. Petersburg Times,* Sept. 14, 2005.

50. "Americans Spending More Time Following the News," Pew Research Center for People and the Press, Sept. 12, 2010.

51. Ibid.

52. Danny Shea, "Fox News Audience Just 1.38% Black," *Huffington Post,* July 26, 2010, http://www.huffingtonpost.com/2010/07/26/fox-news-audience-just-13_n _659800.html.

53. Ibid.

54. Ratings figures supplied by the Nielsen Company.

55. Robert P. Jones, Daniel Cox, E.J. Dionne Jr., and William A. Galston, *What It Means to Be an American, Attitudes in an Increasingly Diverse America Ten Years after 9/11,* Brookings Institution, Sept. 6, 2011.

56. Ibid.

57. Ibid.

58. Pew Research Center for People and the Press, "Americans Spending More Time Watching the News," Sept. 12, 2010.

59. Michael Wolff, *The Man Who Owns the News* (New York: Random House, 2008), 45; Jesse Holcomb, Amy Mitchell, and Tom Rosenstiel, "The State of the News Media 2011," Project for Excellence in Journalism, Mar. 14, 2011.

60. Tom Junod, "Why Does Roger Ailes Hate America?" *Esquire,* Jan. 18, 2011.

61. Rick Perlstein, *Nixonland: The Rise of a President and the Fracturing of America* (New York: Scribner, 2008), 331.

62. Josh Barbanel, "Roger Ailes: Master Maker of Fiery Political Darts," *New York Times,* Oct. 17, 1989.

63. Kaaryn Gustafson, *Cheating Welfare: Public Assistance and the Criminalization of Poverty* (New York: New York University Press, 2011), 35.

64. Bernard Weinraub, "Campaign Trail; A Beloved Mug Shot for the Bush Forces," *New York Times,* Oct. 3, 1988.

65. Tali Mendelberg, *The Race Card: Campaign Strategy, Implicit Messages and the Norm of Equality* (Princeton, N.J.: Princeton University Press, 2001), 142.

66. Jane Hall, "CNBC Chief No Stranger to the Tube," *Los Angeles Times*, Oct. 18, 1993.

67. "Rush Limbaugh TV—Bo Snerdly as Maya Angelou," YouTube video, 4:25, from a segment originally aired on *Rush Limbaugh The TV Show* on Jan. 21, 1993, posted by ConservatismAlive on May 13, 2009, http://www.youtube.com /watch?v=VJYkn_irWeg.

68. Rush Limbaugh, "Rush and Roger Ailes Speak at Boy Scouts Awards Dinner," RushLimbaugh.com, Nov. 11, 2009, http://www.rushlimbaugh.com/daily/2009 /11/11/rush_and_roger_ailes_speak_at_boy_scouts_awards_dinner.

69. Junod, "Why Does Roger Ailes Hate America?"

70. Eric Alterman, *What Liberal Media?* (New York: Basic Books, 2003), 2.

71. Michele McPhee and Sara Just, "Obama: Police 'Acted Stupidly' in Gates Case," ABC News, July 22, 2009.

72. Ibid.

73. Emily Guskin, Mahvish Shahid Khan, and Amy Mitchell, "Media, Race and Obama's First Year," Journalism.org, July 26, 2010, http://www.journalism.org /analysis_report/media_race_and_obama%E2%80%99s_first_year.

74. Pew Research Center, "Obama's Ratings Slide Across the Board," People-Press .org, July 30, 2009, http://www.people-press.org/2009/07/30/section-2-henry -louis-gates-jrs-arrest/.

75. Bill O'Reilly, "Discussion with Geraldo Rivera," *The O'Reilly Factor*, Fox News Channel, July 30, 2009.

76. Eric Deggans, "Fox News, Pat Buchanan Get Thumbs Down," The Feed (blog), *Tampa Bay Times*, July 25, 2008, http://www.tampabay.com/blogs/media/2008 /07/fox-news-and-pa.html.

77. "Racism," Oxford American Dictionaries, 2010.

78. "Colmes Claimed that Imus 'Satirized' Rutgers Women's Basketball Team," Media Matters, Oct. 17, 2007, http://mediamatters.org/research/200710170004.

79. David Carr, "With Imus, They Keep Coming Back," *New York Times*, Apr. 9, 2007.

80. Bob Garfield and Brooke Gladstone, "Morning Sickness: Transcript," *On the Media*, NPR, Apr. 13, 2007.

81. Bill O'Reilly, "Talking Points Memo," *The O'Reilly Factor*, Fox News Channel, Apr. 8, 2008.

82. Monica Williams, "Colorblind Ideology Is a Form of Racism," *Psychology Today*, Dec. 27, 2011.

83. Ronald Brownstein, "The Next America," *National Journal*, Mar. 31, 2011.

CHAPTER FOUR

1. Juan Williams, interview with the author, Feb. 2012.

2. Jeremy W. Peters, "If Reply Was Spontaneous, the Question Was Not," *New York Times*, Jan. 19, 2012.

3. Juan Williams, interview with the author, Feb. 2012.

4. Karen Tumulty, "Newt Gingrich Wins South Carolina Primary," *Washington Post*, Jan. 21, 2012.

5. Juan Williams, interview with the author, Feb. 2012.

6. Tali Mendelberg, interview with the author, Feb. 2012.

7. Dylan Byers, "What Newt Said about Food Stamps," *Politico*, Jan. 6, 2012.

8. Dave Weigel, interview with the author, Jan. 2012.

9. Byers, "What Newt Said about Food Stamps."

10. Howard Kurtz, interview with the author, Feb. 2012.

11. Ted Robbins, "Santorum's Support Builds Ahead of Iowa Caucuses," NPR.org, Jan. 2, 2012.

12. Edward Schumacher-Matos, "Santorum, Race and the Limits of Journalistic Fairness," NPR.org, Jan. 18, 2012.

13. John King, "Interview with Rick Santorum," USA (blog), CNN.com, Jan. 4, 2012.

14. Schumacher-Matos, "Santorum, Race and the Limits."

15. Keith Woods, interview with the author, Feb. 2012.

16. Dan Rather, interview with the author, Jan. 31, 2012.

17. Jerry Markon and Alice Crites, "Paul Pursued Strategy of Publishing Controversial Newsletters, Associates Say," *Washington Post,* Jan. 27, 2012.

18. Dan Rather, interview with the author, Jan. 31, 2012.

19. Studio 20 NYU, "The GOP Debates, What Questions Do Journalists Like to Ask?" *Guardian,* Feb. 16, 2012.

20. Jay Rosen, interview with the author, Mar. 2012.

21. Linda Tropp, interview with the author, Nov. 2008.

22. Dave Weigel, interview with the author, Jan. 2012.

23. Dave Weigel, interview with the author, Mar. 28, 2012.

24. Dave Weigel, "Newt Gingrich's Dog Whistle, Now Audible to Anyone Who's Ever Seen a Dog," *Slate,* Mar. 23, 2012.

25. Lucy Madison, "Santorum Targets Blacks in Entitlement Reform," CBSNews.com, Jan. 2, 2012.

26. Juan Williams, interview with the author, Feb. 2012.

27. Julie Burton, interview with the author, Feb. 23, 2012.

28. Rachel Joy Larris and Rosalie Maggio, "The Women's Media Center's Media Guide to Gender Neutral Coverage of Women Candidates and Politicians," Women's Media Center, Mar. 2012.

29. Ibid.

30. Ibid.

31. Julie Burton, interview with the author, Feb. 23, 2012.

32. Eric Deggans, "Why Are So Many Bigshot Political Reporters Apologizing Now?" *Huffington Post,* Feb. 14, 2008.

33. Ken Layne, "Sarah Palin's Advice for Lady Politicians: Ignore Mean Old Media," Wonkette.com, July 5, 2009.

34. "Sarah Palin: *Newsweek* Cover Showing My Legs, Sexist," *Huffington Post,* Nov. 17, 2009.

35. Diana Carlin and Kelly Winfrey, "Have You Come a Long Way Baby? Hillary Clinton, Sarah Palin, and Sexism in 2008 Campaign Coverage," *Communication Studies,* Sept./Oct. 2009.

36. Julie Burton, interview with the author, Feb. 23, 2012.

37. Brent Bozell, "Stop the High-Tech Lynching of Herman Cain," NewsBusters.org, Oct. 31, 2011.

38. Ta-Nehisi Coates, "On Looking Like a Ghetto Crackhead," *Atlantic,* Jan. 20, 2012.

39. Eric Deggans, "Is This a High Tech Lynching? Hardly," *St. Petersburg Times,* Nov. 6, 2011.

40. Ann Coulter, *Demonic: How the Liberal Mob Is Endangering America* (New York: Crown Forum, 2011), 173.

41. Brent Bozell, "Omnipresent Obama," Creators.com, Sept. 23, 2009.

42. Kevin Liptak, "Cain: Racism Not Holding Anyone Back," CNN.com, Oct. 9, 2011.

43. Michael Norton and Samuel Sommers, "Jockeying for Stigma," *New York Times*, May 22, 2011.
44. Ashley Killough, "Cain Charges Some in the Black Community of Racism," CNN.com, Oct. 11, 2011.
45. Wolf Blitzer, interview with Herman Cain, *The Situation Room*, CNN, Sept. 28, 2011.
46. Tali Mendelberg, interview with the author, Feb. 2012.
47. Tali Mendelberg, Jane Junn, and Erica Czaja, "Race and the Group Bases of Public Opinion," *New Directions in Public Opinion*, May 25, 2011.
48. H. Roy Kaplan, interview with the author, Nov. 2008.
49. Eric Deggans, "President Obama's Birther Announcement Reveals Bitter Truths about Politics, Media and Race Relations," The Feed (blog), *Tampa Bay Times*, Apr. 27, 2011.
50. Eric Deggans, "Let's, Um, Try Talking about Race," *St. Petersburg Times*, Nov. 30, 2008.

CHAPTER FIVE

1. Jaimie Etkin, "People's Choice Awards 2012," *Huffington Post*, Jan. 12, 2012.
2. Transcript, *2 Broke Girls* press conference, Television Critics Association summer press tour, Jan. 11, 2012.
3. Josef Adalian, "CBS Exec Says *2 Broke Girls* Will Be Dimensionalized," *New York*, Jan. 11, 2012, http://nymag.com/daily/entertainment/2012/01/2-broke-girls-less -racist-cbs.html.
4. Alan Sepinwall, interview with the author, Mar. 2012.
5. Eric Deggans, "Does CBS' *Rob* and *2 Broke Girls* Prove Stereotypes Are Back in Primetimes, Long as You're Not Black?" The Feed (blog), *Tampa Bay Times*, Jan. 12, 2012, http://www.tampabay.com/blogs/media/content/does-cbs-rob-and-2 -broke-girls-prove-stereotypes-are-back-primetime-long-youre-not-black.
6. Eric Deggans, "Why Do So Few Black or Brown Actors Snag Lead Network TV Roles?" *St. Petersburg Times*, Nov. 14, 2010.
7. Ibid.
8. "In Face of Threats, Fox and CBS Join Pledge to Promote Diversity," *New York Times*, Feb. 4, 2000.
9. Josh Reims, interview with the author, July 2010.
10. Don Reo, interview with the author, Aug. 2010.
11. Ibid.
12. "*Undercovers* Review Revue," Speakeasy (blog), *Wall Street Journal*, Sept. 22, 2010, http://blogs.wsj.com/speakeasy/2010/09/22/undercovers-review-revue/.
13. Bill Carter, "NBC Cancels *Undercovers*," Arts Beat (blog), *New York Times*, Nov. 4, 2010, http://artsbeat.blogs.nytimes.com/2010/11/04/nbc-cancels-undercovers/.
14. Christina Radish, "J.J. Abrams Talks," Collider.com, Jan. 12, 2011, http://collider .com/j-j-abrams-interview-star-trek-2-super-8/69744/.
15. Shawn Ryan, interview with the author, Jan. 13, 2012.
16. "Blair Underwood Filmography," Internet Movie Data Base, http://www.imdb .com/name/nm0005516/.
17. Blair Underwood, interview with the author, July 2010.
18. Ibid.
19. Rakesh Kochhar, Richard Fry, and Paul Taylor, "Wealth Gaps Rise to Record Highs between Whites, Blacks, Hispanics," Pew Research Center, July 26, 2011, http://www.pewsocialtrends.org/2011/07/26/wealth-gaps-rise-to-record-highs -between-whites-blacks-hispanics/.

20. Eric Deggans, "Shirley Sherrod's Public Fight against Racism May Help Us All," *St. Petersburg Times*, Aug. 1, 2010.
21. Marlon Riggs (director/producer), *Color Adjustment*, California Newsreel/PBS, 1992.
22. Ibid.
23. Donald Bogle, *Primetime Blues: African Americans on Network Television* (New York: Farrar, Straus and Giroux, 2001), 20, 31.
24. Riggs, *Color Adjustment*.
25. Bogle, *Primetime Blues*, 7.
26. Ibid., 115, 142.
27. Aniko Bodroghkozy, "Race, Gender and Contested Meanings," in *Critiquing the Sitcom: A Reader*, ed. Joanne Moreale (Syracuse, NY: Syracuse University Press, 2002), 138.
28. Christopher John Farley, "That Old Black Magic," *Time*, Nov. 27, 2000.
29. Riggs, *Color Adjustment*.
30. Ibid.
31. Catherine Squires, *African Americans and the Media* (Boston: Polity, 2009), 221.
32. Pamala Deane, "Sanford and Son," Museum of Broadcast Communications, http://www.museum.tv/eotvsection.php?entrycode=sanfordands.
33. Eric Deggans, "The Struggle to Get Past Stereotypes," *St. Petersburg Times*, July 22, 2001.
34. Ibid.
35. Eric Deggans, "Revisiting *Roots*," *St. Petersburg Times*, Jan. 18, 2002.
36. *Roots: Celebrating 25 Years*, press materials, NBC, 2002.
37. Deggans, "Revisiting *Roots*."
38. Ibid.
39. *Roots: Celebrating 25 Years*.
40. Ibid.
41. Ibid.
42. Tim Brooks and Earle Marsh, *The Complete Directory to Prime Time Network and Cable TV Shows* (New York: Ballantine, 2007), 288.
43. Warren Littlefield with T. R. Pearson, *Top of the Rock: Inside the Rise and Fall of Must See TV* (New York: Doubleday, 2012), 46.
44. Darnell M. Hunt, "The Cosby Show," Museum of Broadcast Communications, http://www.museum.tv/eotvsection.php?entrycode=cosbyshowt.
45. Eric Deggans, "Behind Bill Cosby's Punchlines Is a Man with a Message," *St. Petersburg Times*, Mar. 21, 2010.
46. Brooks and Marsh, *Complete Directory to Prime Time*, 357, 503.
47. Kristal Brent Zook, *Color by Fox* (New York: Oxford University Press, 1999), 4.
48. Brooks and Marsh, *Complete Directory to Prime Time*, 1616.
49. Zook, *Color by Fox*, 4.
50. Deggans, "The Struggle to Get Past Stereotypes."
51. Brooks and Marsh, *Complete Directory to Prime Time*, 1621.
52. Robert Seidman, "Cable Debut of *The Game* Ranks as #1 Ad Supported Scripted Series Premiere in Cable History," TV by the Numbers, Jan. 21 2011, http://tv bythenumbers.zap2it.com/2011/01/12/cable-debut-of-the-game-ranks-as-1-ad -supported-scriptes-series-premiere-in-cable-history/78387/.
53. The Nielsen Company, "The State of the African American Consumer," Sept. 2011, http://www.nielsen.com/us/en/insights/reports-downloads/2011/state-of -the-african-american-consumer.html.
54. Eric Deggans, "For Lehane, It's Not TV, It's *The Wire*," *St. Petersburg Times*, Oct. 1, 2006.

55. Kathleen McGhee-Anderson, interview with the author, 2010.
56. "The Hollywood Writers Report: Recession and Regression," Writer's Guild of America, 2011, 5.
57. Eric Deggans, "The House that Perry Built," *St. Petersburg Times,* June 6, 2007.
58. Ibid.
59. Tom Umstead, interview with the author, Mar. 2, 2012.
60. David Zurawik, "On TV, No Longer Black and White," *Baltimore Sun,* Aug. 12, 2007.
61. The Nielsen Company, "State of the Media: U.S. TV Trends by Ethnicity," Mar. 2011.
62. Ibid.
63. Sabrina Tavernise, "Minorities Lead Growth in Biggest Cities," *New York Times,* Aug. 31, 2011.
64. Ronald Brownstein, "The Next America," *National Journal,* Mar. 31, 2011.
65. "Where We Are on TV: 2011-12," Gay and Lesbian Alliance Against Defamation, Sept. 2011.
66. Diane Farr, interview with the author, Jan. 2011.
67. Ibid.
68. Ibid.
69. Ibid.
70. Greg Braxton, "Buddy System," *Los Angeles Times,* Aug. 29, 2007.
71. Eric Deggans, "Illusion of Inclusion," *St. Petersburg Times,*" Oct. 30, 2011.
72. Shawn Ryan, interview with the author, Jan. 13, 2012.
73. Ibid.
74. Diane Farr, interview with the author, Jan. 2011.
75. Ibid.

CHAPTER SIX

1. Phil Griffin, interview with the author, Jan. 13, 2012.
2. "NABJ Issues Thumbs Down Award to Cable News Networks," NABJ.org, Jan. 6, 2012.
3. Phil Griffin, interview with the author, Jan. 13, 2012.
4. Eric Deggans, "Keith Olbermann Fired by Current TV, Host Promises Lawsuit Amid Dueling Press Releases," The Feed (blog), *Tampa Bay Times,* Mar. 30, 2012.
5. Bob Butler, "2011 NABJ Diversity Census," NABJ.org, 2011.
6. "NABJ and Rep. Bobby Rush Hosts CBC Panel on Lack of Blacks among TV Newsroom Managers," NABJ.org, Oct. 4, 2011.
7. Bob Papper, "RTDNA/Hofstra Survey Finds Mixed News for Women and Minorities in TV, Radio News," RTDNA.org, 2011.
8. "Total and Minority Newsroom Employment Declines in 2011 but Loss Continues to Stabilize," ASNE.org, Apr. 4, 2012.
9. Ibid.
10. Aly Colon, interview with the author, Apr. 7, 2012.
11. "Total and Minority Newsroom Employment Declines."
12. Ibid.
13. "NABJ Issues Challenge, Offers Assistance to Newsroom Leaders Committed to Diversity," NABJ.org, Apr. 4, 2012.
14. Melissa Harris Perry, interview with the author, Jan. 2012.
15. Don Lemon, interview with the author, Mar. 2012.
16. "Coverage of Jackson's Death Seen as Excessive," People-press.org, July 1, 2009.

17. Don Lemon, *Transparent* (Las Vegas: Farrah Gray, 2011), 182.
18. "Public's Top Stories: Whitney Houston, Election, Economy," People-press.org, Feb. 22, 2012.
19. "Whitney Houston Funeral Coverage," CNN, Feb. 18, 2012.
20. Don Lemon, interview with the author, Mar. 2012.
21. Eric Deggans, "Media 'Linsanity' Raises Question: Why Haven't We Learned from Past Fights over Race Portrayals?" The Feed (blog), *Tampa Bay Times*, Feb. 20, 2012.
22. Richard Prince, "NY Times Avoids 'Armor' Phrase in Jeremy Lin Stories," The Root.com, Feb. 23, 2012.
23. *Meet the Press*, PBS, Dec. 8, 2002.
24. Ibid.
25. *Reliable Sources*, CNN, Dec. 14, 2002.
26. Eric Deggans, "New Study Finds 'Brownout' on Sunday Talk Shows: Hispanics Underrepresented, Black People and Women Too," The Feed (blog), *Tampa Bay Times*, Feb. 10, 2012.
27. Frances Martel, "Liz Trotta: Black Anchors Covering Trayvon Martin 'Can Only Hurt Their Credibility' with Personal Stories," Mediaite, Mar. 31, 2012.
28. David Boroff and Rheana Murray, "Sex Assault in Military: 'What Did They Expect?'" *New York Daily News*, Feb. 13, 2012.
29. Martel, "Liz Trotta."
30. Don Lemon, interview with the author, Mar. 2012.
31. Lyne Pitts, interview with the author, Mar. 2012.
32. Mark Whitaker, interview with the author, Mar. 2012.
33. Ibid.
34. Eric Deggans, "CNN Suspends Roland Martin after Controversial Tweets, Raising More Questions than Answers," The Feed (blog), *Tampa Bay Times*, Feb. 8, 2012.
35. James Crugnale, "Dana Loesch Endorses Taliban Desecration by Marines: 'I'd Drop Trou and Do It Too,'" Mediaite, Jan. 13, 2012.
36. Dylan Byers, "After Remarks, CNN Stopped Booking Loesch," *Politico*, Feb. 13, 2012.
37. Mark Whitaker, interview with the author, Mar. 2012.
38. Eric Deggans, "With Debut of Melissa Harris-Perry, MSNBC Continues Slow Diversification of Anchor Ranks," The Feed (blog), *Tampa Bay Times*, Feb. 13, 2012.
39. Jesse Holcomb, Amy Mitchell, and Tom Rosenstiel, "Cable: CNN Ends Its Ratings Slide," *The State of the News Media 2012*, Project for Excellence in Journalism, Mar. 19, 2012.
40. Alex Weprin, "The Top Cable News Programs in Q1 2012 Were . . ." TVNewser (blog), Mediabistro, Mar. 28, 2012.
41. Patrick J. Buchanan, "A Brief for Whitey," Buchanan.org, Mar. 21, 2008, http://buchanan.org/blog/pjb-a-brief-for-whitey-969.
42. Amanda Terkel, "Buchanan Mocks Sotomayor for Learning English by Reading Children's Books," ThinkProgress.org, June 1, 2009.
43. Patrick J. Buchanan, "How to Handle Sonia," HumanEvents.com, July 14, 2009.
44. "Patrick Buchanan: Unrepentant Bigot," ADL.org, Feb. 27, 2012.
45. Phil Griffin, interview with the author, July 2010.
46. Patrick J. Buchanan, *Suicide of a Superpower* (New York: St. Martin's, 2011), vii.
47. Color of Change, "275,000 Call on MSNBC to Fire Pat Buchanan," press release, Nov. 9, 2011.
48. Eric Deggans, "Pat Buchanan's Dropped by MSNBC, Which Finally Acknowledges His Bigotry," The Feed (blog), *Tampa Bay Times*, Feb. 17, 2012.
49. Brian Stelter, "With Book, Buchanan Set His Fate," *New York Times*, Feb. 26, 2012.

50. Patrick Buchanan, "The New Blacklist," Buchanan.org, Feb. 16, 2012.
51. Buchanan, *Suicide of a Superpower*, 2.
52. Chris Matthews, *Hardball*, NBC News, Feb. 16, 2012.
53. *The Rachel Maddow Show*, MSNBC, July 16, 2009.
54. Patrick J. Buchanan, *Right from the Beginning* (New York: Regnery, 1990), 131.
55. Patrick Buchanan, "Whitey Need Not Apply," syndicated column, Aug. 1, 2008.
56. Juan Williams, "Racial Code Words Obscure Real Issues," *The Hill*, Jan. 30, 2012.
57. Juan Williams, interview with the author, Mar. 2012.
58. Kelly McBride, "GLAAD Creates Database of Anti-Gay Commentators," Poynter. org, Mar. 30, 2012.
59. Aaron McQuade, "Bias Is Not Balance: GLAAD Pushes for More Transparent Punditry," Mediaite, Mar. 14, 2012.

CHAPTER SEVEN

1. Rush Limbaugh, "From Kids on Bus to Kanye West: Race Rules All in Obama's America," RushLimbaugh.com, Sept. 15, 2009.
2. Rush Limbaugh, "Butt Sisters Are Safe from Newt and Rick," RushLimbaugh. com, Feb. 29, 2012.
3. David Boroff, "Rush Limbaugh: Women Who Want Health Coverage for Birth Control Should Make Sex Videos," *New York Daily News*, Mar. 2, 2012.
4. "Women's Health and Contraception Hearing," C-SPAN.org., Feb. 23, 2012, http://www.c-spanvideo.org/program/HealthandC.
5. Nicholas Graham, "Rush Limbaugh: I Love the Women's Movement, Especially When I'm Walking Behind It," *Huffington Post*, Apr. 6, 2010.
6. Zev Chafets, interview with the author, Feb. 2012.
7. Elspeth Reeve, "All the Ads Pulled from Rush Limbaugh's Show," *Atlantic Wire*, Mar. 6, 2012.
8. Dave Cook, "Obama: Rush Limbaugh Slur Disturbed Me as a Father," *Christian Science Monitor*, Mar. 6, 2012.
9. M. J. Lee, "Rush Limbaugh: Sponsors Are Like French Fries," *Politico*, Mar. 7, 2012.
10. Stephanie Miller, interview with the author, Mar. 8, 2012.
11. Eric Deggans, "Why Rush Is a Slicker Race Baiter than Imus," The Feed (blog), *Tampa Bay Times*, May 2, 2007.
12. Zev Chafets, *Rush Limbaugh: An Army of One* (New York: Penguin, 2010), 155.
13. Ibid.
14. David Ehrenstein, "Obama the 'Magic Negro,'" *Los Angeles Times*, Mar. 19, 2007.
15. Michael Inbar, "Rush Limbaugh: I Love to Yank Media's Chain," *Today*, NBC News, Oct. 12, 2009, http://today.msnbc.msn.com/id/33244211/ns/today-today _news/t/rush-limbaugh-i-love-yank-medias-chain/#.T9AY9b_42lg.
16. Rush Limbaugh, "A Statement from Rush," RushLimbaugh.com, Mar. 3, 2012, http://www.rushlimbaugh.com/daily/2012/03/03/a_statement_from_rush.
17. Jay Rosen, "Audience Atomization Overcome," PressThink (blog), Jan. 12, 2009, http://archive.pressthink.org/2009/01/12/atomization.html.
18. Daniel Hallin, *The Uncensored War: The Media and Vietnam* (New York: Oxford University Press, 1986), 53–54.
19. Jay Rosen, "Audience Atomization Overcome," PressThink (blog), Jan. 12, 2009, http://archive.pressthink.org/2009/01/12/atomization.html.
20. Dylan Byers, "Mike Huckabee Takes Aim at Rush Limbaugh," *Politico*, Apr. 7, 2012.
21. "Michael Savage: 'Most' Latinos in America Are 'Illegal,'" Media Matters, June 22, 2011.

22. Michael Harrison, interview with the author, Mar. 1, 2012.
23. "The Top Talk Radio Audiences," *Talkers*, Sept. 2011.
24. Cenk Uygur, "A Challenge to Rush: Prove Your Ratings," TheYoungTurks.com, Mar. 4, 2012, http://www.theyoungturks.com/story/2012/3/4/223053/2435/Diary /A-Challenge-to-Rush-Prove-Your-Ratings.
25. Ron Rodriguez, "Radio Today 2011," Arbitron, 2011.
26. Ibid.
27. Ibid.
28. Bob Neil, interview with the author, Feb. 27, 2012.
29. "Killer Joe," *Time* magazine, July 29, 1966.
30. Eric Deggans, "A Look Back at Bob Grant and Charges of Racism," *Asbury Park Press*, Nov. 22, 1994.
31. Jim Naureckas, "50,000 Watts of Hate," *Extra!*, Jan./Feb. 1995.
32. Bob Grant, "Media's Destructive Power," BobGrantOnline.com, Nov. 16, 2010; Bob Grant, "The End of America as We Knew It," BobGrantOnline.com, Jan. 19, 2011.
33. Alexander Zaitchik, "As If Limbaugh and Beck Weren't Bad Enough, the Grand-daddy of Hate Radio Is Back On the Air," AlterNet.org, Aug. 24, 2009.
34. Lawrie Mifflin, "Bob Grant Is Off Air Following Remarks on Brown's Death," *New York Times*, Apr. 18, 1996.
35. Steve Rendall, "The Fairness Doctrine: How We Lost It and Why We Need It Back," *Extra!*, Jan./Feb. 2005.
36. Zev Chafets, *Rush Limbaugh: An Army of One* (New York: Penguin, 2010), 44.
37. Zev Chafets, interview with the author, Feb. 2012.
38. Lewis Grossberger, "The Rush Hours," *New York Times*, Dec. 16, 1990.
39. Dan DiLoreto, interview with the author, Feb. 23, 2012.
40. Richard Gehr, "Mouth at Work," *Newsday*, Oct. 8, 1990.
41. Lewis Grossberger, "The Rush Hours," *New York Times*, Dec. 16, 1990.
42. *The Rush Limbaugh Show*, RushLimbaugh.com, Sept. 21, 2011.
43. Gehr, "Mouth at Work."
44. Grossberger, "The Rush Hours."
45. Bob Neil, interview with the author, Feb. 27, 2012.
46. Susan J. Douglas, "Letting Boys Be Boys," *El Dorado Sun*, June 27, 2000.
47. Lionel Lebron, interview with the author, Feb. 2012.
48. Ibid.
49. Dan DiLoreto, interview with the author, Feb. 23, 2012.
50. Gabe Hobbs, interview with the author, Feb. 2012.
51. Celia Viggo Wexler, "The Fallout from the Telecommunications Act of 1996," Common Cause Education Fund, May 9, 2005.
52. Ibid.
53. Gabe Hobbs, interview with the author, Feb. 2012.
54. Department of Justice, "Justice Department Approves Clear Channel's Acquisition of Jacor Communications after Parties Agree to Divestitures," press release, Justice.gov, Apr. 22, 1999.
55. Eric Boehlert, "Radio's Big Bully," *Salon*, Apr. 30, 2001.
56. Gabe Hobbs, interview with the author, Feb. 2012.
57. Danny Shea, "Stephen Colbert Rips Glenn Beck: Building His Career on 9/11," *Huffington Post*, Sept. 13, 2009.
58. Gabe Hobbs, interview with the author, Feb. 2012.
59. Ibid.
60. Mark Leibovich, "Being Glenn Beck," *New York Times*, Sept. 29, 2010.

61. Gabe Hobbs, interview with the author, Feb. 2012.
62. Dan Shelley, "Former News Radio Staffer Spills the Beans on How Shock Jocks Inspire Hatred and Anger," *Milwaukee Magazine,* Nov. 17, 2008.
63. Ibid.
64. "Talk Radio Has Minimal Influence on U.S. Presidential Election," America.gov, Feb. 13, 2008.
65. "O'Reilly: FBI Should Arrest the 'Clowns' at Air America Radio for Being Traitors," MediaMatters.org, June 22, 2005.
66. Jon Sinton, interview with the author, Mar. 5, 2012.
67. Julia Angwin and Sarah McBride, "Inside Air America's Troubles: Optimisms and Shaky Finances," *Wall Street Journal,* June 21, 2004.
68. *America Undercover: Left of the Dial,* HBO, Mar. 31, 2005.
69. Angwin and McBride, "Inside Air America's Troubles."
70. Jon Sinton, interview with the author, Mar. 5, 2012.
71. Dee-Ann Durbin, "Clear Channel Adopts Liberal Programming," Associated Press, Feb. 17, 2005.
72. Gabe Hobbs, interview with the author, Feb. 2012.
73. Ibid.
74. Lionel, interview with the author, Feb. 2012.
75. Jon Sinton, interview with the author, Mar. 5, 2012.
76. Stephanie Miller, interview with the author, Mar. 8, 2012.
77. David Edwards, "Sharpton: Dr. Laura's N-Word Rant Was Despicable," *Raw Story,* Aug. 13, 2010, http://www.rawstory.com/rs/2010/08/13/sharpton-dr-lauras-nword-rant-despicable/.
78. Eric Deggans, "Dr. Laura, Heal Thy Self-Delusion," *St. Petersburg Times,* Aug. 19, 2010.
79. Bob Neil, interview with the author, Feb. 27, 2012.
80. Jordan Zakarin, "Kiss FM, Legendary NYC Urban Radio Station, Goes Off the Air," *Hollywood Reporter,* Apr. 30, 2012.
81. Jon Sinton, interview with the author, Mar. 5, 2012.

CHAPTER EIGHT

1. Lynette Rice, "'Big Brother' Contestant Chima Simone Kicked Off the Show; She Claims She Quit," *Entertainment Weekly,* Aug. 15, 2009.
2. Chima Simone, interview with the author, Jan. 2012.
3. Andy Dehnart, "Jessie Evicted after Jeff Used the Coup D'etat," RealityBlurred.com, Aug. 14, 2009, http://www.realityblurred.com/realitytv/archives/big_brother_11/2009_Aug_14_jeff_coup_jessie_out.
4. Chima Simone, interview with the author, Jan. 2012.
5. Andy Dehnart, "Braden Evicted after Tie, Despite Producers Pathetic Sanitizing of His Bigotry," RealityBlurred.com, July 17, 2009, http://www.realityblurred.com/realitytv/archives/big_brother_11/2009_Jul_17_braden_out_producers_censor.
6. Ibid.
7. Chima Simone, interview with the author, Jan. 2012.
8. Rose Rosen, interview with the author, Jan. 27, 2012.
9. "First Impressions," *Real World San Diego,* MTV, Sept. 28, 2011.
10. Courtney Rubin, Simon Perry, and Todd Peterson, "Brigitte Nielsen Weds Italian Beau—Again," *People,* July 8, 2006, http://www.people.com/people/article/0,1211403,00.html.
11. Lola Ogunnaike, "A Ladies' Man Everyone Fights Over," *New York Times,* Oct. 1, 2006.

12. Eric Deggans, "Stepping Up to Celebrity Status," *St. Petersburg Times,* Feb. 17, 2007.

13. Ibid.

14. "Simon vs. L.A.—Finale Night 2," *The X Factor,* Fox, Dec. 22, 2011.

15. "Nicole vs. Paula: The Cry Off," *The X Factor,* Fox, Dec. 22, 2011.

16. Jethro Nededog, "Nicole Scherzinger Opens Up about *X Factor* Firing," *Hollywood Reporter,* Feb. 7, 2012; Frank Digiacomo, Carson Griffith, and Adam Caparell, "Paula Abdul Felt 'Used' after Being Fired from *X Factor,* Say Sources," *New York Daily News,* Feb. 23, 2012.

17. Jennifer Pozner, interview with author, 2010.

18. Jennifer Pozner, *Reality Bites Back* (Berkeley, CA: Seal, 2010), 8.

19. Bill Carter, "After Wedding Fiasco, Fox Vows No More Exploitation," *New York Times,* Feb. 25, 2000; Eric Deggans, "Who Wants to Hear More about Rick Rockwell?" *St. Petersburg Times,* June 27, 2000.

20. Rick Rockwell, interview with the author, June 2000.

21. Carter, "After Wedding Fiasco."

22. Ibid.

23. Hal Boedeker, "Fox Tempts Fate with Temptation Island," *Orlando Sentinel,* Jan. 8 2001.

24. Rebecca Reisner, "*The Bachelor*'s Mike Fleiss on Coming Up Roses," *Bloomberg Businessweek,* Jan. 13, 2009, http://www.businessweek.com/managing/content /jan2009/ca20090113_071334.htm.

25. Chris Harrison, teleconference call with reporters, Feb. 9, 2012.

26. Karen Parr-Moody, "Clarksville's Kacie B. Sent Home without *The Bachelor* Rose," *Leaf-Chronicle,* Feb. 21, 2012.

27. Chris Harrison, teleconference call with reporters, Feb. 9, 2012.

28. "CNY Woman Opens Up about Her Time on *The Bachelor,*" 9wsyr.com, Feb. 7, 2012, http://www.9wsyr.com/news/local/story/CNY-woman-opens-up-about -her-time-on-The-Bachelor/lRl3QNsgREWTmaXly51JWA.cspx; Amy Kaufman, "*The Bachelor* Recap: Don't Tell Ben Flajnik How to Kiss," Show Tracker (blog), *Los Angeles Times,* Feb. 7, 2012.

29. Chris Harrison, teleconference call with reporters, Feb. 9, 2012.

30. Pozner, *Reality Bites Back,* 13.

31. Jennifer Pozner, interview with author, 2010.

32. James Poniewozik, "How Reality TV Fakes It," *Time,* Jan. 29, 2006.

33. Ibid.

34. Eric Deggans, "Waiting to See If the Glass Slipper Fits," *St. Petersburg Times,* May 13, 2003.

35. "How to Spot Reality TV Editing Tricks: The Reaction Shot," Videojug.com, 2007, http://www.videojug.com/film/how-to-spot-reality-tv-editing-tricks-reaction -shots.

36. Jennifer Pozner, interview with author, 2010.

37. "New Americans in Michigan," Immigration Policy Center, Jan. 11, 2012, http:// www.immigrationpolicy.org/just-facts/new-americans-michigan.

38. Joel Stein, "The New Quiz Show Scandal—Reality Television," *Los Angeles Times,* Dec. 5, 2004.

39. Ibid.

40. Jennifer Pozner, interview with author, 2010.

41. Eric Deggans, "The Truth about Reality Television Might Leave You Feeling Guilty," *St. Petersburg Times,* Nov. 7, 2010.

42. Jennifer Pozner, interview with author, 2010.

43. Scott Nowell, "Your Cheatin' Art," *Houston Press,* Oct. 17, 2002.

44. Bill Carter, *Desperate Networks* (New York: Doubleday, 2006), 75.

45. "Survivor Finale Grabs 51-Million Viewers," *Advertising Age,* Aug. 25, 2000.
46. Mark Burnett, interview at CBS Summer Press Tour, July 23, 2000.
47. Scott Pelley, "Let the Games Begin," *60 Minutes,* CBS, Jan. 9, 2001, http://www.cbsnews.com/stories/2001/01/08/60II/main262358.shtml.
48. Bill Carter, "Co-Chief of NBC Entertainment Departs," *New York Times,* July 27, 2009.
49. Pelley, "Let the Games Begin."
50. Eric Deggans, "Shows Miss Chance to Explore Realities of Race," *St. Petersburg Times,* July 31, 2000.
51. "Reality Check," *TV Guide,* June 27, 2004.
52. Deggans, "Shows Miss Chance."
53. Ibid.
54. Ibid.
55. Eric Deggans, "TV Reality Not Often Spoken Of: Race," *St. Petersburg Times,* Oct. 22, 2004.
56. Benjy Sarlin, "Former Apprentice Contestant: Trump 'Doesn't Like Educated African Americans Very Much,'" Talking Points Memo, May 9, 2011, http://tpmdc.talkingpointsmemo.com/2011/05/former-apprentice-contestant-trump-doesnt-like-educated-african-americans-very-much.php.
57. Deggans, "TV Reality Not Often Spoken Of: Race."
58. Ibid.
59. Ibid.
60. Ibid.
61. Eric Deggans, "The White Guy from Wichita Tries to Explain Race-Based *Survivor,*" The Feed (blog), *Tampa Bay Times,* Sept. 8, 2006.
62. Ibid.
63. Edward Wyatt and Stuart Elliott, "GM Drops Survivor but Says Racial Format Isn't the Reason," *New York Times,* Aug. 31, 2006.
64. Deggans, "The White Guy from Wichita."
65. Ibid.
66. Robert Bianco, "Divisive *Survivor* Exploits Ethnic Cliches," *USA Today,* Sept. 15, 2006.
67. Yul Kwon, interview with the author, Apr. 18, 2012.
68. Jeff Probst, teleconference interview with the author and other journalists, Sept. 7, 2006.
69. Lanford Beard, "Men Suing the Bachelor Discuss Their Case," *Entertainment Weekly,* Apr. 18, 2012.
70. "Warner Horizon Television, statement emailed to author, Apr. 20, 2012.
71. Lynette Rice, "*The Bachelor* Creator on His Long-Running Franchise: 'The Romance Space Is Ours,'" *Entertainment Weekly,* Mar. 15, 2011, http://insidetv.ew.com/2011/03/15/the-bachelor-creator-ashley-h/.
72. Greg Braxton, "*The Bachelor, The Bachelorette* Creator Defends All-White Cast of Title Role," *Los Angeles Times,* Mar. 18, 2011.
73. Shawn Ryan, interview with the author, Jan. 2012.
74. Jeffrey M. Jones, "Record-High 86% Approve of Interracial Marriages," Gallup.com, Sept. 12, 2011, http://www.gallup.com/poll/149390/record-high-approve-black-white-marriages.aspx.
75. "Evolving Attitudes about Interracial Marriage," Good Infographics, May 19, 2011, http://www.good.is/post/infographic-evolving-attitudes-about-interracial-marriage/.
76. Ratings information provided by Brad Adgate at Horizon Media, May 26, 2011.

77. Eric Deggans, "Ranking Reality," *St. Petersburg Times*, Sept. 3, 2001.
78. Girl Scout Research Institute, "Real to Me: Girls and Reality TV," fact sheet, Oct. 13, 2011, http://www.girlscouts.org/research/pdf/real_to_me_factsheet.pdf.
79. Ibid.
80. Patricia Erens, *Issues in Feminist Film Criticism* (Bloominton: Indiana University Press, 1991), 33.
81. Parents Television Council, "Reality on MTV: Gender Portrayals on MTV Reality Programming," Dec. 7, 2011.
82. Ibid.
83. Ibid.

CHAPTER NINE

1. Soledad O'Brien, "Interview with Mitt Romney," *Starting Point*, CNN, Feb. 1, 2012.
2. Kristin Seefeldt, Gordon Abner, Joe A. Bolinger, Lanlan Xu, and John D. Graham, "At Risk: America's Poor during and after the Great Recession," Indiana University School of Public and Environmental Affairs, Jan. 2012.
3. Ibid.
4. Soledad O'Brien, "Interview with Mitt Romney," *Starting Point*, CNN, Feb. 1, 2012.
5. Elicia Dover, "Newt Gingrich's NAACP Food Stamp Remarks Stir Controversy," ABCNews, Jan. 6, 2012, http://abcnews.go.com/blogs/politics/2012/01/gingrichs-naacp-food-stamp-remarks-stir-controversy/.
6. Elizabeth Lower-Basch, "Congress: Don't Kick Workers When They're Down," *Huffington Post*, Feb. 8, 2012, http://www.huffingtonpost.com/elizabeth-lower basch/unemployment-benefits_b_1260174.html.
7. Pam Fessler, "Is There Truth in Gingrich's Remarks on the Poor?" NPR, Dec. 7, 2011.
8. Newt Gingrich, "A New Strategy against Poverty," Spotlight on Poverty, May 15, 2008, http://www.spotlightonpoverty.org/news.aspx?id=f530de1e-6ee9-40ab-ae 23-7ef3a79cba15.
9. Ibid.
10. Robert Rector and Rachel Sheffield, "Understanding Poverty in the United States: Surprising Facts about America's Poor," the Heritage Foundation, Sept. 13, 2011.
11. E. J. Dionne, "The Politics of Economic Opportunity," panel discussion organized by Spotlight on Poverty and Opportunity, Jan. 17, 2012.
12. Melissa Harris-Perry, interview with the author, Jan. 2012.
13. Greg Kaufmann, interview with the author, Feb. 17, 2012.
14. Melissa Harris-Perry, interview with the author, Jan. 2012.
15. Mark Jurkowitz, interview with the author, Feb. 10, 2012.
16. Economic Policy Institute, "The Great Recession: Job Loss," *The State of Working America*, Feb. 14, 2011.
17. Andrew Tyndall, "Year in Review 2011," Tyndall Report, Jan. 2, 2012.
18. Pam Fessler, interview with the author, Feb. 16, 2011.
19. Melissa Harris-Perry, interview with the author, Jan. 2012.
20. Andrew R. Cline, "Citizens or Objects: A Case Study in News Coverage of Poverty," *Poverty and Public Policy*, vol. 3, no. 4. (2011).
21. Robert Entman and Andrew Rojecki, *The Black Image in the White Mind* (Chicago: University of Chicago Press, 2000), 94.
22. Ibid., 105.
23. Martin Gilens, interview with the author, Feb. 15, 2012.

24. Martin Gilens, *Why Americans Hate Welfare: Race, Media and the Politics of Anti-poverty Policy* (Chicago: University of Chicago Press, 1999), 92.
25. Ibid., 114.
26. Ibid., 123.
27. Ibid., 114.
28. Ibid., 3–4.
29. Martin Gilens, interview with the author, Feb. 15, 2012.
30. Dawn Turner Trice, "Welfare Issue Makes Political Comeback," *Chicago Tribune*, Jan. 22, 2012.
31. Pam Fessler, interview with the author, Feb. 16, 2011.
32. Trice, "Welfare Issue Makes Political Comeback."
33. Arloc Sherman, Robert Greenstein, and Kathy Ruffing, "Contrary to 'Entitlement Society' Rhetoric, Over Nine-Tenths of Entitlement Benefits Go to Elderly, Disabled or Working Households," Center on Budget and Policy Priorities, Feb. 10, 2012.
34. Bob Butler, "TV Station Takes Four-Year-Old Child's Quote Out of Context," Mije.org, July 27, 2011, http://mije.org/health/tv-station-takes-four-year-old -childs-quote-context.
35. Ibid.
36. "The Hidden America," CBSNews, June 26, 2011, http://www.cbsnews.com/8301 -504803_162-20074138-10391709.html.
37. Beth Davalos, interview with the author, Mar. 8, 2012.
38. Ibid.
39. Scott Pelley, "Hard Times Generation Update," *60 Minutes*, CBS, Dec. 11, 2012.
40. Beth Davalos, interview with the author, Mar. 8, 2012.
41. Pam Fessler, "A Daily Fight to Find Food: One Family's Story," NPR, July 19, 2010.
42. Pam Fessler, interview with the author, Feb. 16, 2011.
43. Byron Pitts, interview with the author, Mar. 8, 2012.
44. Shanto Iyengar, "Framing Responsibility for Political Issues: The Case for Poverty," *Political Behavior*, vol. 12, no. 1 (1990): 21–22.
45. Ibid.
46. Ibid.
47. Jane Feinberg, "How Framing Influences Citizen Understanding of Public Issues," FrameWorks Institute, 2009.
48. Brian Williams, *In His Own Words: Brian Williams on Hurricane Katrina*, NBC, Oct. 27, 2005.
49. Eric Deggans, "Katrina Aftermath Coverage: Where's the Big Picture?" The Feed (blog), *Tampa Bay Times*, Feb. 27, 2006, http://www.tampabay.com/blogs/media /content/katrina-aftermath-coverage-wheres-big-picture.
50. Eric Deggans, "Katrina Has Failed to Kindle Dialogue on Race and Class," *St. Petersburg Times*, Mar. 1, 2006.
51. Eric Deggans, "NBC Anchor Brian Williams on New Hurricane Katrina Documentary," The Feed (blog), *Tampa Bay Times*, Aug. 20, 2010, http://www.tampa bay.com/blogs/media/content/nbc-anchor-brian-williams-new-hurricane -katrina-documentary-im-going-make-you-sad-and-im-goi.
52. Ibid.
53. Eric Deggans, "Add to Katrina's Toll Race-Tinged Rhetoric," *St. Petersburg Times*, Sept. 14, 2005.
54. Ibid.
55. Pam Fessler, interview with the author, Feb. 16, 2011.

CHAPTER TEN

1. Eric Deggans, "Students Join a Few Original Freedom Riders on the Ride of Their Lives," *St. Petersburg Times,* May 29, 2011.
2. Ibid.
3. Ernie Suggs, "Restored Ebenezer Baptist Church Opens Friday," *Atlanta Journal-Constitution,* Apr. 14, 2011.
4. Bernard Lafayette, interview with the author, May 2011.
5. Ibid.
6. Eric Deggans, "Isolating Our Points of Viewing," *St. Petersburg Times,* July 31, 2005.
7. Shanto Iyengar and Kyu S. Hahn, "Red Media, Blue Media: Evidence of Ideological Sensitivity in Media Use," *Journal of Communication* vol. 59 (2009): 26–29.
8. Marc Fisher, "Polarized News Market Has Altered the Political Process in South Carolina Primary," *Washington Post,* Jan. 20, 2012.
9. Stephanie Rosenbloom, "Love, Lies and What They Learned," *New York Times,* Nov. 21, 2011.
10. Ibid.
11. Edward Glaeser and Jacob Vidor, "The End of the Segregated Century," Manhattan Institute, Jan. 2012; John R. Logan and Brian Stults, "The Persistence of Segregation in the Metropolis: New Findings from the 2012 Census," Project US2010, Mar. 24, 2011.
12. Ibid.
13. Rinku Sen, interview with the author, Apr. 7, 2012.
14. Erik Eckholm, "Reports Find Racial Gap in Drug Arrests," *New York Times,* May 6, 2008.
15. Rinku Sen, interview with the author, Apr. 7, 2012.
16. Shanto Iyengar, interview with the author, Mar. 30, 2012.
17. Richard P. Eibach and Joyce Ehrlinger, "'Keep Your Eyes on the Prize': Reference Points and Racial Differences in Assessing Progress toward Equality," *Personal and Social Psychology Bulletin,* Jan. 2006.
18. Ibid.
19. Ibid.
20. H. Roy Kaplan, *The Myth of Post-Racial America* (New York: Rowman & Littlefield, 2011), 203.
21. Linda Tropp, interview with the author, Apr. 5, 2012.
22. Ibid.
23. Shankar Vedantam, "See No Bias," *Washington Post,* Jan. 23, 2005.
24. Ibid.
25. Shanto Iyengar, interview with the author, Mar. 30, 2012.
26. Rinku Sen, interview with the author, Apr. 7, 2012.
27. Ibid.
28. Edward Herman and Noam Chomsky, *Manufacturing Consent: The Political Economy of the Mass Media* (New York: Pantheon, 1988), lviv.
29. Ibid., 26.
30. Brad Knickerbocker, "Who Is Saul Alinsky and Why Is Newt Gingrich So Obsessed With Him?" *Christian Science Monitor,* Jan. 28, 2012.
31. Ibid.
32. Meghan Ashford-Grooms, "Houston Group Says Martin Luther King Jr. Was a Republican," PolitiFact Texas, Jan. 17, 2011.

33. Richard Hofstadter, "The Paranoid Style in American Politics," *Harper's Magazine,* Nov. 1964.
34. Ibid.
35. Lee Rainey and Aaron Smith, "Social Networking Sites and Politics," PewInternet.org, Mar. 12, 2012.
36. Jeff Jarvis, interview with the author, Apr. 2012.
37. Clay Shirky, interview with the author, Apr. 14, 2012.
38. Dodai Stewart, "Racist Hunger Games Fans Are Very Disappointed," Jezebel (blog), Mar. 26, 2012.
39. Michael Omi and Howard Winant, *Racial Formation in the United States,* 2nd ed. (New York and London: Routledge, 1994), 15.

INDEX